# THE INT

JOHN COWPERTWAIT AND SIMON FLYNN

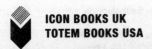

**ICON BOOKS UK**
**TOTEM BOOKS USA**

Published in the UK in 2000 by
Icon Books Ltd., Grange Road,
Duxford, Cambridge CB2 4QF
e-mail: info@iconbooks.co.uk
www.iconbooks.co.uk

Published in the USA in 2001
by Totem Books
Inquiries to: Icon Books Ltd.,
Grange Road, Duxford,
Cambridge, CB2 4QF, UK

Distributed in the UK, Europe,
Canada, South Africa and Asia
by the Penguin Group:
Penguin Books Ltd.,
27 Wrights Lane,
London W8 5TZ

In the United States,
distributed to the trade by
National Book Network Inc.,
4720 Boston Way, Lanham,
Maryland 20706

Published in Australia in 2001 by
Allen & Unwin Pty. Ltd., PO Box
8500, 9 Atchison Street,
St. Leonards, NSW 2065

Library of Congress catalog card
number applied for

Text copyright © 2000 John Cowpertwait and Simon Flynn

ISBN 1 84046 224 8

Design by Sarah Jackson

Printed and bound in the UK
by Cox & Wyman Ltd., Reading

# CONTENTS

# PART ONE

# THE INTERNET DEMYSTIFIED

Welcome to *The Internet from A to Z*, a new approach to understanding the **Internet** and the **World Wide Web.**

The Internet looks set to transform the way we live in the future, and is even now an integral part of the daily lives and routines of many millions of people. One of the effects of the rapid development of new technology is that a new language to describe it usually develops in parallel, sometimes creating entirely new words, sometimes giving old words new meanings and contextual uses. This is clearly the case with the Internet.

While the extension of the English language is an exciting and exhilarating process, the resultant plethora of new words, terms and phrases can undoubtedly confuse the uninitiated. Struggling to come to terms with technical phrases and computer jargon can be an alienating and excluding experience that may convince potential users that the Internet and the World Wide Web are not for them. With *The Internet from A to Z*, we aim to dispel the confusion and break through the jargon. In the dictionary section (Part Two), using simple, non-technical language, we attempt to explain the ideas and concepts behind the main words connected with the **Net** and the Web.

*The Internet from A to Z* aims to bring those on the outside of the Internet experience, inside. Our aim is to provide new and intermediate users of the Net with useful explanations, and to offer pointers to help find a way into and around the new world of information that is accessible via the Internet. Those who are not yet online, but who are interested in finding out more, will also find this book an invaluable source of information. Whatever level of user you are, we hope you find something here that is of interest.

*The Internet from A to Z* is two different books in one. As well as providing a dictionary and reference guide to Internet and World Wide Web terminology in Part Two, in Part One there is a series of introductory essays examining each element of the Internet in turn. We attempt to provide a context for the Internet by explaining what it is, how it has developed and what you can do with it today. We also suggest how the Internet is likely to grow in the years ahead, and predict how that will affect you. We examine the history and development of the Net, and explain how a **network** initially confined to academics and researchers developed into the backbone of the most important communications revolution since the invention of printing. And, in order to get you up and running, we show you how to get connected and rise to the challenge of the changes that are happening in our society.

By examining and describing the basic structure and workings of the Net, and explaining the differences between **browsers**, **search engines**, **media players** and other Internet-specific **software**, we provide a grounding in the principles of using the Internet.

We let you in on the secrets of how to use a variety of search tools to find the information you need on the World Wide Web effectively, and how to communicate with friends and colleagues around the world using **e-mail**. We also explain the differences between **newsgroups**, **mailing lists** and **chat**, and suggest how you might use

In the 'Using the Internet' section, among other things, we help you to find **shopping** bargains on the Web, take part in online **auctions**, book a flight, sell your house, and watch live **broadcasts** of concerts by your favourite bands. We've selected just a few of the thousands of **Websites** that now exist for virtually any subject you could think of. These are suggested as examples of the type of site you may find useful. There may well be hundreds, possibly thousands, of similar sites, so the ones we mention should not be seen as recommendations, although any site mentioned here has been visited by us in the course of researching this book. This section aims to help you discover those parts of the Internet that will be most useful for you. We hope it will enable you to take part in the Internet revolution on your own terms.

This is not a step-by-step *How-to book*, as it would be impossible to outline all of the steps for all of the software we cover. However, we give you enough rudimentary generic information and direction to get started. A finer level of detail is available in the online help features that can be found in each piece of software, such as browsers, search engines and media players. Integral online help can be an extremely useful consultation tool when you are actually using the software. It is designed to provide answers to technical queries and to show you how to execute specific tasks.

In *The Internet from A to Z* we place the emphasis on *what* you can do with the Internet, rather than the technical details of *how* it is done. We will introduce you to the principles and basic workings of the Net and the Web. However, the best way to find your way around is by throwing yourself into it.

Rather than attempt the impossible and try to take you through each stage step-by-step, we redirect you back to the rich environment of the Internet itself, giving you the confidence to **surf** for yourself. The essence of the Internet is self-determination. We aim to help you embark upon an adventure. This book will open up avenues that can be explored, and will send you on your way at your own pace. *The Internet from A to Z* will not give you all the answers. However, it may help you to formulate some questions. It is a starting point, suggesting further possibilities. We hope to point you in the right direction, so you can begin your journey of discovery.

Using the Net can be frustrating – the connection lines are frequently busy, **links** often don't work, and Websites go missing. That's just how it is. It's best to approach the Internet with a relaxed attitude. Don't expect to understand everything immediately. And don't expect everything to work the first time you try it, either. Along the way you'll experience many unexpected **glitches**, and you'll also discover lots of little tricks to get around them.

When learning about the Internet, trial and error are the order of the day. Take time to experiment. Take risks – **click** on things and see what happens. Technically, there's little to fear, and technophobes should bear in mind that it\rquote s virtually impossible to cause problems by pressing the wrong keys. If the computer screen locks and you can't get the cursor to respond, then usually the best way out is to restart the computer and continue from where you left off.

The more you use the Net, the more self-explanatory it becomes. Don't feel pressured. Enjoy the experience.

# SOME NOTES ABOUT USING *THE INTERNET FROM A TO Z*

One of the great wonders of the Web is that you can adapt the way both browsers and some Websites look on-screen to suit your own requirements. You can make changes to layout and colour (see pages 61–3), but also to **content**, tailoring it to contain information specifically slanted to your interests. Many sites now offer this **configuration** option, often called 'Myxxxx' (xxxx being the site name of the Website), or simply using a command called 'personalise this page'. However, one of the off-shoots of this degree of customisation is that it can make it difficult to lead you through a step-by-step on-screen learning process. The screen descriptions and reproductions shown in this book will not necessarily be identical to the ones on your screen, as the chances are that they will have been subject to some degree of tailoring – by you as the user, by the way your browser's display controls are configured, or by the Website publisher. They will be similar, but slightly different. Therefore, screenshots shown in this book should be used for guidance only.

The research for *The Internet from A to Z* was carried out using Microsoft's **Internet Explorer** browser, since this is the browser used by the majority of people using the Internet for the first time. For this reason, Internet Explorer is used as the primary reference in the browser section, although the vast majority of what is written also applies to the other major browser, **Netscape Navigator**.

The technology of the Internet advances apace. Please bear this in mind when reading *The Internet from A to Z*. It may be that what was considered to be the latest development at the time of writing has been superseded by the time you are reading this. Later technological developments will be covered in subsequent editions of this book.

Similarly, content on the Web is **dynamic**, and changes occur at an exhilarating speed. Occasionally, Websites that are referred to in this book will have evolved in design, changed their nature or expanded their content, and in rare cases may even have disappeared completely. This is the nature of the Web, so please be aware of this on the occasions when discrepancies occur between the information in this book and what you locate on the Web.

While you've been reading this introduction, you've probably wondered why certain words have been printed in bold. These words can be found in Part Two of *The Internet from A to Z* – the dictionary section. Here, as well as the words highlighted in the text of Part One, you'll find a vast number of other words connected with the Net and the Web, as well as words associated in a general sense with computing technology. Most of the dictionary entries contain a 'links' section showing a list of other words associated with the main word that is being defined. By looking up the entries for each of the words in the links list, and then the words in the links lists for those words, you can read around the subject matter connected with the initial word, surfing through the dictionary by word association.

## Waiver

All of the information contained in this book is believed to be correct at time of going to press. The information in this book is provided for guidance purposes only. The authors or Icon Books cannot be held responsible for any errors, omissions or factual inaccuracies.

## Thanks

John Cowpertwait would like to thank Jocelyne Dudding, Robin Cowpertwait, Jackie Maguire and Dragan Nikolic for their help, advice and comments during the writing of this book.

Simon Flynn would like to thank David Flynn, Charlotte Robinson, Duncan Heath, Andrew Furlow, and Media Paradigm for all of their help. Thanks also to Sarah Jackson for her wonderful efforts regarding the design of the book.

## Profiles

John Cowpertwait has worked with information technology for over 20 years. He has worked in a marketing management capacity for major software companies, including Micro Focus (now Merant) and Lotus Development. He works as a marketing consultant and is also a visiting lecturer in Arts and Broadcasting at the Department of Arts Policy and Management, City University, London.

Simon Flynn started using the Internet whilst studying Chemistry at Bristol and Philosophy at York. He worked briefly at IBM before joining a publisher and becoming involved in Website development and e-publishing.

# THE INTERNET: AN INTRODUCTION

This section asks 'What is the **Internet**?', then takes us through a brief history of the **Net**, looking at its past, its present and what's likely to happen in its future.

## What is the Internet?

This seemingly simple question is actually extremely difficult to answer. Where you are standing will determine your viewpoint. To a business person or long-term investor, the Internet probably represents a great business opportunity, a means of making money both through stock flotations and through future sales operations. To a short-term speculator it may be a bubble that has already burst. For many retailers, **e-commerce** will provide a means of exponentially expanding business, taking sales beyond the limitations of geography.

For others, the Internet is primarily a new media space: a means of publishing and presenting information – about people, products, services, international affairs, hobbies, science and technology, the arts, pets, celebrities and so on. Anything and everything. The old media, represented by newspapers and magazines, television and radio, and the new media space offered by the Internet, are converging. The paradigms and conventions of old media formats are mixing and merging with the new possibilities of presentation and distribution created by the developing electronic media. For example, existing newspapers now generally have Websites that mimic, in part, their old layout: **articles** are reproduced, news items are paragraphed and are accompanied by photographs with captions. However, news sites are beginning to combine newer technology with their more conventional style of presentation, by running short accompanying video soundbites for example. And media distribution is no longer restricted by the constraints of printing, binding and packaging.

In the not so distant past, the means by which people published information may have been in the form of a newsletter, bulletin or fanzine produced using a typewriter, glue and scissors, and a photocopier. Then along came the possibilities afforded by **desktop publishing**. The Web combines the worlds of desktop publishing with an international network, broadening access to anyone with a computer and a **modem** connection. With access to the Net, everyone has the opportunity to become a publisher. The Web presents opportunities to provide information on a worldwide level unlike those that have existed before. Anyone can establish a **Website** for any reason and, provided it is an open site, anyone else can visit it. This is as much about distribution as it is about the ability to present information.

As well as information, all sorts of **digital** products can also be distributed over the Internet. Anything that can be electronically digitised can now be transported over the Internet, including text and images, moving images and sounds. **Software programs** themselves are regularly distributed over the Net. Many of the pieces of software needed to function on the Net can now be downloaded from it and automatically installed on users' computers. Because the Internet is a global network the distribution reach has extended beyond anything imaginable just a few years ago.

It's no over-statement to say that the Internet has revolutionised the world of communications. It is a global public communications network. For next to nothing, connected people can communicate with others all over the world almost instantaneously. Gone are the days of sending letters, which could take a week or more to reach someone on the other side of the world. People won't stop writing to each other with pen and paper altogether of course, but **e-mail** offers an alternative, cheaper, quicker and infinitely more flexible means of doing so. Add to the e-mail explosion the impact and implications of instant messaging services, **chat rooms**, electronic mailing lists and **newsgroups**, and the picture gets even bigger. Soon, communicating telephonically via the Internet will become commonplace. Voice connections are possible now, but the advent of newer broader, more efficient, telephony technology will make them an everyday occurrence for all of us.

So, the Internet is simultaneously an international shopping arcade, a new media space, a global communications network, an interactive forum for the exchanges of idea, opinions and information, and a software distribution mechanism. To the average user, the Internet can be any, all, or none of these things. It depends on how you approach the Internet and how you use it. How people both generally and as individuals take advantage of the Internet is constantly changing.

Culturally, the Internet has already influenced our language, the way we think and speak, and how we communicate. For many, it enshrines a Utopian vision where national boundaries tumble, restrictions are lifted and censorship is eradicated. The reality, of course, is not quite as simple: there are still restrictions and controls in place. However, it is possible to maintain a high degree of freedom of expression. The Net provides a means by which an alternative, relatively uncensored, supply of information can be distributed via Websites and newsgroups.

For many, the Internet is a manifestation of the times in which we live, encapsulating a multi-cultural, multi-tasking, pluralistic, cut-and-paste, sampling, twenty-four-hour, seven-days-a-week lifestyle of blurred boundaries and self-determinism. The Net can be perceived as a great leveller, or in a broader sense it can be seen as divisive. The digital divide is one of the issues that we are now facing as access to computers and skill-sets separates those who are Internet-literate and those who are not.

On the Net you can be anything and anyone you wish to be. And no one owns the Internet. Companies control telephone lines, **ISPs** (Internet Service Providers) control **access**, **content providers** own some of the material published on the Net, but no *one* organisation owns or controls the whole. The Internet's impact on our societies has only just begun. In many shapes and forms, it is here to stay.

## A short history of the Net

What is shocking and simultaneously thrilling is how recent the explosion of the Internet into general use is. It was only in 1994 that the **multi-media** element of the Internet, the **World Wide Web**, really began to expand, and it was as recently as 1996 that it exploded. According to one calculation, in 1994 there were an estimated 3,000 Websites; by 1995 there were 25,000; by 1996 250,000; by 1997 1.2 million; and by 1998 4.2 million. Estimates for the year 2000 vary between 10 and 11 million sites.

### The Internet then

The Internet is the latest development in a relatively long progressive history of communications technology, encompassing the telegraph wire system (1844), cables (1866), the telephone (1876), radio (1915) and satellite (1957).

Spurred on by the former Soviet Union development of the first successful satellite, Sputnik, the United States of America formed the Advanced Research Projects Agency, which began to set down what would become the foundations of the Internet. The story goes that during the Cold War the Americans wanted to develop a communications network that could withstand a nuclear attack from the East. This is now dismissed as a myth by some technology historians, but there is a poetic irony in the idea that what was designed as a result of global divisions is now instrumental in bringing us closer together.

Whatever the motivations, in 1964 the US research and policy organisation, the RAND corporation, published a document outlining the principles of **packet switching**, on which the Internet was to be based. The idea was that, rather than having a centrally controlled network, the Internet would comprise of numerous decentralised independent equal-status control **nodes**. This would produce a sustainable network in the event of sections of the network ceasing to function. The chances of all the nodes going down together would be remote, so some parts of the **system** would always be up and running, and messages could still find a route through. Messages were broken down into small '**packets**', which would be routed independently around the system and automatically reassembled when they reached their destination. At the same time **protocols** were developed that switch information around a network until it finds a route through.

It was not until 1968 that the first wide area network (**WAN**) to employ packet switching was tested. The tests were carried out by the National Research Laboratory in the UK. The Pentagon funded a more ambitious project in the US shortly after, which resulted in a four-node network being established in 1969 called **ARPANET** (Advanced Research Projects Agency network). The network slowly grew and the first public demonstration took place in 1972 linking forty machines. Networks could accommodate many different machine-types as long as they could all handle packet switching protocols.

Initially used for US government and military information exchange, the network was soon expanded to incorporate university research sites. The first international connections to ARPANET were established with University College, London and the Royal Radar Establishment in Norway in 1973. At this time links were laborious to establish, connections were slow and the information shared primarily textual.

The first e-mail software was developed in 1972, and users quickly discovered a taste for sending personal messages, as well as large **documents**, over both short and long distances, using electronic mail. The invention of the e-mail **mailing list** quickly followed, which meant one message could be simultaneously sent to many recipients.

In 1974, the development of a more sophisticated protocol standard, **TCP/IP**, led to further expansion of the networks. TCP (Transmission Control Protocol) was an improved version of the protocol that converted messages into small **data** packets when they were sent, and reassembled them at their destinations. **IP** (Internet Protocol) took care of **addresses**, ensuring that packets went to the appropriate places over multiple nodes and networks. TCP/IP is integral to the success of the Internet. Providing networks supported it, they had the potential to all communicate together. TCP/IP software was placed in the public domain and was therefore accessible to anyone who wanted to use it. The result was that while networks continued to develop separately, many incorporated support for TCP/IP standards, enabling them eventually to link together in what today we call the Internet.

The development of discrete networks continued throughout the 1970s. **Telnet** was established in 1974 as the first public packet data service. In 1976 AT&T Bell Laboratories developed a **UNIX-to-UNIX protocol (UUCP)** that opened up networking to a wider academic community, as most university computer systems used the UNIX operating system. The **Usenet** newsgroup network was created in 1979, and by the early 1980s the number of separate networks was increasing exponentially.

At the same time, the personal computer revolution was starting to take a hold in the commercial sector as the microchip developed, and processing power and data storage capacity increased. As businesses moved towards using personal computers, the use of e-mail and telephony conferencing on private networks began.

When ARPANET adopted the TCP/IP protocol in 1982, the Internet can be said to have been established. By 1983,

ARPANET had become big enough to require splitting into two sections – one for military use and one for civilians. The following year **domain name servers** were introduced which created a categorisation of user types distinguishing between education, governmental, commercial and international users.

**JANET** (Joint Academic Network) was introduced by the British government in 1984, followed by the establishment the following year in the US of the National Science Federation network (NSFNET). In 1986, a stronger US **backbone** infrastructure for the Internet was laid down by NSFNET, linking supercomputers, providing high data transmission speeds and standardising communication protocols (TCP/IP). NSFNET encouraged international co-operation, established funding routes and enabled agreements between different networks.

At this time the policy of use for the Internet was still primarily limited to research and education, and excluded commercial activity. However, commercial networks were being developed in tandem which also adhered to TCP/IP protocols. Initial discussions had taken place between government, academic and private sector commercial companies in 1985, and by 1987 the first commercial Internet company was established. Its main attractions were e-mail, chat, newsgroups and computer games facilities. **IRC** (Internet Relay Chat) software was written in Finland in 1988, the same year that the first fibre-optic cable linking the US and Europe was introduced. IRC came to prominence in 1991 during both the Gulf War and the Russian *coup*, when it was used to transmit eye-witness accounts outside the restrictions of conventional media. The fascinating IRC **logs** of these events have been preserved as historical documents.

**Graphical User Interface** (GUI) business **applications** software for personal computers began to appear on the market around 1988. The development of GUI products, such as **word processors**, desktop publishing **tools** and **hypertext** packages that were used on personal computers, occurred at the same time as the growth in the numbers of **LAN** and WAN networked personal computers in the commercial environment. Personal computers had gone from being essentially stand-alone machines to computers linked to each other in company-wide networks, transmitting data and sharing **hardware** externals such as printers. These have become known as **intranets** and continue to exist outside of the Internet.

While the Internet is perceived primarily as a US initiative, due to much of the information it carries being of American origins, many of its recent critical developmental stages can be traced back to Europe and research into particle physics. **CERN** (Conseil European pour la Récherché Nucléaire), the world's largest research laboratory, became the largest Internet site in Europe in 1990. It was hugely influential in the spread of Internet techniques worldwide. However, its most significant contribution to the development of the Internet was an offshoot of its main concerns and resulted from a desire to find an improved way of distributing information among high-energy physicists.

It was at CERN in 1989 that Englishman Tim Berners-Lee developed the concept of the World Wide Web based on distributed computing techniques. In a move that was ultimately to transform the use of the Internet, he conceived a system that would make the distribution and retrieval of networked GUI hypertext documents much simpler. In 1990, the first piece of **browser/editor** Web software was developed with the ability to view, edit and send linked hypertext documents over networks. In a critical move, the software was placed within an **FTP (file** transfer protocol) **site**, which meant that anyone could freely download it.

The protocol used by the browser software, **HTTP** (Hypertext Transfer Protocol), simplified the writing of addresses and also automated search and call-up procedures. As a result, the process of sending information was drastically improved. At the same time, **HTML** (Hypertext **Markup Language**) was developed, which created the ability to produce and link attractive graphics-based Websites which were easily accessible through a new generation of Web browsers.

In 1990, ARPANET was wound up and the same year, as the amount of information on the Internet grew, **Archie**, the first Internet **search engine**, was developed in Montreal. The Internet's commercial restrictions were finally lifted in 1991, giving companies access to the network, but, as it was still highly complex to use, the Internet remained primarily a tool of research and academia.

As the Internet expanded, the idea of an aspirational '**Information Superhighway**' seeped into the general public consciousness after the term was coined by US vice-president Al Gore, whose High Performance Computer Act 1991 provided funds for research aimed at improving the Internet's US infrastructure.

However, it was not until 1993 when **Mosaic**, an advanced GUI Web browser, was developed at the National Center for Supercomputing Applications (NCSA) that the Internet's user base started to broaden. Backed by twenty-four-hour support, simple to install and relatively easy to use, Mosaic became the blueprint for the browsers that run on the Web today. Its improved graphical capabilities and general features made it accessible to a broad user base and, importantly, it was available to run on **Windows**, the dominant PC operating system. Mosaic was the first widely used piece of Web software, and by 1994 several thousand copies had been installed.

Seizing this lead, the browser developers left the NCSA to establish a new corporation and developed a faster, more easy-to-use browser, **Netscape Navigator**, making Netscape Communications at that time the fastest-growing software company in history. This led to a further explosion in users and can be seen as the beginning of the continuing rush by businesses to establish a Web presence.

The success of Navigator was a concern to Microsoft, which, while it had been instrumental in spreading the growth of the personal computer, had not predicted the explosion in Internet use. It developed its own Web-browser, **Internet Explorer**, and in a move subsequently adjudged to be anti-competitive in the US courts, tied it into the Windows operating system. Internet Explorer was first incorporated into the 1996 OEM release of **Windows 95**, which was made available to manufacturers for pre-installation on new computers. Subsequent versions of Windows also included Internet Explorer. As Windows 95 and **Windows 98** installations increased, Internet Explorer became the dominant browser, pushing Navigator into second place.

From the mid-1990s, inexpensive high-specification multimedia PCs became generally available which led to a growth in the development of personal Websites developed by individuals, clubs, schools and families. This, combined with an escalating business Web presence, meant that the Internet was no longer primarily the domain of the academic and scientific community, and computer-literate e-mail and newsgroup users, but was now accessible to *all* computer users.

## The Internet now

From being a well-kept secret, preserved for the use of technologically aware computer users, the Internet has quickly become part of our everyday lives. The reception given by the media to the Internet has been instrumental in this process. More and more people used the Internet from 1994 onwards due to easier access via the GUI browsers. Interest increased as individuals and businesses began to realise that the Internet was not going to be a short-lived phenomena and the implications of this new way of publishing information became clearer. As businesses began the scramble to get **online**, the Web and the Internet began to seep into the public consciousness via the media.

For a time, the media seemed to see the Internet as a threat, a possible replacement for themselves. However, as it became clear that the Net was likely to complement, even expand, media empires instead of nullifying them, the various components of the mass media began to embrace the new technology. The process went hand in hand with the digital television revolution, the opening up of **broadband** to local regional TV channels. In many ways the Internet is a logical next step in the evolution of the media that began in the 1980s with the movement of the UK newspaper industry from Fleet Street to Wapping, and the subsequent satellite television revolution. As the markets were opened up, a degree of de-regularisation and de-unionisation of the media industries took place. Now, with the Internet, everyone can be a reporter, critic or journalist.

Around 1996–97, newspapers and magazines began publicising their Web addresses, television programmes indicated their own Websites at the end of programmes, and advertising in both TV and print carried a Website locator. The word 'dotcom' became ubiquitous, as the old media promoted the new media.

In the last few years the notion of the World Wide Web has become synonymous with the abstract multi-media space of the Internet – inhabited by documents, sounds, videos, all types of information – while the Internet itself is seen as the supporting infrastructure network of cables and wires. Although dependent upon it, the Web popularised the Internet because it made sending and receiving information easier, more practicable and ensured the Internet was accessible to people who *didn't* have programming language-level computer skills.

While elements of the Internet do remain distinct from the Web, such as Usenet newsgroups, which can be accessed via a **newsreader** independently of the Web, there is a convergence happening whereby the Web is becoming the entry point for access to all of the Internet. Usenet, for instance, can also be entered via both Websites and an Internet browser, and other previously discrete Internet functions, such as e-mail and chat, can now also be reached via the Web.

As more and more information becomes available to users of the Internet it has become vital to be able to **navigate** around and locate the information required – hence an explosion in the number of search facilities now available.

From the humble beginnings of Archie, a wealth of different search and location processes have developed. Huge **meta-** and **multi-search** sites now trawl the Web *en masse* by simultaneously engaging hundreds of different engines, while **directory** sites allocate hand-picked Websites to carefully selected categories and guide the user to relevant information through a series of stages. There are also thematic search engines, covering sites only within one topic, such as music files or **shopping**.

## The Internet future

The potential of the Internet is huge. The sheer range of activities in which it is instrumental is already vast, but in the future this will expand exponentially as finance and creative energy fuel its further development.

e-commerce is one area that many of the companies which have invested heavily in the Internet are hoping will take off. Accordingly, there are vast numbers of shopping and commercial sites that will help users find the right product for them, usually at a substantial discount from prices available in the high street. Banks and financial institutions are ensuring that Internet credit card **security** is improved, so users can shop in safety on the Net.

For the present, a relatively small number of us use the Internet for shopping, buying houses and cars, booking flights and holidays, and managing our financial affairs, but the likelihood is that in a few years this will be the norm. Traditional methods are not likely to disappear overnight, but they will become relatively less important.

In terms of entertainment, there are already thousands of Internet radio stations that you can choose to listen to while you surf. Although receiving video broadcasts over the Net can still prove a disappointment over low speed connections, this looks set to change fairly quickly as communications technology advances in big strides to permit better quality pictures to be distributed to more people.

In the future, more of us will be accessing the Internet more frequently for more reasons, as the cost of accessing the Internet continues to fall. With cheaper computers, free access and low- or no-cost phone calls, an increase in the number of access points in public places, and access via mobile phones and television sets, the user base looks as if it is set to expand even further.

# GETTING CONNECTED

This section takes a look at the equipment you need to get connected to the Internet, then runs through operating systems, the connection process and getting online. It concludes with a selection of ISP sites.

## What equipment do you need to get connected to the Internet?

If you work in an office environment, the chances are that you are already connected to the Internet via your office computer. Many other users **connect** via **Internet cafés** or public-access connection points such as libraries, or at school. There's currently lots of talk in the media about being able to connect to the Internet via many exotic routes, such as mobile phones and television sets. However, the main growth area for Internet connectivity is via home computers. In this section we will deal with the means by which most users will still, initially at least, make the connection onto the Internet for their own use – a desktop or laptop computer.

### Recommended specification

It is recommended that you have the following.

- A telephone line with 56 **kbps modem** (or **ISDN/ADSL** line).
- 400 MHz **Pentium III** (or equivalent) computer with:
    - 64 MB **RAM**
    - 1 GB free **hard disk** space
    - **Windows 98 operating system**
    - **CD-ROM** drive

  – Soundcard and speakers
  – 2 MB RAM video card.
- **ISP** (Internet Service Provider) access arrangements.

*Minimum specification*

Below is probably the minimum specification you can get away with. Although it will allow you to get connected, it means you will have difficulty accessing audio and video material, and the connections will be achingly slow. Overall, it will be a frustrating experience accessing the **Net** using equipment with this level of specification and isn't to be recommended. You will probably come across suggestions that you can access the Internet with computers with an even lower specification than that shown below. While in theory this is probably true, in practice it just isn't worth it.

- A telephone line with 28.8 kbps modem.
- 100 MHz 486 computer with:
  – 16 MB RAM
  – 200 MB free hard disk space
  – **Windows 95** operating system
  – CD-ROM drive.
- ISP access arrangements.

## Operating system

There are various levels of **software** on your computer. The base of your system is the operating system (OS). There are a number of PC operating systems available, such as **Linux** and **UNIX**, and **Apple** Mac computers have their own OS. The most popular OS is Microsoft **Windows**. If you bought your computer system since 1995, the chances are that Windows was supplied with it.

The OS is the link between all the applications software and your machine. It allows software that does specific things to communicate with the workings of your computer. It also allows you to organise the **files** on your machines into folders, and provides a few useful but relatively insignificant applications like a calculator, a clock, and so on. You don't have to know the workings of the OS; it is just there in the background, getting on with things.

As with all pieces of commercial software, over time new features and facilities are added to Windows. These are made available to the public as upgrades, and are indicated by a version name or number. When you are accessing the Internet you need one of the most recent versions of the OS, which are Windows 95, **Windows NT** or Windows 98. The version before these is Windows 3.1. It is possible to access the Internet using this, although we do not recommend it. You can **upgrade** your software from an earlier version to a later one by contacting your dealer or Microsoft direct. Microsoft is currently working on a new version of its operating system – **Windows 2000**.

Linux is worth considering as an independent alternative to Microsoft's Windows if you are feeling adventurous and technically able. However, for novice computer users, the new streamlined installation procedure is still a daunting prospect. It's freely downloadable over the Internet and is being adopted as the OS for an increasing number of 'netpliances', low-cost Internet-**active devices**.

## Connecting to the Internet: modems, ISDN, ASDL, cable and satellite

If you are working from home the most likely way that you will connect to the Internet is using your residential telephone line and a modem. Which of the three types of available modem you use will depend on your computer. An internal modem slots inside the back of your machine. These can be used on desktop computers and it is possible to insert internal modems by removing the back of your computer. If you are not particularly confident about doing this, it's probably best to get your computer dealer to do it.

The more likely options are either an external modem or, if you are using a laptop, a **PCMCIA** modem card. An external modem is the cheapest option and can be used with either a desktop or a laptop. The downside is that, being external, it takes up room, requires a separate power supply and is not very portable. Certainly the best option if you are working from a laptop is the PCMCIA card. It's similar in size to a credit card and slots easily into the side of the laptop. Modems are powered by the computer and have an external lead that connects to standard **analogue** telephone lines. The slowest modem that is usable to any degree of satisfaction on the Web is 28.8 kbps, although life will be much better with a 56 kbps modem. There are now a few alternatives on the market that provide more reliable connections and a much faster service: ISDN (Integrated Services Digital Network), a digital telephone service that works over standard telephone lines, can transmit data at up to four times faster than a modem. The increases in speed over standard analogue lines are not that impressive and ISDN looks to be under strong competition from newer services in the pipeline. BT's ISDN service, Highway, converts single phone lines into a digital system with two lines, which means you can **surf** and use the phone at the same time, but there is a line conversion charge and increased line rental charges. You also need to replace your modem with an internal ISDN card or an external ISDN terminal adapter supporting either 64 kbps or 128 kbps.

BT is currently pushing BTopenworld, its new broadband **ADSL** (Asymmetrical Digital Subscriber Line) connection ISP service for home and business users. Like Highway, this system uses existing phone lines and you can make voice or fax calls when you are surfing the Internet. ADSL promises to be up to sixteen times faster than ISDN services. Home users are offered a service at 512 kbps, just over nine times faster than a 56 kbps modem; for business users it's up to forty times faster at 2 **mbps**. The service is structured as an ISP service and includes unlimited access to the Web for a fixed fee with no additional Internet call charges. Unique content is promised, including quality streaming video and clear stereo sounds from Websites that, when accessed with a low speed connection, would be mainly text based. This service is likely to push the **multi-media**, interactive and broadcasting dimensions of the Internet to another level.

Although not yet generally available, for those who can have cable access to television and phone facilities, cable Internet access may also be a viable option. Cable access offers faster connections than standard telephone lines, so it's worth enquiring with your supplier.

An exciting developing means of accessing the Internet is via the broadband technology of satellite connections under the 'Internet via the Sky' initiative (more information at www.teledesic.com). This interesting example of European technological co-operation is currently available with Europe Online via the Astra satellite, and requires the installation of a satellite receiver card into your PC and a satellite dish. At the moment the receiver card covers data only, but in the future an option will be available allowing the reception of free-to-air television and radio programmes. Europe Online's Website (www.europeonline.com) gives details of dealers throughout Europe.

## How to get online

There are a number of ways that you can do this using any of the following Internet Service Provider (ISP) options.

### Internet Service Providers

Between your computer and the Internet is the ISP, which provides your hook into the Internet. Your computer connects, usually via a telephone line and modem, to the ISP's server, which supplies your high-speed link to the Internet. As well as providing Internet access, ISPs often also offer a number of **e-mail** addresses and Webspace in which to site your own Webpages. As they provide your main means of accessing the Internet, ISPs are highly significant and the one you select can influence your whole Internet experience.

Historically, UK users have been asked to pay an access fee to connect with the Internet, in addition to having to pay local rate telephone charges for the duration of the connection period. This has made using the Internet a relatively expensive exercise compared with costs in other high-usage Internet regions. In the USA, for example, users have had greater access to the Internet due to the way the telephone system is set up. Unmetered access, or toll-free telephone calls, for unlimited usage of the Internet in return for a fixed fee charge per month has been the norm in the US.

As Internet usage in the UK has taken off, market and government pressure has been on the UK telephone companies to come up with more equitable arrangements for customers. Recent government legislation designed to develop greater competition and to drive down prices has opened-up the telecommunications market. The rise of the Internet has been a welcome impetus to this process, and we are now witnessing the fracturing of British Telecom's previous near monopoly as more and more telephone companies evolve by getting into the Internet game.

## Free-access ISPs

Over the past year a new breed of free-access ISPs has emerged. These free-access ISPs no longer charge a fee for access to the Internet, but users still pay for the local-rate telephone calls that connect their computers to the Internet.

This situation has become the norm, with hundreds of free-access ISPs being set up by all sorts of commercial concerns, from media organisations such as the BBC (freebeeb.net, a joint venture with Thus – formerly Scottish Telecom – the company that runs the pay-ISP Demon), retail outfits such as Tesco, Waitrose and WH Smith, to sports organisations, particularly football clubs.

Commercial interests are the motivating force at work here and it's the big retailers who have led the way. Dixons, the hi-technology goods retailer was the first to establish a free-access ISP in the UK – Freeserve – distributing the software through its complex network of multi-branded technology outlets. Freeserve is now an independent stock-listed company under the Dixons Group umbrella. Other commercially orientated concerns with retailing interests have followed Dixons' example.

By providing free access to the Internet, commercial companies are forming a direct relationship with users who will usually route into the Net through the site of their ISP, and will thus be subject to the editorial influences and advertising messages to be found there. Users are usually also customers, and sales potential, either through traditional routes or the evolving e-commerce framework, is a major reason why retailers provide free Internet access.

These retail-orientated ISP sites are generally professionally designed, well maintained and easy to navigate. They provide stable and reliable access to the Internet for the minimum of effort, and at no charge except local phone calls. However, some people may prefer not to be so closely allied to one particular retailer, or wish to escape the consumerist ethos inherent in the smooth commercialism of these sites. Many opt for one of the less overtly consumerist free-access ISPs.

### Paid-entry online services

The very select band of ISPs that continue to charge for access justify doing so by positioning themselves as providing essential exclusive members-only information via their entry **portal** (for more details on portals, see page 121). This is a sensible route onto the Internet only if you need access to that information and it is not available elsewhere on the Net for free.

These ISPs have also been the traditional route onto the Net for non-technical Web users. The best-known ISP in this arena is **AOL** (America Online). Its blanket marketing approach has turned it into one of the best-known names connected with Internet access. At one stage it was difficult to avoid coming into contact with one of its seemingly ubiquitous CDs delivered to your door via personally addressed mailshots or cover-mounted on Net magazines.

AOL positions itself as a family orientated service and has been successful in seizing a large slice of the user base. In several ways it is now similar to the many other portal-style ISPs, with much of its content being available to anyone who visits its site, with a few extras for members. In response to the threat to its user base from free-access ISPs, AOL has established Netscape Online, a free-access service for the 'value conscious', which uses the Netscape Navigator browser.

The business community is also served by AOL in the guise of **CompuServe**, which continues to provide specialised information for corporations and professionals, such as large-scale **databases**, specialist forums and communication tools. One of the benefits of CompuServe accounts is that they can be accessed from most international cities by busy executives away from the office.

There are some special interest sites that charge for entry to subscriber-only material as part of an ISP role. For example, the members-only Bowie.net is targeted at the loyal band of David Bowie enthusiasts who are willing to pay for exclusive access to rare audio and video clips (and the like). As this site is also providing Internet access via a **server** it is an ISP service, rather than a pay-for-entry special interest subscriber site.

Anyone still paying to access the Internet must seriously ask themselves why they continue to hand over good money for something that most people now get for free. A reasonable answer might be a requirement to have access to unique information sources. However, unless you feel strongly attracted by the additional services and information that the ISPs who charge for Web access provide, then there seems little sense in opting for one of these services.

## Free access, free calls

In recent months, the arena has hotted up even further, with a third generation of ISPs arriving on the scene offering Internet access arrangements that go beyond the model of the USA. They provide both free Internet access and, by linking up with telephone service companies, free Internet access telephone calls. As a result, the ISP market is currently in exciting turmoil. Almost daily there are new offers from a newly established ISP. These deals may be subject to certain terms and conditions, which may include free calls being limited to certain off-peak times of the week (usually weekends, or evenings and weekends).

The competition for customers in telecommunications is not limited to Internet access. Hand in hand with this goes an opportunity for the telecommunications companies to gain voice customers. Each supplier is vying for position, with the free-access free-call ISPs trying to grab as many customers as they can, as quickly as they can, to ensure they have a viable future. The new telephone companies are trying to seduce customers away from BT with reduced-rate call charges for voice connections. Some deals require you to switch phone companies altogether (including line rental), while some of the newer offers require a **plug-in** adapter to be used to route your voice and Internet calls away from your current telephone supplier.

In response, many of the free-access ISPs are rising to the challenge and restructuring their charges, with the provision of limited periods of free Internet calls earned by prior usage. Other deals include free Internet calls in return for a monthly commitment to a minimum amount being spent on voice calls made via an associated telecommunications company, or 'free' access for a small up-front monthly or annual payment. The resultant plethora of charging structures is reminiscent of the confusion that surrounds mobile phone tariffs and users may end up having multiple phone bills, with a number of different companies sharing the tariff pie.

At one end of the scale one ISP is charging £11.75 per month just to access the Net, with telephone line rental and local call charges on top of that. Another ISP is offering a 'deal' that provides unlimited off-peak Internet access and calls for an astonishingly high £49.99 per month. At the other end of the scale, one ISP is offering free access and free Internet calls twenty-four hours a day, seven days a week, for spending a minimum of £5 per month on national and international voice calls at rates heavily discounted from BT's. And there's all sorts of deals in-between.

There's so many special deals being offered that it is impossible to list them all here. It's a matter of shopping around. Some of the best-sounding deals are inevitably subject to some stringent conditions and when you get into the fine detail of the small print, some of these deals are not all they're initially cracked up to be. Having said that, there are some impressive bargains to be had. For the moment at least, the Internet continues to be one of those rare places where you don't only get what you pay for.

However, bear in mind that many of these companies are start-ups and the level of service may be variable. A measure of service is how quickly you get connected to your ISP's server when dialling. Some ISPs have a dismal record in this area, and in some cases a minimum call charge is levied each time your computer tries to connect, as calls are actually getting through to the server, but it is unable to respond. Those 5p minimum call charges levied by the telecoms company each time this happens soon add up.

Monthly magazines about the Internet along with the daily press and broadcast media, are useful sources of immediate information, often preparing tables indicating the comparative performances of different ISPs. If you have online access already you can also key in 'free-access ISPs', or something similar, to the search engines of your preference to see what they come up with. You can also check the Websites listed on pages 41 and 42 for more information.

Keep your eyes and ears open. Gather the fine details, do some comparisons and calculations, then make your choice. Before you commit yourself, remember to read the small print; make sure you understand what kind of agreement you are entering into, and what, if any, restrictions it binds you to and for what period.

You may feel that initially it's sensible to spend a period with an ISP that does not require you to make any big commitments. As well as giving you time to sample the Internet and make an assessment of the ISP's service, this will also enable you to observe your own Internet habits and usage patterns. Then you can locate a service that best matches your needs, providing free Internet calls at a time of the day or week that will deliver most benefit to you. You may wish to sample more than one free ISP, although only one at any given time can be the **default** ISP that your computer dialler automatically contacts when you enter the Internet. Check the terms and conditions of your agreement regarding using more than one supplier at once for accessing the Internet, because ISPs are becoming stricter about this as the competition increases.

### After you've signed up

Once you have signed up with an ISP, it will provide you with its version of a browser. This will usually be Netscape Navigator or Microsoft Internet Explorer and may be subtly branded by them in some way, such as the addition of the ISP logo. This software is available either via a CD that you insert into your computer's

CD-ROM drive (then following the installation instructions) or, if you are on the Internet already, by **downloading** the software via your telephone connection. In both cases, the installation process should be automatic and trouble free. If it isn't, it's usually best to simply try another ISP. The fact that there are problems at this early stage may indicate the level of service to come, and if you phone the support lines the chances are they will charge you a premium rate for doing so. Assuming the installation has gone well, you should now be able to surf forth upon the Internet!

## ISP listing

The Websites listed here give just a selection of the many ISP sites available.

### 24/7 free access and no Internet call charges

    www.4unet.co.uk/callnet.co.uk
    www.lineone.net
    www.ntl.com
    www.visualdepth.com
    www.worldonline.com

### Free access plus some free Internet call periods

    www.greatxscape.co.uk
    www.screaming.net
    www.veryfree.net
    www.x-stream.com

### Free access, charged local calls

    www.btclick.com
    www.freebeeb.net
    www.freeserve.com
    www.madasafish.net
    www.netscapeonline.co.uk

www.publiconline.com
www.tesco.net
www.virgin.net
www.waitrose.com
www.whsmith.net

## Charged access, free Internet call periods

www.altavista.co.uk.
www.bt.com/adsl/
www.btinternet.com
www.clara.com

## Charged access, charged Internet calls

www.demon.net

## Paid-entry member services

www.aol.com
www.compuserve.co.uk
www.davidbowie.co.uk

## Information about free ISPs

A number of sites aim to monitor the ISP market and may be worth a look.

www.sevenoaks.strayduck.com
A site listing some of the UK call-free access deals.

www.12free.co.uk
An amiably amateurish site with some useful information.

# HOW IS THE INTERNET STRUCTURED?

The **Internet** is composed of a number of distinct areas, each with differing functions. The three most popular aspects of the **Net** are the **World Wide Web**, **e-mail** and **newsgroups**. Historically, each of these areas was a clearly defined entity in its own right. In recent years however they have merged, with the Web the dominant element. e-mail and newsgroups (and associated activities such as online chat and discussion lists) can now be reached via the Web. Each area requires its own set of instructions to function; therefore each area has its own **software** products. On the Web in particular, there has been a bewildering proliferation of product and brand names in recent years. You will come across a plethora of trendy and dynamic names and logos, and will probably wonder what they are and what they do. Brand and/or product names that you may see in connection with the Internet include **Hotmail**, **Outlook Express**, RealTime, Netscape, **Internet Explorer**, **AOL** and so on. There are hundreds, maybe thousands.

In this section we will examine how the Internet is structured, what types of software **applications** and **tools** there are, and how some of them are used. We will explain the differences between the various levels of software tools (for example, **browsers**, **search engines**), and sub- or inner-applications, known as **Plug-ins** and **ActiveX controls** (for example, **RealPlayer** and **Shockwave**).

## The World Wide Web

Here we will take a look at the structure of a **Website**, **Web-pages**, and the components of Website addresses or **URLs**.

## Structure of a Website

Websites are at the heart of the World Wide Web. A Website is a location managed by an individual, group, organisation or company that provides information about specific areas of interest, products, services, general knowledge and so on. The Web has millions of Websites, each of which contains many Webpages. These pages use text, graphics, animations, and sometimes **multi-media** elements like video options and sounds. Websites often contain **links** to other Websites. Connecting between Websites by clicking on these links is known as 'surfing' the web.

## The Website

Webpages are collected together in Websites. Websites contain all the pages developed by an individual or company about a certain topic. Each Website has an opening, or home, page. Often the **homepage** will provide a site map or Website content listing. This is often situated in a box on the left of the

screen, although it can be sited elsewhere. By clicking on entries within this listing, you will be connected with pages relating to each entry. You will usually be provided with an option to return to the homepage from each of these pages. A typical homepage looks like the one shown on page 44.

## *The Webpage*

Websites contain Webpages. They vary in size from just a few interlinked pages to corporate sites containing hundreds of elaborately constructed pages. A Webpage will often appear the same size and dimensions as the full-screen browser window on which you view it. It can also be a different size and shape. If the Webpage is bigger than your full-screen browser window, or the viewable area of the browser window on your screen, you can use **scroll**-bars found at the right-hand side and sometimes at the base of the screen to bring the information into view (see example below). Clicking on the arrows on the scroll-bars will move the information up and down, or left and right, to enable you to view it.

Scroll bars

*The components of Website addresses or URLs*

Each Website has a specific location on the Internet. A unique Web address or URL (Uniform Resource Locator) is allocated to each Webpage, which enables your browser to locate it. For example, a sample page of the Icon Books Website has the URL:

http://www.iconbooks.co.uk/new/intro.html

'http://' stands for hypertext transfer protocol and indicates that the location you are seeking is on the Web, rather than one of the other areas of the Internet.

'www.iconbooks.co.uk' is the domain name for Icon Books.

| Address | http://www.iconbooks.co.uk/ |

'www' stands for World Wide Web. This shows that the site is a Website, although this is not always used.

'iconbooks' indicates the company's Website homepage. As is often the case, the key part of the **domain name** in this instance is also the company name. The domain name could actually represent anything – a product, a service or something more inventive. If you wish to locate a particular site, but don't know the address, you can often work it out with a bit of applied guesswork, particularly for larger companies. For example, you may guess that the retailer WH Smith's site might be 'www.whsmith.co.uk'. This would take you to the WH Smith online homepage.

'.co.uk' the '.co' extension means that the site belongs to a <u>co</u>mpany. This usually suggests that it will be followed by '.uk', which means it hails from the UK. American companies and multi-nationals usually use '.com' to stand for <u>com</u>mercial and rarely use a country extension, although companies outside the US now sometimes also use .com. URL **extensions** are a means by which you can identify the type of category into which a Website falls, although they are becoming increasingly confused. Other extensions include:

.ac – academic institutions (other than US)
.edu – educational institutions (usually US)
.gov – governmental sites
.mil – military establishments
.net – Internet industry companies
.org – non-profit making organisations, such as charities.

The country extension indicates where a site is hosted. You can usually work out what the country extension stands for. 'eu' looks likely to become a new extension denoting European companies. A few examples are as follows.

.ar – Argentina
.at – Austria
.au – Australia
.br – Brazil
.ca – Canada
.ch – Switzerland
.de – Germany
.fi – Finland
.fr – France
.it – Italy
.mx – Mexico
.nl – Netherlands
.nz – New Zealand
.pt – Portugal
.th – Thailand
.tw – Taiwan
.uk – United Kingdom

'/new/intro.html' this is the file path that will take you to a particular page within the Icon Books Website. In this instance it is the introduction to the 'What's New' section.

'.html' indicates that the site is written in hypertext markup language, the computing language that is used to compose most Websites.

## Website design

Like most things, Website designs are of variable quality. If you think of the Web in terms of a publishing analogy, then there are examples of every level from the equivalent of amateur fanzines to expensive glossy coffee-table books – and every stage in between. As there's arguably less pleasure to be gained from a finely designed Website than the physical presence of a quality book, the key is to look through the design to the content. Often, good content is marred by poor navigation techniques which make it hard to locate information.

In many recent, expensively designed Websites, form often triumphs over content. Seductively eye-catching images take an age to download on older computers. Once you have downloaded them, you have to move beyond the initial page almost immediately in order to gain any useful information. **Animated** images and bright colours can be attractive, but can also become distracting and lessen site usability.

As the techniques of Webdesign have become more sophisticated over the past four or five years, designs have generally improved – although there are many instances of animation technology, flipping text and suchlike being used purely because they are there, rather than for any practical reason of improved communication. Because of this, many of the corporate sites leave you with a feeling of being short-changed. Corporations have the finance to afford the 'best' design techniques, but often provide an essentially empty experience.

Corporate Websites often leave the impression that they were created out of a desire to have a Website as the latest element of a corporate communications strategy. But they don't contain anything new or essential; they are merely recycling old forumulaic information. Not surprisingly, corporate Websites toe the company line in the same way that corporate magazines tend to, presenting the information from an angle that places that company in the best light. Some of the best sites are still the amateur ones produced by enthusiasts rather than by professionals. Their unique content is often worth suffering some of the less competent design skills for.

## Building your own Website

In the past you may have been able to produce a newsletter using a typewriter and a photocopier or, more recently, a computer, **desktop publishing** package and a laser printer. However, the chances of more than a few hundred, or at most a few thousand, people seeing your efforts were remote, due mainly to the issue of distribution. It was difficult and expensive to get your newsletter in front of people – production and mailing costs were usually prohibitive.

With the Internet those problems have disappeared. Digital technology and electronic distribution mean that each page only has to be produced once and can then be infinitely reproduced all over the world at the touch of a button, wherever computers are connected to the Internet.

There are millions of pages on the Web produced by individuals, rather than product or service companies. With the Net anyone has the potential to be a widely read writer and publisher. Additionally, Websites are able to be much more sophisticated than newsletters (with links to sound and audiovisual files, and other sites), and can include graphics and photographic material.

In order to make your own Website available over the Net, you need a **host**. This will take the form of a computer that is permanently connected to the Web which will act as the host server for your Website. Many ISPs provide free Webspace to those who are registered with them, and there are a number of free **online content** and host communities that provide help with constructing and uploading sites, and **hosting** them, such as Yahoo!GeoCities, Moonfruit and Tripod.

Using one of the community sites means that your Website URL may be rather convoluted and will probably include the name of the community site. Similarly, if you use your ISP as the host, the URL for your Website will probably include the name of the ISP. However, they may be able to host your site with a unique domain name of your choosing, but they may charge an additional fee for this service. The domain name can be important if you are trying to attract the maximum number of visitors to your site. Many people prefer to use a separate domain name because it makes the site seem more professional than if it is preceded by an ISP or Web host service name. It will also make the site easier to find. In order to have the right to use a domain name you have to lease it from one of the domain name registration companies such as NetNames.

You can add lots of facilities to your site to make it attractive to users by taking advantage of the free tools that are available to you. Facilities such as search tools and graphics can be added at no cost. They can add value to your site by making it more user-friendly. Check out The Free Site to see what's around.

The simple way to get your Website constructed is to prepare the textual and graphical material, design the pages, test them and then **upload** them to the host service. One of the easiest ways to start is by using your **word processor** to create your pages. Later versions of most of the leading packages, including Microsoft **Word** and WordPerfect, now allow you to save documents as **HTML** (Hypertext Markup Language) files necessary for the Web. Alternatively, both Internet Explorer and Navigator come with limited authoring packages in **FrontPage**

**Express** and Composer respectively, which are a great starting point for the novice.

When you have successfully established your Website using a word processor or start-up authoring package, you may wish to advance to more sophisticated dedicated authoring software such as Macromedia's **Dreamweaver**, Microsoft's FrontPage or SoftQuad's HotMetal Pro, which are specifically designed to produce Websites.

To upload your Webpages either contact your host, or consult the Windows Web Publishing Wizard under Internet Tools.

For help with constructing and uploading sites, and hosting them, check out the following.

    www.geocities.yahoo.com
    www.hotmetalpro.com
    www.macromedia.com
    www.microsoft.com/frontpage/
    www.moonfruit.co.uk
    www.netnames.co.uk
    www.thefreesite.com
    www.tripod.co.uk

## The browser

A browser allows you to enter and find your way around the Internet. While you are on the Internet, the browser, like the **operating system**, will always be functioning in the background, providing the framework in which you work. It enables you to retrieve and display pages from the Web, save page locations for future reference, link to search facilities and save information from the Web permanently.

In the past, browsers were primarily used for viewing Webpages. Nowadays however, browsers also interface with activities such as e-mail, chat and multi-media. There are two main browsers – Microsoft's Internet Explorer and Netscape's Navigator – although there are others available such as **Neo-Planet** and Opera. For more comprehensive details of different browsers, consult Browserwatch. Internet Explorer and Navigator work in much the same way and generally have similar, but not identical, commands and layouts. Most of the examples and terminology in this book relate to Internet Explorer, as it is the most popular browser.

If you are working on a computer purchased in the last few years, a browser will usually have been supplied with it. Internet Explorer has been bundled with Windows for some time. If not, your ISP (see 'Getting connected', pages 34–42) will supply you with a browser either on its installation CD or by downloading it on to your computer over the Internet when you sign up. Often, the ISP flavours the browser it uses with its own logos and other customised elements; however, the browser will usually be either Internet Explorer or Netscape Navigator. As with Windows, there are a number of different versions of each browser available reflecting the stages in their development over the years. It's usually best to try to use the latest version of browsers where possible. These can be downloaded over the Net.

For more information about browsers check out the list that follows.

www.browserwatch.Internet.com
www.home.cnnnet.com/Internet/o-3773.html
www.neoplanet.com
www.opera.com

The latest versions of Internet Explorer or Netscape Navigator can be found at:

www.home.netscape.com/computing/download/index.html
www.microsoft.com/ie/default.htm

*Getting to know your browser*

Browser windows tend to look slightly different according to factors such as which machine you are viewing them on, which ISP you are using or how your browser has been **configured**. However, the following description should give an indication of how your screen will look.

At the very top of the screen will be a text description of the site you are visiting. Underneath this is a series of text commands. Clicking on any of these commands will produce a **drop-down menu** with a series of options. You can view your **'Favorites'** in this way, as well as the invaluable online browser 'Help' section, and the menu for 'Internet Options' under 'Tools'.

In the right-hand corner of the very top line on screen you will see three **buttons**. These buttons are useful if you wish to simultaneously **open** a number of browser windows. Clicking on the '-' button will diminish the browser window you are working on, keeping the session alive but enabling you to work within another window at the same time. The 'overlapping square' button will reduce the window in size, but not make it disappear entirely, so it sits on top of other windows you are working with. Clicking on the 'X' button will close that particular window.

You can multi-task on the Web; rather than just doing one thing, you can work in a number of different windows at once or, for example, download a piece of software in the background, while surfing the Net or sending an e-mail in another. This is an important aspect of the Web; it means you can work on a number of tasks at the same time, which, as well as saving time, will be significant if you are paying for your access calls. However, opening too many windows may slow down your machine, stall it or **crash** it. It will depend on the combination of power and **memory** that you have on your computer.

Under the browser button bar (described on page 54) is the Address bar. This contains the letters 'http://' which signify that you are trying to find a Website rather than another type of Internet location. The quickest way to reach a Website for which you already have the URL is to type it in here and press 'enter'. This should take you directly to the site.

## *The browser bar*

To gain a thorough understanding of your browser, a good first step is to familiarise yourself with the navigation buttons in the bar near the top of your browser's window. These may vary according to the size of your screen, the particular browser you are using or how your browser is configured. A typical Internet Explorer browser bar would contain the following.

- Back and Forward: the two buttons at the top left are two of the commands you will use most frequently when surfing the Net. They take you back and forth between Webpages you have visited during your current session. The small down button next to the Back button shows you pages you have recently visited, between which you can move using the two buttons, or you can go directly to one of the sites by clicking on it.
- Stop: this button is used for halting the process of loading a Webpage. You would use it if the downloading process was happening too slowly, or if you decide that you no longer wish to **load** a particular page.
- Refresh: a page may fail to appear on the screen in its entirety. Refreshing the screen may correct the problem. It will also ensure that the page is up to date.

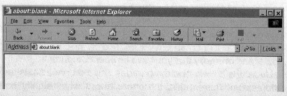

- Home: this button will take you to the page you have designated as your homepage, which is the first page you see when you start the computer.
- Search: this takes you to the **default browser** search engine from which you can make a Websearch.
- Mail: links to your mail program. You can send Web links and pages within e-mails using this feature.
- Print: this will enable you to print out the current Webpage. To do this you have to have the correct printer **drivers** installed on your machine.

Two of the buttons on the browser – Favorites and History – will become very important to any regular user of the Internet and they deserve special mention.

### Favorites (or Bookmarks)

Naturally, as you surf through Webpages you are likely to find information that you would like to be able to revisit time and time again. You can store links to these Webpages in the 'Favorites' section (called '**Bookmarks**' in **Netscape Navigator**). When you are on a Webpage you wish to store, you simply click on 'Favorites' and a bar will appear on the left of your screen, giving you the option to 'Add' the page to your list (see the example on page 56). The link will be directly to the page on which you are sited. If you wish to provide yourself with a quick link to a whole Website, rather than a single page, then it's best to 'Add' the Website homepage, so your 'Favorite' link will be to there. From the homepage you will have links to all the pages within the Website.

You can put your Favorites into groups by using the 'Organize' facility (see page 56). You can group Websites into category folders and sub-folders. Your Favorites store will probably become one of your most valuable locations. It will enable you to return quickly to pages and sites you treasure without having to relocate them in the great mass of the Web.

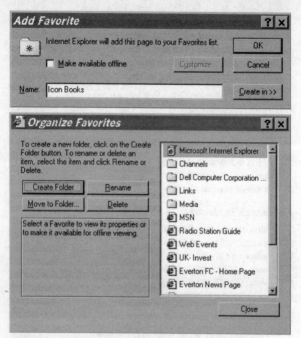

*History*

Other means of locating pages you have previously visited are also available. For instance, the 'History' button allows you to revisit all the pages you have visited on previous occasions. The History file stores the URLs for all these pages, and you can set the duration for which these are stored by adjusting the settings within 'Internet Options', 'Tools', from the pull-down file menu at the top left of the browser screen. Webpage URLs can be kept for anything from a day to a few months (the days indicator actually extends to 999 days, but it's unlikely you'll want to keep anything this long!). You can view them according to a number of criteria – that is, by date, site, site most visited and order visited.

History can be a useful tool for relocating Webpages you didn't save as Favorites (see the example below). However, if your computer is used by other people, you may feel that you do not want a ready log of the pages you have been visiting to be immediately available for scrutiny, perhaps in a family or corporate environment. Remember that Webpage addresses are accessible back in time to the maximum period specified by you. You have the option to 'Clear History' whenever you like by visiting 'Internet Options'.

The Webpages you have visited are also stored as Temporary Internet Files in the **cache**. The cache is the store of the locations you have visited that is kept on your machine. The machine retains these as it makes accessing frequently visited Websites much faster. However, it also means that there is a record on your computer of all the sites you have visited. Only when the cache is cleared are these removed from your

computer (and even then a computer expert may well be able to retrieve them). Clearing the cache periodically will also have the benefit of speeding up your computer. You can clear this record of your viewing habits in Internet Explorer by selecting 'Tools', 'Internet Options', 'General', 'Temporary Internet Files', 'Delete Files'.

## Browsing offline

Most of the Webpages that you have previously visited will be available to you **offline**. You can visit them by using your browser without connecting to the Internet. You do this by clicking on 'Work Offline' under the 'File' menu. When you are working offline, this may be indicated by a small computer **icon** with a red cross through its connection lead, visible in the bottom right-hand corner of your screen.

To view Webpages you recently visited, use your History files. The majority, but not all, of these will be available to you offline provided you have not recently cleared out your cache. If you try to connect to a page where the link has not been downloaded, and is therefore not available for offline reading, a small no-entry icon will appear. To read those pages you have the option of connecting to the Net.

You can search the pages stored as History files by clicking on the word 'Search' at the top of the column of files. A search box will appear, into which you type the word or phrase that you wish to find. Then press 'Search Now' and the Webpages you have visited will be automatically searched.

A means of managing your offline browsing is by using 'Favorites'. Rather than just revisiting sites offline by using the means available through 'History', you can also make arrangements to view your Favorite Websites offline in the group categories in which you have arranged them.

When designating a Webpage as a 'Favorite', you will have the option to make it available offline. This means you will be able to access and view it when you are not connected to the Internet. The current version of that page will be stored on your disk for you to open without logging on to the Net. When you are saving pages as Favorites, you will also be given the option to add a limited number of other pages linked to the one you save as a Favorite. Additionally, you will have the option to update pages automatically or at specified times.

By making Favorites available offline, you retain certain Webpages for offline viewing for longer, instead of just for the number of days stipulated by your History folder option.

## Saving Webpages permanently

After tracking down material on the Net, the chances are that you will want to save some of it permanently on your computer. The are a number of ways to do this. A Webpage is made up of several discrete elements, such as graphic images and text. This means you can save each of these elements together or

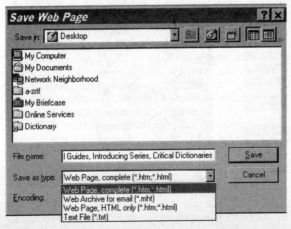

separately. You can save them by using the 'File', 'Save As' commands from the pull-down menu. To save only the text, save as type 'Text File (*.txt)'. You may only wish to save part of the text. To do this, position the cursor over the text and **highlight** it, then copy and paste in the normal way (see page 59).

Rather than saving just the text you may wish to save the whole Webpage, including both text and images. To do this save as either 'Webpage, complete' or 'Web Archive for e-mail'. If you are interested in the html coding you can right-click on the background and select 'View Source'. The source document for the entire Webpage can be saved as before, but this time selecting Save As 'Webpage, HTML only'.

To save only images, position the cursor over the image and click the right **mouse** button. From the menu select 'Save picture as' and save the file to the destination of your choice. You have a number of options with images, including saving the picture as your desktop wallpaper.

Providing you have the correct plug-ins to display them, you can also save files other than text or graphics ones, including sound and video files. Use the right mouse button to do this. You should save the file to disk. When you open it, the file will either play or display automatically, depending on the multi-media programs you have available, or you will be asked to designate a **program** that is suitable for this type of file

## Plug-ins and ActiveX controls

Plug-ins and ActiveX controls are software applications that permit multi-media facilities to be used over the Web. It is these that distinguish the Web from the other Internet facilities like e-mail and **discussion groups**, which are still primarily text and static graphics (although you can send Webpages by e-mail). They provide additional capabilities to the browser, usually related to audio-visual activities, which will use your computer's sound and video card. You will be able to listen to online radio, watch video clips or listen to music samples using these plug-ins. For more information about multi-media on the Web see 'Broadcasting', 'Music' and 'Media players' in 'Using the Internet' (pages 149–67).

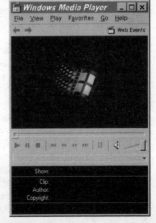

Plug-ins can be down-loaded free of charge from the Web, either from the manufacturer's Website or from a site displaying audio-visual material that requires them. They are generally memory-hungry, so if you're short of machine memory, think about whether you need these or not. Some audio-visual material will work with a selection of different plug-ins. Check out the following.

- Apple **QuickTime** (www.apple.com/quicktime/)
- Beatnik (www.beatnik.com)
- Microsoft Windows Media Player (www.microsoft.com)
- RealPlayer (www.real.com)
- **Shockwave** and Flash Players (www.shockwave.com)
- **WinAmp** (www.winamp.com)

Another widely used plug-in is **Adobe Acrobat**, which is not multi-media based, but is designed to allow texts from incompatible formats to be displayed using different, usually incompatible applications. Acrobat files have the .pdf (Portable Document Files) extension. To read them you will have to download the free Adobe Acrobat Reader. Visit www.adobe.com for more information.

Many plug-ins have optional cost upgrades that you may wish to utilise as you become an expert user and want extra functionality. However, the basic free versions are suitable for everyday use.

Images and sounds can take time to download and may slow down your Web browsing, especially if you have an older model computer. To speed up your surfing, you do have the option to browse the Web using text only, eliminating images, sounds or video. However, while videos appear relatively rarely on the Web, sounds are increasingly common and images are ubiquitous – and you may feel you are not receiving the full Web experience if you limit yourself to text.

Alternatively, you may feel that it's the textual information that is most important for you, and that the image and sound files merely clutter the process of reaching your key data. If you do feel it's worth having the option to turn images on and off, the Web accessories pack for Internet Explorer provides a

**toolbar** image on/off toggle. You can also turn off 'Play' animations, sounds, videos and 'Show' pictures within the 'Advanced' tab of 'Internet Options' from the 'Tools' menu, turning them back on again when you need to.

## Tailoring your own Web use

You are provided with the means to customise your personal interface into the world of information that the Internet offers. By doing this you can ensure that your laptop, desktop computer or other Internet accessing equipment provides you with the facts, data and information that may make your life more fulfilling and more productive.

A number of tools and services are provided to help you to extract the information you need, such as Web browsers (see pages 51–9), search engines (see pages 108–13), directories (see pages 114–18), portal sites (see pages 121–23) and so on. They help you reach the information that is relevant to you. By taking the information they deliver and managing it, you are taking the process of individualising your Net experience a stage further.

As a means of controlling that information the History function helps to track and trace Websites you have visited, and the Favorites option permits your browser to memorise Webpage and site addresses so you can always find them quickly during your Web sessions. Saving Webpages, sites and sounds enables you to extract information from the Web and utilise it elsewhere, perhaps as reference material, in reports, or for sending to friends or colleagues.

You can go even further in personalising your Internet workspace by adapting the way your browser looks and feels specifically for your own tastes.

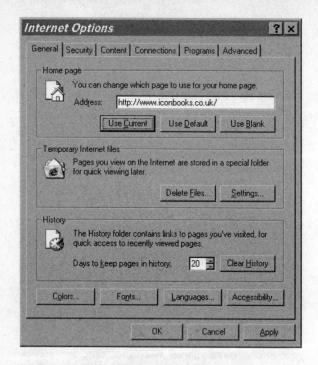

*Configuring your browser*

There's a fair amount of flexibility built in to your browser. You can make alterations to the settings if you wish to make it more convenient for your own use. For instance, you can select any page on the Web as your homepage. This is the page that you see each time you start a session. It is also the page you return to when you press the 'Home' button on your browser's button bar.

Many people choose to have a blank screen when they first **logon**. This has the advantage of avoiding the tempting distractions of your browser's standard homepage, and also means you don't have to spend time waiting for text and graphic images to download. Others choose their most used e-mail site, or a favourite sports or culture site. Your home-page can be changed by going to 'Tools', 'Internet Options', 'General', 'Homepage' – you can then designate a page of your choice, select 'Use Current', or select 'Use Blank' (see the example on page 64).

Using the same 'Internet Options' under 'Tools', you can adapt the way Websites are displayed according to your own tastes. For example, you can change the **fonts** and back-ground colours within Websites that have not directly specified them. Be selective about the changes you make, as it can render some sites unreadable. If in doubt return to the default 'Use Windows Colors' by ticking the box option. Times New Roman is the standard font for Webpages and Courier New for plain text. There are also options for you to specify lan-guages other than English to be used as the default. Whether you use this option successfully or not will depend on the language support offered by each Website. You can get infor-mation about the latest browser accessories and extensions that will enable you to tailor your browser to a greater extent, including the Internet Explorer Web Accessories pack, at:

www.microsoft.com/windows/ie/webAccess/ie5tools.asp

## Moving around the Web: hypertext linking

'Surfing the Web' is the process of clicking on **hypertext** links, the connections between Webpages that are acti-vated, by a click of the mouse button. This is the essence of the World Wide Web and it is also where it gets its name from. Web-like formations are created as you weave your way around the Net, linking from one site to another, each site leading to another one.

The links usually appear on screen in the form of underlined text, coloured text or iconised graphics within Webpages. When your cursor (or mouse arrow) passes over a link, the cursor will change into the shape of a hand, and usually a small box of text will appear next to the hand indicating where the link will take you. Clicking on links leads you to different locations within the same Webpage, different pages within the same Website or to a different site altogether, as well as opening sound or audio-visual files.

As you place the cursor over hypertext links you will find either the URL for the link or an alternative text message supplied by the link in the left-hand side of the **status bar** that runs across the length of the bottom of your computer screen.

## Restricting access to the Net

While the Internet is home to interesting, exciting and educational information, as it is an open environment there is also a fair amount of objectionable material to be found on Websites, over **IRC channels** and within newsgroups. If you wish to protect yourself, your family or your employees from seeing this material there are a number of measures you can take.

### Using your browser to restrict Net access

The first and most obvious step is to adjust your browser's settings so that it filters out material about subjects you may find offensive or may not wish to be subjected to. Both Internet Explorer and Netscape Navigator employ a filter system. You can also establish a list of approved sites and limit specified sites to **password**-only entry. To set the filter ratings in Internet Explorer, select the following from the pull-down 'Tools' menu: 'Internet Options', 'Content' and 'Enable' the 'Content Advisor' (see example opposite).

When you enable the Content Advisor you will be asked to create and confirm a password. This gives the password holder the right to adjust the level of content that can be viewed through the browser. Each time the levels are adjusted you will need to type in the password. Within Content Advisor 'Settings' you have four sections:

- Ratings
- Approved Sites
- General
- Advanced.

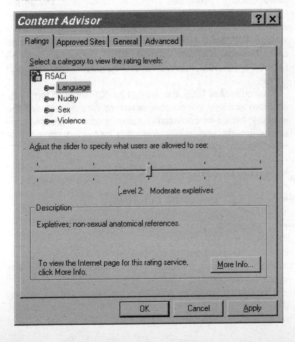

The Ratings section gives you the option to establish the levels of material you are prepared to permit in four areas: Language, Nudity, Sex and Violence. These can be set on a sliding scale through five levels, 0–4, using a slider bar. For example, the range for Language is from level 0 'Inoffensive slang; no profanity' to level 4 'Crude, vulgar language or extreme hate speech' (see page 69).

The ratings system used was established by the **RSAC**i (Recreational Software Advisory Council, Internet), which is managed by the ICRA (Internet Content Ratings Association) (www.icra.org), which has offices in Washington, DC (in the USA) and Brighton (in the UK). It is a voluntary system supported by the Internet industry. Founding members include AOL, Bell Canada, Bertelsmann Foundation, BT, Cable and Wireless, Demon Internet (UK), Deutsche Telekom Online Service, IBM, Internet Watch Foundation, Microsoft and Novell.

Formed in May 1999, the remit of the ICRA was to formulate an internationally acceptable online ratings system for the industry, based on consultations with children's groups, consumer groups, universities and other interested parties. The RSACi ratings system aims to:

• be voluntary and internationally acceptable
• protect free speech
• be culturally non-specific and objective
• be user- and provider-friendly
• be adaptable.

By advocating responsible self-regulation the industry is diminishing the disturbing possibility of government legislation in this difficult area.

The system relies on content providers voluntarily having their sites rated. To date more than 130,000 Websites have been rated, with the majority of the top 100 sites that account

The RSACi ratings system

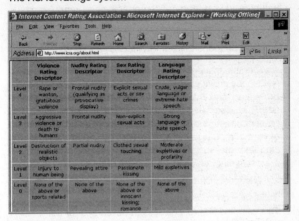

| | Violence Rating Descriptor | Nudity Rating Descriptor | Sex Rating Descriptor | Language Rating Descriptor | |
|---|---|---|---|---|---|
| Level 4 | Rape or wanton, gratuitous violence | Frontal nudity (qualifying as provocative display) | Explicit sexual acts or sex crimes | Crude, vulgar language or extreme hate speech | |
| Level 3 | Aggressive violence or death to humans | Frontal nudity | Non-explicit sexual acts | Strong language or hate speech | |
| Level 2 | Destruction of realistic objects | Partial nudity | Clothed sexual touching | Moderate expletives or profanity | |
| Level 1 | Injury to human being | Revealing attire | Passionate kissing | Mild expletives | |
| Level 0 | None of the above or sports related | None of the above | None of the above or innocent kissing; romance | None of the above | |

for 80 per cent of all Web traffic having been assessed. Any site that relies on high volume traffic, including commercial sites, has an incentive to register as there is the option to **block** out all unregistered sites.

## Using blocker and filter software packages

There are a number of software packages available on the market that purport to add a further layer of protection. These packages are customisable and provide blockers for a much broader area than that offered by the browser options.

Take a look at the following.

> www.cyberpatrol.com
> CyberPatrol provides filtering based on Cyberlists with tailorable filtering levels. Time-setting and user-group profile features enable precise filtering for different users at specified times of the day.

www.cybersitter.com
Established in 1993 as a filter for AOL and CompuServe, CyberSitter expanded to the Net in 1995. It provides a menu of blocking options, including occult, online casinos, weapons dealers, banner ads and **MP3**s.

www.netnanny.com
Net Nanny provides a high degree of digital privacy and protection, and is available in a network version, NNPRO. Associated products include: PC Nanny (to prevent unauthorised access to files and specified areas of your computer) and Biopassword (whereby a unique algorithm measures your personal keystroke rhythm to create an electronic signature embedded within your logon and password).

www.safesurf.com
This uses the first ratings system developed for the Internet. It is also available via Internet Explorer.

www.surfwatch.com
As well as offering the usual blocks, Surf Watch (from JSB software) prohibits fifteen other areas: Astrology/Mysticism, Entertainment, Games, General News, Glamour and Intimate Apparel, Hobbies, Investments, Job Search, Motor Vehicles, Personals and Dating, Real Estate, Shopping, Sports, Travel and Usenet News.

## Freedom of speech and access to information

One of the problems with blocking and filtering software is that it also tends unintentionally to prohibit Websites containing references to items tangentially related to the undesired material, rather than just the material itself – therefore becoming a form of border-line censorship. Sites that may be prohibited include, for example, those dealing with medical problems such as breast and testicular cancer, references to reproduction, nude art, anti-drug information sites, gay resources material, HIV and AIDS information, sexual assault and rape information, and sexually transmitted diseases. It is easy to imagine how blocking and filtering software can be employed to support a suppressive agenda. Ironically, using Internet Explorer with the content advisor enabled led to difficulties entering ICRA's own Website during the course of writing this book, underlining the fact that these systems are by no means perfect.

One of the questions that has to be asked when the primary cause of concern is the protection of children, is how old they should be before the filter blocking is relaxed or stopped. For younger children, responsible parenting is perhaps one answer, with parents making the decision when to allow greater access. Parents can take measures other than using software filters to lessen the likely exposure of their children to potentially harmful material, such as surfing the Net together with younger children or placing the computer in a position in the home where the screen is clearly visible. You can always keep an eye on the History and Temporary Internet Files if you are concerned about what your children have been reading.

Discussing offensive material openly and educatively with older children, rather than just prohibiting it, may be another approach. Nothing could be more guaranteed to make something attractive to a child than banning it, and many kids are more aware of how to by-pass prohibitors than parents. Similarly, coaching children to be sensible when communicating over the Web by suggesting that they should not release sensitive information (such as their real names, addresses and telephone numbers when using chat rooms and e-mail) will also help. Being Net-wise is similar to being street-wise, and cosseted children may be more at risk than those who gain an understanding of the difficulties and dangers they may experience on the Net. Check out the Websites on page 72, which discuss some of these issues in more detail.

www.cdt.org
The Center for Democracy and Technology supports
user empowerment technology, but opposes
governmental attempts to set a national standard
defining inappropriate material or restricting
adult access.

www.censorware.org
The Censorware Project publishes essays about the
issues surrounding freedom of speech and Net access.

www.ciec.org
A site preserved from 1997 when the Citizens Internet
Empowerment Coalition – a broad group of Internet
users, library groups, publishers, ISPs and civil liberties
groups – fought for the future of first amendment and
free expression in the information age by opposing the
Communications Decency Act, which the US Supreme
Court found unconstitutional.

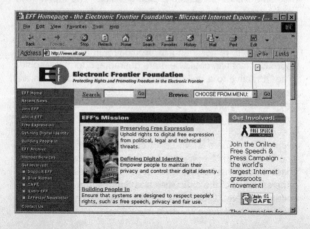

www.eff.org
The Electronic Frontier Foundation intelligently explores
concerns about the protection of rights and freedom of
expression on the Internet (see 'homepage' opposite).

www.peacefire.org
Formed in 1996, Peacefire represents the interests of
people under the age of eighteen in the debate over
freedom of speech on the Net. An interesting 'Blocked
site of the day' feature highlights what can go wrong with
blocking software. There's always another side to the
coin; Peacefire analyses each of the major censorware
packages in turn and points out what can go wrong
with them.

### Family-safe ISPs (USA)

In the USA, some ISPs are promoting themselves as being
family orientated, offering access to a sanitised filtered and
blocked version of the Internet.

Here are some examples.

    www.killporn.com
    www.safeisp.cjb.net
    www.smutstopper.com

Other related Websites include the two featured below and
those on the next page.

    www.childnet-int.org
    Childnet International looks after the interests of children
    using the Net.

    www.cyberangels.org
    Discussion and information site tackling the issues
    of online safety, cyber-stalking and laws relating to
    the Internet.

www.getnetwise.org
This is a coalition of Internet industry corporations and
public interest organisations brought together to inform
parents and families about the Internet. It contains very
useful advice for parents facing questions about the
Internet from children.

www.w3.org/PICS/
**PICS** (Platform for Internet Content Selection), based
at MIT, is the platform on which other rating services
and filtering software have been built. RSACi is
PICS-compliant.


## How to communicate better: Internet e-mail

Electronic mail is one of the original functions of the Internet
and is probably the main reason why most people become
Internet users. Increasingly, e-mail is a part of our everyday
lives. One of the most visible up-takes has been in interactive
media activities such as radio and TV phone-ins, and newspaper letters pages, where e-mail offers a viable alternative to the
telephone and the fax. Along with Website addresses, e-mail
addresses form the Internet contact details that appear on
marketing materials such as ads, brochures, newspapers and
magazines.

e-mail has been around for many years. Before it became
generally available via the Web, however, it was restricted to
those individuals who were part of a **LAN** (Local Area Network)
or a WAN (Wide Area Network), or those who used the Internet
in one of its original incarnations – as a form of academic
exchange and discussion. By the 1980s, as a result of the proliferation of the desktop personal computer, e-mail had
become part of office suite business application products and
was therefore used to link individuals within organisations in a
closed community.

As client/server technology advanced, it became possible to expand this community to include organisations or individuals connected with the host company. So, for example, a business was able to link up online with its partners, suppliers and customers using a series of inter-connections between computers. As the Internet is a large series of inter-connected computer networks, it's now possible to link everyone in that network system, and messages can be exchanged between them using e-mail software.

The main advantage that e-mail has over conventional mail is speed. It may occasionally take a few hours for your message to find its way to its destination, which may be as far away as the other side of the world or as close as the next room, but at its fastest this can be achieved in a just few minutes. Compared to the unreliable '**snail mail**' of old, this is clearly a major benefit. Also, it costs only as much as you have to pay for the phone connection, which may well be nothing.

e-mail does have limitations – for example, you are not able to physically enclose things with your message. Having said that, this can often be achieved if the material you want to enclose is digitised or can be scanned into your computer. In the past, e-mail systems were text-based, but now they have graphical user interfaces and can communicate images, sounds and videos.

### How do I get an e-mail address?

e-mail addresses are available from a whole host of sources and many sophisticates run multiple e-mail accounts provided by a number of different suppliers. This can be useful for separating the different types of mail you are likely to receive – for example, hobby or sports mail to one account, social mail to another, business mail to a third account and so on. However, if you run too many accounts things can get very confusing, not to mention time-consuming. For the initiate, it's best to start with one account, or maybe two, and develop from there. Your ISP should supply you with one 'or more' e-mail addresses. You'll be asked to select an e-mail address of your choice when you sign up. You can also get e-mail addresses from a variety of other sources: they are widely available on the Internet.

## About e-mail

Whichever e-mail option you choose, the composition of your address and the basic facilities on offer are likely to be very similar.

### The components of e-mail addresses

e-mail addresses are much less complex than Webpage URLs. A typical e-mail address will consist of three parts: the '@' sign, and information before and after it. For example:

Joe.Bloggs@iconbooks.co.uk

'Joe.Bloggs': this is the **username** of your account. It may not be your actual name, as you may prefer to use a nick-name or other word(s) as your username. You will use the username to **login** to your e-mail account. Other variations of the username could look like this:

JoeBloggs<br>
joebloggs<br>
joe_bloggs ... and so on.

'@': the ubiquitous 'at' sign, which appears in so many marketing guises these days. From being one of the least used signs on the computer keyboard, '@' has been elevated to one of the most significant. It links the account username with the domain name.

iconbooks.co.uk: this is the domain name, indicating the server that handles your incoming and outgoing e-mails. In this case, it is the same as the company name used on the Icon Books Website, but often the domain name may be the address of your ISP – for example, Freeserve. So, the address may look like this:

Jobloggs@freeserve.co.uk

## Using e-mail

e-mail systems are generally easy to use, and all of them tend to incorporate the following standard functions.

- They save an e-mail before it is sent in draft format.
- They keep a copy of the e-mail sent.
- They send to people other than the main recipient (carbon copy or .cc).
- They send to people other then the main recipient without the main recipient or carbon-copied recipients knowing (blind carbon copy or **.bcc**).
- They forward a received e-mail to someone else, with or without an appended message.
- They file received e-mails in folders.
- They send copies of an e-mail to multiple recipients.

How you use these facilities will vary according to your needs and wishes. Some systems allow you automatically to route e-mail from certain sources into pre-designated folders, effectively doing some of the filing for you. Like most things on the Net, it's best to get up and running, and work out which of these functions you will use most as you go along, rather than trying to adhere to a pre-planned system.

## Creating e-mails

To create a new e-mail click on 'Compose' or 'New Message' (or similar) and start typing; it's as simple as that. When you've finished typing your message, click 'Send'. Depending on the system you are using, you may get an acknowledgement on

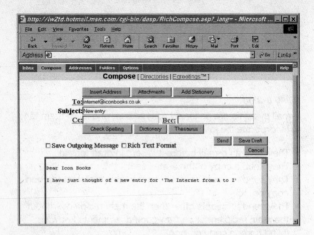

screen that the mail has been sent. If you requested to keep a copy you will find it in the appropriate 'Sent Mail' folder.

To respond to an e-mail, you have the option to use 'Reply'. This will create a response with the heading 'Re:' plus the title of the message to which you are responding. You have the option of including all of the original e-mail in your reply or just part of it. You can edit the message you received by highlighting the unwanted text, then cutting – like you would in a word processor. You have the option of appending your own message at the beginning of the e-mail. Alternatively, you may wish to respond to particular sections of the e-mail. You can do this by inserting your replies within the original text at lines decided by you. The original text will be differentiated from the new text you are adding by the e-mail program, usually using quote tags (a '>' at the beginning of each line of original text), so the person to whom you are replying won't get confused about who said what. You can also forward, and sometimes redirect, an e-mail you have received to an individual or a group. Forwarding means you add a comment of your own. Redirect simply re-sends the e-mail. This is one of the good things about e-mail, but it's also potentially one of the worst. Remember that everything you write to one person could potentially be sent to others either intentionally or otherwise – accidents do happen. So, take care what you write in an e-mail, and think about the consequences if someone other than the intended recipient happened to see it.

Another thing to consider is that e-mail systems within companies are easily monitored by the 'powers that be'. So, if you are concerned that your boss may be reading e-mails sent by you to friends, loved ones or the recruitment agency, and you want to avoid potential problems, consider what you write.

You can use your word processor in conjunction with your e-mail. This will enable you to spend more time on your messages, rather than being under the time pressure that may result if you have to pay for your Internet calls or if someone else is waiting to use the computer. You can type out a message in a word processing package such as Word, then cut and paste it into the **body** of the e-mail you are sending. You can also cut and paste from e-mail messages into a word processor file. Because of limited time online and e-mail storage space limitations, it is courteous to keep e-mails reasonably brief and attach long documents as separate files.

## Managing your e-mails

You will receive e-mails into an **'In' box**. From here you read them, then choose either to delete them, store them in a folder, or keep them in your 'In' box. The e-mails will be coded in some way indicating whether they have been read or not.

It's best to try to keep your e-mails up to date and sorted out. Be stern with yourself and delete as many as you can as often as you can, otherwise you'll find they build-up unnecessarily. In any case, it probably won't take you long to work out that you don't need to keep copies of many e-mails. The essence of the

Internet is its instantaneousness. Over-storing and archiving works against the grain of this dynamic environment. Every now and again there will be an e-mail you wish to keep for reference. For the rest, if you keep them for a few weeks and revisit them, you'll be amazed how the world has moved on.

## Signature files

This is effectively a store of your e-mail sign-off information, like the signature at the bottom of a letter. It is automated so you don't have to type it each time. It is up to you how you sign your e-mails. Some people use witty strap lines, quotations and even logo-like images, effectively creating their own marketing presence. Others just provide their office or house address details and telephone or fax number. You can be selective about when you add your **signature** files; for instance, you may want to think carefully before including details of your home address in your signature file when sending e-mails to people you don't know.

## Address books

Most e-mail systems allow you to create and maintain a directory of your e-mail contact addresses. Optimal information such as home and business addresses, telephone, fax and mobile numbers, and birthdays, can also be stored here. Nicknames can be allocated to each address. This allows you to quickly add e-mail addresses to your messages either by clicking on the appropriate nicknames from a menu, or by typing the nickname directly into the message 'To' box. The full e-mail address will usually be added automatically in both cases. Nicknames can also be allocated to group mailing lists.

## Personal mailing lists

You can create your own mailing lists using your **address book** directory. Personal mailing lists are useful when you want to send a message to several people simultaneously. You can create multiple group lists and contacts can be included in more than one group.

## Sending a Webpage as an e-mail.

Sending Webpages via e-mail is one of its most useful facilities. It takes the blurring of the boundary between the Web and e-mail to another level. Finding a Website of interest can be exciting; being able to send it to others is a joy. From the Webpage, there are two options: you can use the drop-down file menu 'Send', 'Page by e-mail', or click on the mail icon on the browser tool bar and 'Send Page'. Alternatively, you can send a Webpage address as a **live** link by selecting 'File', 'Send', 'Link by e-mail', or mail icon 'Send a link'.

## Sending file attachments

It's simple to attach computer files to e-mails. Most types of files can be sent via e-mail, including spreadsheets, word processor documents, graphics, sound and audio-visual files. The command is usually '**Attachments**' or 'Send File' … or something similar. You will then be asked to specify the file you want to attach. If you don't know its exact name, there may be a browse option for you to locate it within your computer file listings. Once located, it can take anything from a few seconds to a few minutes to attach, depending on the size of the file. You may then have the option to attach other files to the same message. Once you have completed the attachment process you are free to send the file (or files). Before doing so, you will usually have the option to write an e-mail message in the normal way, which will be delivered with the attachment.

Assuming the recipient of your e-mail has the correct soft-ware to view the type of file you have sent (this may be an issue for some of the more obscure audio-visual file formats), it will be a matter of detaching the file and saving it to disk or viewing it immediately. Saving to disk is usually the best option. If you are sending large attachments, it's always best to check that the recipient has the available disk space.

A downside of e-mails is that they are one of the most effective ways of spreading computer viruses. Attachments such as Word files can sometimes contain viruses, and while receiving an e-mail with an attachment containing a **virus** is not enough to contaminate your computer, downloading the attachment may be. One way of beating this problem is by scanning attachments with a virus checker before downloading. Many e-mail packages include virus-checkers that offer a scanning option, which you should always take. For example, Hotmail automatically scans all attachments using the virus checker **McAfee**.

## e-mail and the spread of viruses

One of the Internet's founding principles and still one of its great strengths is that it is an open system with no true regulation. Unfortunately, this means that the Net is also open to cyber-terrorism in the form of virus software, which strikes unpredictably and with great effect causing e-pidemics. Viruses can range from those causing short-term mischievous problems limited to individual computers to potentially disastrous strains causing whole systems to collapse. Viruses now spread extremely quickly because of the huge growth in the number of servers in the ever-expanding Internet network.

The Melissa virus of 1999 resulted in many consumers taking steps to protect their computers with anti-virus software packages. Worm-type viruses that grow organically spreading out through e-mail systems are currently the vogue. A recent virus to strike was the 'Love Bug', so called as messages were headed I LOVE YOU. Dubbed 'the killer from Manila', the virus is thought to have emanated from the Philippines, and quickly surpassed 'Melissa' in the number of machines and the speed with which it attacked, bringing down many e-mail systems globally at the beginning of May 2000.

This particular virus reincarnated itself in new strains, including one that appeared in e-mail 'In' boxes as an e-mail joke promising to be 'very funny', another purporting to be a Mother's Day order confirmation and a third with a heading in Lithuanian, translating as 'Let's go for a coffee tonight'. The virus targeted users of Microsoft Outlook running under Windows, and deleted image and music files before mailing itself to every destination in victim's address books. The Houses of Parliament, the Pentagon and the White House were all reported to have been affected, along with millions of other users and business e-mail users across the world. The bug was assessed to have cost business millions of pounds in fixes and lost trade due to computer **downtime**.

It was interesting to note the concern with which this was reported in medias new and old, a reflection of how all-pervasive e-mail systems have become in the global economy. Anti-virus detection software developers reacted quickly to post downloadable updates to their software on the Internet in an attempt to hold the spread of the virus.

Precautions that can be taken include ensuring that all e-mail attachments are scanned before downloading and taking extreme care when downloading software from unknown sources. Anti-virus software packages that can be installed on your computer system include McAfee and Sophos, Dr Solomon's AntiVirus and **Norton AntiVirus**. These should be kept up to date by downloading from the official developer sites as new viruses appear frequently. Check out the following Websites.

www.mcafee.com
This Website is now personalised to each user's experience and requires that you register.

www.norton.com
Latest information from Symantec about its internet security and protection software.

www.uk.sophos.com
This is a well-designed Website with product to match
from Europe's leading developer of corporate anti-virus
**solutions**.

www.antivirus.com
Trend Micro Inc provides enterprise-wide virus
protection tools.

## Which type of e-mail should I choose?

e-mail systems fall into two categories: **POP3**-based and Web-
based. Your ISP is likely to provide POP3 e-mail, which has the
reputation of being **robust** and reliable. Web-based systems
offer the advantages of **portability** and flexibility. There's
nothing to stop you having accounts with both types of system.
With POP3, you can be restricted to your own computer, where
the e-mails are archived and stored using e-mail management
tools. Web-based e-mails, however, enable you to use any
Internet-connected computer to access your account via the
browser.

### POP3 e-mail systems

When you register for a free POP3 e-mail account you are
setting up a post-box with the supplier, who will retain your
e-mail messages for you on a remote server until you collect
them. In order to read your mail you need to use software
that works with your browser and will arrange for the downloading of your mail on to your own computer. Once the
messages have been downloaded, they are deleted from the
server.

### e-mail management software

Your browser will usually incorporate a piece of software to
manage your e-mail accounts. In the case of Internet Explorer,

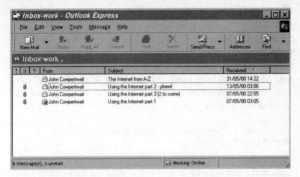

this is known as Outlook Express. For Navigator, it's Messenger. If you want to maintain a degree of distance from your browser supplier there are alternative packages produced by independent developers, such as **Eudora** and **Pegasus**. These can be downloaded from the Internet free of charge.

e-mail management software is resident on your computer's hard drive. It enables you to direct all your individual e-mail accounts to one location, where you can read and manage them centrally. The software enables you to **sort** and organise your e-mails into electronic customisable folders, grouping relevant messages together. You can also read and compose offline, connecting to the Internet only when you wish to send and receive messages, potentially saving Internet call charges and freeing up your telephone line.

You can send an e-mail at any time, even when you are surfing the Web, by clicking on the Mail icon button on the browser toolbar. This will produce a Compose box linked to your e-mail management system.

The real benefit of using computer-based e-mail management tools is the storage facilities they provide compared with Web-based systems. You can receive, store and archive e-mails limited only by your computer's capacity.

*Checking POP3 accounts on the Web*

Theoretically, you now no longer need an e-mail management package to check your POP3 accounts. A number of services have been developed that allow you to pick up messages via the Web anywhere in the world. These can be useful if you are absent from your computer for a short period and don't have a Web-based e-mail account, but they are not particularly reliable and lack sophistication, for the moment anyway.

*Web-based e-mail systems*

Web-based e-mail systems combine in one facility the services provided separately by an ISP e-mail address and a computer-based e-mail management system such as Outlook Express. Instead of getting your address from one provider and your e-mail management tools from another, both services are provided by one source.

Web-based e-mail allows you to check your mail from more than one computer. As mail is stored centrally on the **Web e-mail** supplier's server, you don't even need to own a computer or have a contract with an ISP. You can check your e-mail account at any time from any computer that is connected to the Internet, wherever it is located. This is why services like Hotmail are highly popular with people on the move, such as international travellers or students who don't want to be tied to their college accounts. Visitors to any Internet café will note that the majority of those connected to the Web are using e-mail, making contact with family and friends. Internationally, many libraries and tourist offices provide Internet access points, and there are numerous other Internet access options.

Some people adopt Web-based e-mail accounts because of issues of privacy and security. If you are currently sharing your computer with other people, Web-based e-mail offers improved security. An e-mail management program stores your e-mails on the hard disk of your computer. With Web-based e-mail systems, unless you have chosen to download your messages into an e-mail management program, they will be located on the e-mail host's server, which lessens the possibility of other people gaining access to them.

If you use a company e-mail at work for personal e-mails, as well as confusing business and social activities, you are also leaving yourself open to possible surveillance by the company. Establishing a Web-based e-mail for your personal use will separate business from pleasure, and achieve an increased level of privacy.

One of the problems associated with ISP mail accounts is that if you change your ISP, or if ISPs merge and change names, your e-mail address will probably change. This brings obvious problems, such as having to inform all your contacts of your new e-mail details. Similarly, you will probably loose access to an e-mail account that is provided by your place of work or study when you change jobs of finish your academic pursuits. Web-mail should not carry these potential difficulties as accounts purport to be permanent and are transportable. Wherever you work, study or travel your e-mail address stays the same.

An advantage of Web-based accounts is that you have the option, but not the necessity, of using a computer-based e-mail management system, which means you can access your Web e-mail account through the management system and pull-down and store on your computer important e-mails that you wish to keep or when storage capacity becomes an issue with your Web-based system. Many Web-based e-mail systems now offer the option of redirecting your **POP** mail accounts to your Web account. By doing this you can also use Web-based mail as a central collecting point for other e-mail addresses you may have, further enhancing the attraction of Web-based systems.

While most e-mail systems, whether they are Web-based or computer-based, have similar facilities, some Web-based mail

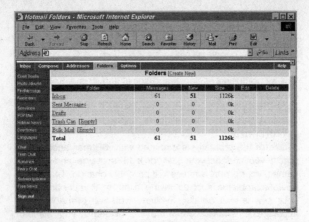

systems also provide an **auto-reply** service. This service will automatically reply on your behalf with a message written by you if there are any periods when you will not be able to access your account. If you are on the move, another very useful feature of Web-based e-mail systems is the 'address book' feature. If you keep this up to date, you will always have access to contact information, so lost address books will become a thing of the past.

One of the arguments against Web-based e-mails is that the adverts they carry are annoyingly intrusive. Try out the systems before you agree with this conclusion. After a time you'll probably hardly notice the limited banner ads. Another issue with Web-based e-mail services is security. There have been a few noticeable hacks into Web-based e-mail systems recently, so security clearly remains an issue for some of these systems. However, one assumes that with every significant hack security improves.

A word of warning: no computer system is failsafe, and that includes Web-based e-mail systems. While writing this book, the author suffered ten days of not being able to access his account with the most popular **Webmail** package. Access was eventually restored, but a number of e-mails containing important information were not, despite the host company's assurances that all received messages were restored. The moral is where important information is concerned take copies and back ups.

As the costs of being online decrease, Web-based e-mails are likely to grow in popularity as users seek to lessen their dependence on computer-based systems, preferring the flexibility that Web-based storage offers. To keep Web-based accounts alive and current, most operators insist that accounts are visited at least once within a fairly generous minimum period, usually between ninety days and six months.

One drawback of Web-based systems is the limited storage they offer. For example, Hotmail provides only 2 MB of space. When this becomes full it starts deleting e-mails. However, other Web-based e-mail services such as O2O offer up to 5 MB, which, it claims, is enough to store '1,000 e-mails' – although that will depend on the size of the individual e-mails. One of the disciplines developed by using only Web-based e-mail systems is a ruthless approach to deleting old e-mails due to the stringent memory limitations.

If you are using a Web-based e-mail system you can have the best of both worlds, managing your messages from within your computer-based system when you have access to your own computer, and using the e-mail accounts from their Web locations if you are on the move.

## *So, which type of e-mail should I choose?*

It depends on your individual circumstances and the hardware facilities at your disposal. If you do not have a computer of your own and you access the Web at work, college or through Internet cafés, then a Web-based e-mail system would seem to be the best option. If you do have your own computer, then a combination of Web-based and POP mail accounts would cover all requirements, providing maximum flexibility and improved privacy.

### e-mail developments

Everything on the Internet changes quickly, but, at the time of writing, e-mail systems seem to be developing faster than most things, and a number of the longer-established systems are undergoing upgrading and redesigning with many new facilities being added. There's further evidence of the merging nature of much of the Internet's functionality with Mailing Lists, News-groups, and Messaging and Chat facilities now becoming part of the services offered by e-mail systems.

### Mail forwarding services

Mail forwarding services (such as BigFoot) forward messages to an existing mail address. Their only real advantage is that they let you select a new, possibly more permanent, e-mail name and address to the one you already have. If you change POP3 e-mail accounts frequently there is an advantage in that the name you give out to those who want to send you mes-sages remains the same, as you simply change the address to which your mail is forwarded. However, as you are placing another link in the mail chain, there may be delays in getting the mail to you, and you are also subject to a greater margin of error relating to network or service problems.

### Computer-based e-mail management tools

You might like to check out the following.

Eudora (www.eudora.com)
This respected program from Qualcomm is now available in three modes: Sponsored, a full-featured option that includes a series of static on-screen ads; Paid, the same as Sponsored, but without the ads; and Light, which

includes no ads, but has a reduced a number of features. **Macintosh** versions are available.

Messenger (www.netscape.com)
This is provided with Netscape's Navigator browser and offers a high degree of integration.

Outlook Express (www.msn.com)
This is provided with Microsoft's Internet Explorer; it is the e-mail manager of choice for many Microsoft devotees.

Pegasus (www.pmail.com)
This is a long-standing independent alternative.

## Web-based e-mail systems

The following are worth further scrutiny.

020 (www.020.co.uk)
This is a new stylish tagline-free service, which allows you to collect mail from existing accounts and reply as though the mail is sent via them. Storage of 5 MB is available.

Another (www.another.com)
Make e-mail fun. Choose your own username, *and* select up to 20 different domain names.

Eudora Webmail (www.eudoramail.com)
This is a Web-based version of the Eudora desktop system.

Hotmail (www.hotmail.com)
This is the largest Web-based e-mail system. Now part of Microsoft, it features close integration with Outlook Express. Beware: there is a limitation of 2 MB storage.

Hushmail (www.hushmail.com)
If you're worried about the security of e-mails, or your

privacy, this service may be of interest. It provides a fully encrypted system within which users can send secure e-mails to each other.

Mail City (www.mailcity.lycos.com)
This is part of the Lycos network. It provides 4 MB storage.

Yahoo! Mail (www.yahoo.com)
This is Web-mail provided courtesy of Yahoo!

### Other e-mail services

You may also like to consider the following.

www.bigfoot.co.uk
This provides a permanent e-mail address, backed up by forwarding and distribution services.

www.e-mailaddresses.com
This independent site provides a great list of e-mail services, with links and lots of interesting user comments. It includes details about POP3 Web-based services.

## Spam, glorious spam

It's likely that you'll receive a lot of '**spam**', which is Netspeak for unsolicited e-mails suggesting you visit other Websites or take up certain offers. Inevitably, these e-mails are selling a service or product.

Spam has become such a problem that certain e-mail services now employ spam-blocking techniques to enable you to filter out unwanted mail. Hotmail, for example, has recently been upgraded to include an Inbox Protector, which siphons off spam mail items and places them in a Bulk **Mailbox** where you have the option to browse the incoming messages or place them straight in the Trash can for disposal. These messages are automatically deleted after thirty days – whether they have been read or not. As well as being a useful device, this will protect you from exceeding Hotmail's 2 MB memory limitation due to unwanted spam. Eudora Webmail offers a similar facility whereby you can filter off all mail except that received from pre-approved addresses.

Another way of ensuring spam does not interfere with the daily management of your e-mail accounts is to establish a spam-friendly account. This would be a separate account to the one you use for your daily messages from friends, associates and colleague. When you download software, MP3 files or anything else from the Web, you will usually be asked for an e-mail address. This will be used quite legitimately to send you details of the next software product update or the latest multi-media site that you may be interested in, for example. However, sometimes such e-mail addresses are made available to e-mail distribution lists for spamming purposes, with the result that, along with useful product and service information messages, you may also receive unwanted or unsavoury e-mails. By retaining an e-mail address specifically for these types of messages you will be in a position to stop them polluting your everyday e-mail use.

## Finding e-mail addresses

If you don't know someone's e-mail address, there are a number of directories, often called people finders, that purport to be able to track down your long-lost friends, erstwhile colleagues and forgotten aunts. However, these vary in their effectiveness. It may be that the world of e-mail is so volatile, with people switching addresses and adding new ones so frequently, that it's almost impossible to keep track. One of the difficulties is that the search has to assume that individuals are registered under their real names, whereas this is often not the case. People can use a number of aliases, especially when contacting news and discussion groups. Your mail management software may have links to e-mail databases and most of the significant search engines also have dedicated people finder search options. If you do want to locate someone you could try the following.

Yahoo! People Search (www.yahoo.co.uk)
WhoWhere Internet Directory Search
(www.whowhere.lycos.com)
Bigfoot Internet Directory Search (www.uk.bigfoot.com)

## e-mail culture

e-mail has created a new means of communicating. It's different to conventional letter or memo writing and it's less interactive than the telephone. There's much written about the styles of e-mail writing, suggesting that there exists a special e-mail argot. Well, if you want to include **smileys** such as :-) (happy) or :-( (sad), or TLAs (Three Letter Acronyms) such as BFN (Bye For Now) or IMO (In My Opinion), that's up to you. e-mail can be as formal, as casual or as Web-hip as you wish. Like all forms of communication, what you say and how you say it will depend on whom you are communicating with and will vary accordingly.

The sense of distance and anonymity that e-mail can sometimes engender leads some users to indulge in 'flaming' or creating 'flamograms'. This is writing uninhibited, angry, aggressive e-mails. This is not to be advised, particularly as e-mails are so forwardable. It tends to be the aggressor who looks worst in these situations. Using all capitals in e-mails should be avoided as well, as it tends to make the sender appear VERY AGGRESSIVE!

e-mail can become pretty compulsive, particularly if you work from home. The computer tends to sit on the desk beckoning you to open your e-mail account. Try and be disciplined about using your e-mail, perhaps establishing a few set periods during the day when you check your account, otherwise you can find yourself constantly monitoring your account and letting e-mail consume your working hours.

## Mailing lists, newsgroups, chat and instant messaging

Once they have mastered the rudiments of the Web and e-mail, some Internet devotees turn their attention to the text-based interactive communication aspects of the Internet. Many people never use these mass information exchange and debating forums, but those who do sometimes develop a dedication to them verging on addiction.

It's worthwhile outlining the distinctions between mailing lists, newsgroups, chat facilities and instant messaging.

- Mailing lists: these usually consist of closed networks of individuals who communicate by e-mail and all receive the same messages in their e-mail 'In' boxes. Each e-mail sent by every member of the list is copied to everyone else in the list. To join a list you **subscribe** by submitting your details and engage by either just receiving all the e-mails or receiving them and responding.
- Newsgroups: generally, these are debating forums where people who are interested in the same topics 'post' comments via e-mail. Others in the group may respond to posted comments by **posting** their own e-mail on the same subject. Newsgroup debate is carried out on the newsgroup site, rather than via e-mail.
- Chat: this is carried out in chat 'rooms', a section of the Internet made available for two or more individuals to indulge in live real-time exchanges, again using e-mail facilities.
- Instant messaging: similar to the Short Message Services (SMS) but allows text messages to be sent via mobile phones in that it allows instant short-burst communication.

Like many things on the Net, the divisions between activity areas are being broken down, and you may now find newsgroup discussions and chat rooms available as a facility of your Web browser, e-mail management tool and sometimes Webmail suppliers. The notion of 'Web communities' is currently being promoted at www.communities.msn.co.uk/home by Microsoft. These are defined as 'A private area on the Internet where a group of people can meet, chat, post photos and share information', and seem to be aiming to be a more family friendly space that covers some of the functions of mailing lists, discussion groups and chat.

Let's take a look at each area in more detail.

## Mailing lists

Creating e-mail mailing lists is one of the oldest activities of the Internet. In its original guise, the Net was a forum for the easy exchange of information between the limited groups of individuals who were online, many of whom were part of the academic community. So, many of the longer-standing lists tend to cover esoteric subjects of great interest to just a few people. However, while these types of list still thrive, the list arena has opened up and you can now find mailing lists on just about every topic.

Mailing lists can be a lively interactive means of exchanging views, opinions and information. Alternatively, they may be based on a newsletter or bulletin service from one individual or a small group, aimed at keeping list members informed, but not necessarily soliciting a response.

Joining commercial mailing lists can be a good way of keeping up to date with topics and events. There are mailing lists covering a wide variety of subjects. Increasingly, the marketing departments of organisations are becoming aware of the effectiveness of solicited electronic mail as a means of keeping their contact base informed. The Barbican Arts Centre in London, for example, provides an electronic mailing list to keep audiences aware of events and performances it is holding. As with a traditional mailing list you have the option to receive information or not and can remove yourself from the mailing list.

There are many different types of mailing list. While some are driven by commercial interests, others are simply a means of like-minded people keeping each other informed. These are sometimes referred to as e-groups. Others are driven by the desire to sell you something. This is the area that gets into borderline spam. While spam is generally unsolicited, opt-in lists are those where someone has requested to receive information. Just as with traditional mail, there are list-broking companies who specialise in creating and maintaining these types of list and making them available to organisations for marketing purposes.

You can find pre-existing mailing lists on almost any topic. There are a number of sites that specialise in listing lists, which may vary from interactive discussions by mail to regular newsletters. However, if you join any active lists you are likely to receive a fair number of e-mails which you may find overwhelming. Many list sites let you sample the list via archives before you join. This is also an alternative way of investigating a topic without being submerged by an avalanche of e-mails. Used sensibly, mailing lists can prove a useful means of keeping abreast of developments in areas that you are particularly interested in. Some mailing list sites also contain advice about setting up your own open mailing lists.

You may like to check out the following mailing list Websites.

www.lsoft.com
CataList, a list of public **LISTSERV** Internet lists.

www.onelist.com
This is a free service that allows you to construct and

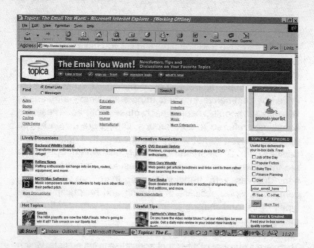

manage new, or join existing, non-commercial e-mail groups. It offers 20 MB of free disk space to store archives and files, and is available in international languages.

www.topica.com (see above)
This is a modern-looking directory-style list service, including Hot Topics instant opinions mail lists. Topica has recently acquired Liszt, the original list listing site.

## Newsgroups

Newsgroups are also referred to as 'discussion forums' or **'Usenet'**. Not all newsgroups are Usenet newsgroups, though. Many more discussion forums are coming online, and Usenet is just one of the newsgroup forums that now exist. Estimates suggest there are between 60,000 and 80,000 open forum discussion groups available.

Newsgroups are groups of people getting together on the Internet to discuss things that are of mutual interest. The original spirit was one of co-operation and collaboration, and this still holds true for many of the groups, although others seem to relish heated exchanges and in-fighting. Taking part in a newsgroup is a bit like instigating a conversation with a stranger in a bar; you go down all the politics, religion and philosophy routes, and gradually other people join in wanting to have their say. You can have a good debate and learn something along the way.

The title 'newsgroups' is a bit of a misnomer. Newsgroups are not concerned with the managed political and marketing 'news' that emanates from the spin-doctors and PR agencies in the general media sense of the word, nor with the 'world news' of events and happenings; rather, they are open platforms for free information and opinion exchange between individuals.

The idea is that information can be made available to everyone without the controls, restriction and censorship that we experience through the bureaucracies, corporate and political controls, and consumerist manipulations of nation, state and society.

What this leads to, of course, is a bit of a free-for-all, although to claim that the newsgroup environment is totally anarchic is over-stating the situation.

Whenever restrictions are lifted you have to take the rough with the smooth and, not surprisingly, there are a significant number of newsgroups that deal with the social taboos of sex, violence and drugs, although if they detect them, some ISPs remove these from their servers.

Newsgroups are divided into topic areas by category name or **hierarchy**, indicating the very broad subject matter they cover. The category name appears at the beginning of the newsgroup name. The list on page 100 shows just some of the categories in use.

alt.
This stands for alternative and was set up in response to the controls that were imposed on some Usenet groups. It tends to cover some of the more wayward sites, including **pornography** groups.

biz.
This relates to business products and services.

comp.
This includes discussions relating to computers and technology, and incorporates consumer advice.

humanities.
Here you'll find both professional and amateur discussions relating to humanities and the arts.

misc.
This indicates miscellaneous discussions about anything not covered by the other categories.

news.
This contains information about the Usenet network.

rec.
A mixture including recreational sports, hobbies, music and so on.

sci.
Professional and lay scientific discussions.

soc.
Social issues, society and socialising.

talk.
Topical debates about current issues.

There are also many regional forums covering many country areas as well as individual US states, also delineated by category names.

Anyone can watch active newsgroups without having to take part or subscribe, a practice known as 'lurking'. In fact, according to the statistics, lurking is what most people do in newsgroups. While the bigger newsgroups have hundreds of participants posting messages, thousands of readers may be enjoying the debate passively, without posting responses. Lurking allows you to see if the discussion contains information useful to you and whether the tone of the newsgroup appeals, if you are thinking about joining in. Alternatively, like the majority, you may just wish to see what's being said.

While most newsgroups are interactive, some are just pin boards where information is posted and read. Some newsgroups are also used for exchanging files of all sorts. If you do download files of any kind from usergroups, you should first take the precaution of scanning them with a virus detector (see pages 83–4). Most newsgroups are unmoderated and don't require membership or fees. Moderated newsgroups are administered by an individual who reviews postings to

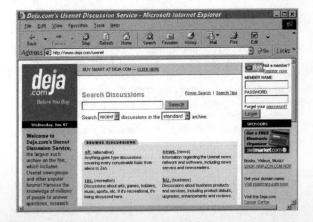

de-duplicate material that's made available, generally manages things, and may occasionally perform a kind of minor censorship role by deleting any inappropriate postings.

News servers host thousands of newsgroups, each of which contains collections of messages. You can join in Usenet newsgroups only if your ISP links to the news server that hosts the newsgroup in which you are interested. When you request to enter a Usenet newsgroup you will be asked for details of your ISP's **NNTP** (Network News Transfer Protocol) server, information that should be available from your ISP's help section.

While you can enter newsgroups directly from the Web via newsgroup search sites, you can also use Outlook Express or Messenger as your newsreader to display a newsgroup. When you use Outlook Express for this purpose for the first time details of all the newsgroups available to you via your ISP's server will be downloaded. These may run into tens of thousands and downloading them will therefore take a few minutes. An alternative to using your e-mail management software's facilities is to use an independent newsreader such as FreeAgent (www.forteinc.com).

Newsgroups are effectively interactive bulletin boards. Messages are posted to a newsgroup, which sends the message to the many news servers that carry that particular newsgroup. People then respond to that message by posting more messages and a response **thread** is created. An **archive** logs all the responses to a particular message, which are visible for everyone to see, and a thread chart shows the pattern of interaction. Each thread has a heading, which should give at least some indication of the topic.

Reading the vast amount of material posted can be a time-consuming activity and there are tools that will help you find the messages containing the information in which you are most interested. As with e-mails, you can read newsgroup messages offline by transferring them to your computer, saving online costs and releasing the phone line. You may choose to synchronise only **message headers**. This will give you the opportunity to select the **header** topics you think are most relevant, then download the messages associated with these for later reading offline.

AOL has good facilities for searching for, and browsing, newsgroups (provided by Deja.com), including an author posting history, enabling you to see the subjects on which a particular author has sent postings and how many postings have been made on each. The more prolific posters' tallies often run into many thousands. Search facilities are available to guide you to newsgroups covering relevant topics in Outlook Express, and many search engines and directories also provide search facilities specifically for newsgroups.

You may like to check out the following newsgroup Websites.

www.deja.com/usenet/
This is a large archive of discussion forums.

www.tile.net
As well as maintaining a list of Usenet newsgroups, tile also maintains a directory of mailing lists.

## Chat and instant messaging

While e-mails sometimes reach their destination in just a few minutes, they can take much longer. With chat, communication is generally still text-based via the keyboard, but it is virtually instantaneous. You are effectively carrying out a real-time textual conversation with a group of people on screen.

**Chat** is pretty ubiquitous on the Internet. Many **portal** and entertainment sites provide online chats with celebrities, perhaps tied in with a television programme, or a new film or music release. Generally controlled in a traditional way with a mediator who intervenes between you and the special guest to select which comments and questions to pass on, these sessions are a slowed-down online equivalent of the studio audience question-and-answer sessions you see on TV.

Conferences and chat forums are often used in business circles, and online services such as CompuServe are traditionally strong in these areas. Businesses often also use live audio and video links in conjunction with online conferencing. However, live chat has moved into the mainstream of the Web and there are now copious opportunities for online chat available to everyone.

There are two main types of chat: Inter Relay Chat (IRC) and Web-chat. Most real-time chat is carried out with IRC channels, although Web-chat is fast becoming the more obvious choice. IRC requires a piece of software to be downloaded, such as **mIRC** (www.mirc.co.uk). Once you've downloaded mIRC, it will offer you a choice of chat channels.

With Web-chat you just locate a site, sign on and go. There's so many options of places on the Web to chat that it's difficult to suggest one, but Yahoo! Chat is easy to find and quick to sign up to. Try typing 'Web chat' into a search engine for more locations.

In a chat situation users tend to protect themselves by using false names, or nick-names, rather than reveal their true identities, unless they're communicating with people they already know. Chat can range from the fairly superficial to the aggressively offensive. However, chat is increasingly becoming less of a computer nerd's or teenager's plaything and is being adopted by business types as they realise its potential as an effective communications tool.

A typical chat-room (or channel), would have between ten and twelve chatterers connected together exchanging short, usually one-line, messages. The nature of the exchange tends to be fast, conducted in Webspeak and can sometimes be confusing. Needless to say, this environment does not necessarily lend itself to in-depth debate. However, it is sometimes possible for two or three people to indulge in serious discussion in an otherwise uninhabited chat-room. Unfortunately there's always the possibility that someone else will join you.

An alternative way to have a more private one-to-one or small group conversation is via Instant Messaging. This has grown in popularity over the last year and is now available as an extra bolt-on to many other services, including MSN Hotmail and Yahoo!. It involves downloading a simple piece of software that signals to you that your contacts are online. For the present, mostly you'll only be able to contact people who are linked up to the same service as you. For example, MSN Messenger users cannot have an instant message chat with Yahoo! Messenger users. Instant messaging is quick and easy to use, and some services also include voice messages and chat. You can choose whether to broadcast that you are generally available for a chat with anyone or limit this information to your own contacts.

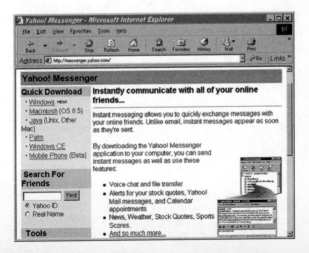

Check out the following Websites for instant messaging services.

AOL Instant Messaging (www.aol.com/aim)
ICQ (web.icq.com)
ichat (www.ichat.com)
MSN Messenger (www.msn.co.uk)
PowWow (www.powwow.com)
Yahoo!Messenger (www.messenger.yahoo.com)

# SEARCHING THE INTERNET

The **Internet** is a major source of information about almost everything. Indeed, it is estimated to have between 800 million and one billion pages of publicly accessible information, so if you are interested in something, whatever it is, the chances are that somewhere on the Internet you will be able to find useful material. As the Internet expands, more and more information is uploaded. This information takes many different forms and shapes. Locating and tracking relevant material has become one of the primary skills needed to use the Internet successfully – hence the proliferation of hundreds of free search **tools** to help you achieve this.

## Search tools

There are a number of different types of tool available on the Internet to help you find information relating to specific areas of interest. All of them allow users to search for keywords or phrases to assist in their searches, although the *method* of locating the relevant information may be different. Undoubtedly, new and alternative ways of searching the **World Wide Web** are currently being developed. For the moment though, the search tools roughly fall into four types.

- **Search engines**.
- **Directories**.
- **Multi-search tools**.
- **Meta-search tools**.

*Search engines*

Search engines are the driving force behind information retrieval on the Internet. They search the full text of **Webpages** automatically and are the main means by which users will, initially at least, locate information on the Web. Search engines do not usually search Webpages alone; they also visit other parts of the Internet (such as **discussion groups**) in search of relevant references.

Search engines constantly collect data using **Net**-scouring **programs** variably referred to as '**spiders**', '**crawlers**', '**bots**' or '**robots**'. These computer programs roam the Net looking for new and updated Webpages. Originators of **Websites** submit the address of the site **homepage** to the search engines together with keyword summaries of **site** contents (**meta tags**). These provide the starting point for the bots, which go on to examine the content of other Websites linked to the submitted sites. The **links** to the secondary link-sites are then examined, and then tertiary links … and so on, to generate an ongoing organically spreading data collection process. The location, title and **contents** of each Website are indexed and added to the search engine's mass of data.

Search engines try to find instances of individual words or phrases (known as the search term). It only takes a matter of seconds for the search engine to deliver a list of Internet sites, ranked by relevance, in which it has identified the presence of the requested search term. The resulting hit list may contain a few, or more likely, hundreds, possibly thousands, of Websites.

An increasing number of these 'hits' seem to have little relevance to the search terms, which may be the result of corrupt meta tagging, whereby in their summary submissions originators include words that are only tangentially relevant to the site's content in an attempt to divert more users to their sites. In order to reduce the number of hits, the search engine may provide options to narrow or broaden the search by, for example, searching only the Web, or limiting searches to sites emanating from a specific geographical or national region, such as Canada or Australia.

Each search engine has an individual way of pulling together the data to which it refers when searching, and will also have a unique way of indexing it. So it's unlikely that the same search terms will deliver an identical result from any two search engines. As each search engine has its own strengths and weaknesses, it's worth sampling a few different ones to find out which most closely suit your needs. You can use as many or as few as you like. Short cuts can be created by adding them to **Favorites** or **Bookmarks** (see page 55).

Several different search engines are currently available. Many of those that have been around since the Web increased in popularity in the mid-1990s are being upgraded to cope with the increase in information and are being redesigned for easier use. The engines are trying to differentiate themselves from each other, so a few varying approaches are being tried out. We're concerned here primarily with search engines designed for Internet use on PCs. **Apple** computers have their own dedicated search engine – Sherlock 2 – which now comes as part of the **Mac operating system**. Those listed below are just a sample, but include most of the more familiar names.

www.alltheweb.com
'Fast' is a search tool using new technology developed in conjunction with **Dell** that promises to **index** the whole Web rather than just a portion, and claims to search 300 million Webpages in under half a second. Fast supports thirty-one languages and includes specific **MP3**, **multimedia** and **FTP** search options.

www.altavista.com
A comprehensive and popular **portal** site with both full-text search and directory facilities providing access to the impressive Babel Fish which translates words, phrases and entire Websites into Spanish, French,

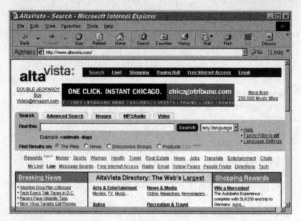

German, Portuguese and Italian. Now part of the CMGI network, as is Lycos.

www.ask.com
www.ask.co.uk
www.ajkids.com

Three **Ask Jeeves!** enquiry sites that forsake keywords, Boolean strings and directory navigation trees to use plain English questions to retrieve evaluated data for the US, UK and kids. Ask Jeeves! compares your questions to the nearest matching questions in its database and also provides material from Web search engines, although it can be a bit hit and miss. The UK site is a joint venture with independent television companies Carlton Communications and Granada Media Group.

Britannica.com
Search engine based around *Encyclopaedia Britannica*. As well as searching Websites and the encyclopaedia itself, this site also trawls magazine and book lists. It is

framed within a standard-style portal offering news, sports and the ubiquitous weather reports.

www.deja.com
Provides a 'precision buying service' with access to information to influence purchasing decisions. Also, and somewhat incongruously, Deja is the destination if you want good access to some 35,000 **Usenet newsgroups** and 18,000 discussion forums. Old democratic values and new commercial aspects of the Internet united under one site.

www.excite.com
Popular portal with an engine that searches conceptually, extending searches to look for ideas closely related to **query** words. The site also includes directory channels. Many international versions, including Australia, Canada, France, Germany and Sweden, are available.

www.euroseek.com (see page 111)
Refreshingly Euro-centric portal, search engine and
directory offering searches in thirty-nine different
European languages. Offers a blended global and
national outlook. Searches can be delimited by
national boundaries (for example, Slovenia or Turkey),
international regions (for example, Scandinavia) and
special domains (such as 'military' or 'government').
The site also covers the US and Asia.

www.findwhat.com
One of a new breed of search engines that charges for
entries. This naturally results in searches dominated by
commercial enterprises trying to sell you something,
which is fine if that's what you are looking for.
Organisations pay for a guaranteed appearance
of their site under certain subject categories.

www.google.com
New breed of non-portal search engine that takes into
account links to other sites when ranking. Simplifies the
search process and seems to deliver the results.

www.goto.com
Search engine facilities and directory-based listings.
Companies can pay to be ranked higher in the listings.

www.hotbot.com/hotbot.lycos.com
Respected portal-style directory and search site which
is part of the Lycos network. A database for over 110
million fully indexed Web documents, which is refreshed
in its entirety every month. Sophisticated advance
search features.

www.lycos.com
A self-styled '**hub**' site providing controlled searches
such as Lycos Pro, MP3, Multi-media, FTP and

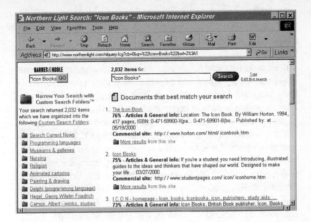

Listening Room. Offers links to a comprehensive
network of associated sites. Part of the CMGI
network.

www.northernlight.com (see above)
Leading search and research engine with exclusive
access to over 6,000 full-text publications. Dynamically
groups results into meaningful category folders and
also provides a useful alert facility whereby
changes to Websites of interest are notified to
you by e-mail.

www.webtop.com
Business-orientated professional search tool using
innovative drag and drop technology that allows you
to search the Web with WebCheck using text
extracted from your own documents and matches
against a computer-compiled concept
database.

## *Directories*

The way in which directories group together Websites under thematic headings means that they tend to be better at finding Websites about specific topics, while search engines can be more useful for locating all the references to a particular theme, object or idea, regardless of what form they take and where they may be located. Also, as the process of compiling a search engine's data is computerised it is likely to be more up to date, but less focused, than that contained in directories.

Data within directories is more structured than it is within search engines. Directories are usually formatted hierarchically into vertical Internet directories or category listings, under general headings such as Business & Commerce, Entertainment, Leisure & Recreation, Science and so on. These headings are shown in the directories' homepage. Sub-headings are reached by clicking on one of the general headings, further dividing the contents into smaller, more manageable portions about ever-more specific topics. You can usually search for a specific **keyword** or phrase during this subdivision process, when you feel you are getting near your target.

Because the sites in directories tend to have been submitted for inclusion, rather than having been located by a search tool robot, directories are less comprehensive than search engines. However, to counter-balance this slight disadvantage, a higher percentage of the results delivered are likely to be relevant. The idea is that the sites are proven to have relevant content and thus search results are of a higher quality than those delivered automatically by search engines.

It's the human presence that makes directory-based search tools different to automated search engines. Sites listed in directories have usually been submitted for inclusion by their originators, although some directories also use bots to find relevant sites. Their submission will usually include a short description containing details of the contents of the site. This information is used to locate the site in the directory hierarchy

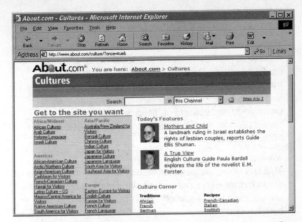

and is often also the data that is searched during keyword or phrase searches in directories (unlike search engines, which will search the entire text). This means directory searches can be more limited by the integrity and accuracy of the submitted details than search engines.

However, the sites are usually reviewed by human editors before they are incorporated into a directory's database, and sites are checked periodically to ensure they are still delivering appropriate information and the nature of their content has not radically changed. The editors prioritise what they consider to be the most useful and relevant Websites, subject to regular revision. Many directories also tend to filter out sites that may be offensive, including those that contain hate speech and are sexually or violently explicit (see the **RSAC**i ratings system on page 69).

You may wish to check out the following.

www.4anything.com
A different approach from this US-centric Webguide

network of four-hosted Webguides under fourteen categories with links to other sites.

## 100hot.com

A guide to the Internet's most popular sites, which is useful if you're interested in keeping up with the sites that everyone else is visiting. The 100hot index identifies and ranks the top 100 Websites in such categories as technology, entertainment, finance, lifestyle and so on based on Web-surfing patterns of a sample of over 100,000 surfers worldwide.

## www.about.com

This site takes the personal side of directory searching a stage further with a network of niche vertical sites that are uniquely led by named expert guides based in over twenty countries.

## www.dmoz.org

Aims to be the biggest hand-built open directory on the Net, compiled by thousands of voluntary **online** editors. Interesting alternative to the mainstream.

## www.galaxy.com

The oldest searchable directory, launched in 1994. In 1999, Galaxy was brought under the umbrella of the Fox/News Corporation corporate umbrella.

## www.go.com

Portal-style with a directory of Websites reviewed by Go Guides. A result of the merger between Infoseek Corporation and Walt Disney Company's Buena Vista Internet Group.

## www.infospace.com

All-purpose directory with UK and Canadian versions.

## www.looksmart.com

Widely used directory of 1.5 million Websites indexed into

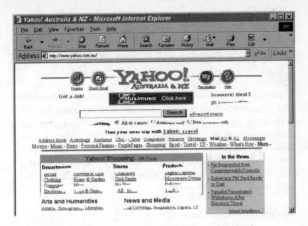

more than 100,000 categories. Provides additional
services, such as hosting LookSmart Live! – an interactive self-help search community monitored by editors.

www.msn.com
www.msn.co.uk
Microsoft network portal directory and search facility.
Can be used from within the **Internet Explorer** browser.
Can also be useful for quick searches, but to get a
broader perspective use other search facilities as well.

www.ukplus.co.uk
UK-centric directory portal owned by publishers of the
*Daily Mail* and London *Evening Standard* newspapers.

www.webcrawler.com
Portal-style directory site and search facility that is part
of the Excite empire.

www.yahoo.com (see above)
Probably the Net's most popular directory-based portal,

now with a whole network of world Yahoo!s, including
Yahoo! UK and Ireland (www.yahoo.co.uk), and Yahoo!
Australia and NZ (www.yahoo.com.au). See also
Yahooligans! Websites for kids (www.yahooligans.com).

## Multi-search tools

These provide access to a number of different search engines
and directories from one site, but deliver the results for each
separately. This is a way of carrying out multiple searches using
different search tools one after the other from one convenient
location. The results are presented separately enabling comparisons to be made between the different search tools, which
may suggest that certain tools are more appropriate for specific research tasks than others.

You may wish to check out the following.

www.1blink.com
Executes individual searches on AltaVista, HotBot,
Yahoo, Excite, Lycos, Thunderstone and Euroseek
search engines.

www.allonesearch.com
All-in-one multi-search site providing access to over 500
search tools for individual searches.

www.gogettem.com
A multi-search tool covering eighteen popular search
engines with a tick option to decide which search
engines are used. Brings up each search engine on
screen in an individual **browser** window to indicate
results. Also lists 2,600 specialist directories.

## Meta-search tools

Meta-search engines sit on top of standard search tools, simultaneously searching two or more. Which search engines and

| Engine | Progress | Matches |
|---|---|---|
| AltaVista | | 10 |
| Direct Hit | | 10 |
| EuroSeek | | 7 |
| Excite | | 10 |
| FAST Search | | 10 |
| Google | | 10 |
| HotBot | | 10 |
| **Infoseek** | | **0** |
| Lycos | | 10 |
| **Magellan** | | **0** |
| **MSN Web Search** | | **0** |
| **Netscape Netcenter** | | **0** |
| **Open Directory Project** | | **0** |
| **WebCrawler** | | **0** |
| **Yahoo!** | | **0** |

Title bar: *Search Progress - Montreal Canada*

how many are simultaneously searched is usually definable by the user within the limitations of the tool.

What makes meta-search tools different to multi-search tools is that the results are merged and purged, to avoid getting the same locations delivered by two or more different search engines. The results are then usually ranked according to relevance. With some meta-search tools the number of results for each individual search facility can be limited so, theoretically, by limiting searches to, for example, ten results for each facility on a five tool search, the overall result should deliver up to the best fifty results matched against a word search. However, in practice this can be difficult to achieve with any degree of accuracy, as only slight differences within meta-tags or different versions of the Webpages being scanned will result in Websites appearing more than once within the results.

The reality is that meta-search engines do not always successfully manage to eradicate multiple listing. However, they can represent an extremely efficient method searching, especially for more advanced but broad searches where users are attempting to compile a wide-ranging list of references to keywords and phrases.

While most meta-searches take place on the Web, some more advanced search tools are managed by **software** that is resident on your computer – for example, Copernic 2000. To use this you have to download the program from the Website. Each time it is connected to the Web it then updates the search engine links it uses to ensure that the data used is the latest (see the screen grab on page 119). It retains the details of the searches made and the search results, which means they can be updated and referred to whenever required. While Copernic 2000 is free and will more than satisfy the needs of most reasonably serious researchers, upgrading to Copernic Plus or Pro provides more features for a small charge.

You may like to check out the following.

search.cnet.com
Search tool of the technology information company
Cnet inc. Claims to search over 700 engines in one go
and includes a list of over 100 speciality search links.
Directory based with keyword searches powered by
infoseek.

www.copernic2000.com
One of the best search tools. Likely to save time and
effort, and deliver results.

www.debriefing.com
Search engines include Yahoo, AltaVista and Excite.
Merges and removes duplicates, and ranks results.
Available in French.

www.dogpile.com
Part of the Go2Net group. Metasearch of Web engines
using MetaCrawler, Usenet sources and FTP archives.

www.infind.com
Searches six engines, removes duplicates and uniquely
groups results into clusters for easy understandability.
French and German options available.

www.mamma.com
Claims to be the largest independent meta-search tool.

www.metacrawler.com
Uses databases of various Web-based search engines,
including AltaVista, LookSmart and Lycos. Includes the
interesting MetaSpy and MetaSpy Exposed features
which allow those who are voyeuristically inclined to
observe live searches being executed.

www.monstercrawler.com
Simultaneously searches Yahoo!, Excite, AltaVista,
GoTo.com, WebCrawler and 7Search.

www.savvysearch.com
Another Cnet meta-search tool. Search engines include
HotBot, Galaxy and Lycos among others.


## Portal and hub sites

Portal sites are routing **nodes** to other Websites. They aim to
point you in the right direction and offer you a few alternative
routes, with diversions, to get there.

There are two kinds of portal site:

- a very specific portal into information about a specific subject area or topic, and
- a general portal that will carry information such as international news, business and stocks, entertainment and e-mail facilities. If horoscopes, weather reports and celebrity gossip are your thing, general portal sites are for you.

Many portal sites now include search facilities, and many search tools have turned themselves into portal sites. Sometimes the search facilities on offer will just be searching the limited range of sites covered by the portal. Alternatively they may offer a route into the wider territory of the Web. Often the search facilities provided will be links from within the portal site to one of the standard search engines.

Similarly, many of the ISP homepages now function as portal sites (see example above). Portals are a hybrid of search engines, directories and ISPs. By providing lots of facilities from one site, under one brand, they are aiming to be the homepages of choice that appear when you **boot** up your computer.

The idea is that by aiming to serve your every need you should only occasionally wish to move beyond their suggested links into the bigger world of the Web and Internet proper. For many, this attempt to harness and contain users contradicts the true spirit of the Internet. While they can be useful first port(al)s of call, portal sites can be considered too controlling and limiting, especially when allied with directory search facilities which are vetted and therefore, by extension, subject to a form of censorship.

The world of the Internet does not stay still for long and development following on from portal sites is the hub site, which takes the notion of the closed portal a stage further. Hubs, rather than being a **gateway** to be passed through on a journey to somewhere else, aim to service your needs from within, protecting you from the rigours and frustrations of the real Internet. Depending on your views, they can be an entrapment, a limitation or a service that saves you time and effort.

In response to the graduation of some of the older search engines to portals and hubs, a new generation of streamlined search tools has begun to appear, such as Google and Northern Lights. These go back to the basic principles of clean, uncluttered searching, with the minimum of distractions and temptations. Your choice will depend on your outlook and your needs.

## Specialist search sites

Most of the search tools mentioned in this section are broad-based in their scope, aiming to provide information about any subject. There is also an increasing number of specialist search tools and sites dedicated to particular themes or topics, catering to audiences with particular areas of interest – for example,

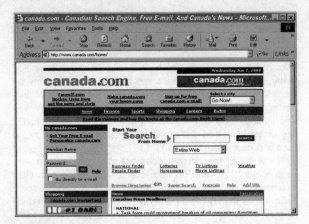

Health or Fishing or Australia. Many of these are driven by commercial concerns. Examples of other **specialist search sites** include research, hobbyist and travel sites. There are also several national and regional search tools, many of them portal sites. As the amount of information to filter and process increases, it is likely that directories with more narrowly defined areas of interest will increase in number, as the example above shows.

## Searching

Having examined the search tools themselves, it's now time to begin searching.

### Searching using search engines

As well as being relevant to search engines, the general principles of searching explained here are also applicable to the other categories of search tools, as they all use search engine technology in addition to their own particular refinements.

Quick searches can also be made directly from within your browser – for example, the **MSN** search facility used by the latest version of Internet Explorer. However, the results from these searches are unlikely to be as rewarding as those made by dedicated search tools.

To locate a search engine from those listed, type the **URL** or Web address of the tool you wish to use in the address bar of your browser and click on 'go' or 'search', or an equivalent. This should take you to the homepage of the search engine you have selected.

Then, in the search box, type in the words or phrase for which you wish to search, and press 'Enter'. Within a few seconds a hit list will appear. Simply place the cursor on one of the links, click, and you should be taken to that Website. You may be fortunate and find the information you need first time. However, the chances are you will get too many results and will need to narrow them down. There are various ways of doing this which are related to the 'search terms' – the words and phrases you choose for your search – and how they are structured (see pages 127–9).

It's important to realise that no one search tool will produce comprehensive results and that some sites may not be included in the search process at all. There can be a number of reasons for this, including sites requesting not to be indexed or being **password** protected. The amount of data being sifted by each search tool will vary enormously from a few million to hundreds of millions of pages. Each search tool will usually produce different results from the same search term, although some engines that share search technologies may produce a similar hit list. So, if you get into the habit of using just one search tool, you could be missing out on valuable information.

It may be useful to gain an understanding of the context of a search tool's database and the data-collection and search methods it employs. Most search tool sites will provide details of this nature in the 'About' section. It's worthwhile reading

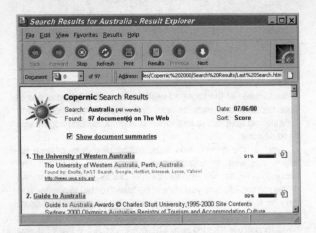

these sections to understand what type of material you are likely to find. Often a statement of intent can be found that will indicate what the orientation of the site is – whether it's broad-based in outlook, or more specifically focused, for example.

The 'About' section is often tucked away at the base of the homepage of the search tool Website. This section also often contains a wealth of background information about who owns, runs and therefore controls the site, and who their partner organisations are. If you are interested in this sort of thing, it's worth taking a look. It may influence the sort of content you are likely to find. You may also find information about whether the site is run independently or is part of a larger corporate concern, which may influence your decision to use it or not.

If you are using standalone search engines or directories, rather than one of the meta-search tools, it may be worthwhile creating links to three or four different engines (using Favorites/Bookmarks in your browser) which have relative strengths and which complement each other.

For really comprehensive search results, an approach combining a meta- or multi-search tool with individual search engines may be appropriate. It's worth checking which stand-alone search engines are covered by the meta-search tools and then using those not covered individually. Also, when using multi- or meta-search tools ensure that the individual search engine data is updated frequently, thus ensuring that searches are not being made on outdated material. The results of your search will probably be referred to as 'matches', 'documents' or 'hits' and will be displayed on screen in batches with the ones deemed to be most relevant at the top (see the example opposite). A way of getting to the next batch, usually between ten and fifty hits, will be shown at the bottom of the screen.

The chances are you will still have to do an element of manual scan searching yourself. It's unlikely that all the results in the hit list will be relevant and you will have to go through them hand or **mouse** picking the best ones. You are the final judge of whether they are useful or not. You should not have to scan through more than the top thirty or forty (often far fewer) to find something worthwhile.

## Search terms

Most search tools provide search instructions and advice which will make your searches more effective. These can usually be found under 'Help' or 'Search tips' on the homepage of the search tool's Website. They may suggest things like adding more words, checking spelling and entering your key phrase in a particular way. Following these suggestions should improve the yield of your searches.

Some engines will also indicate more advanced search methods such as how to narrow down your search if you received too many hits by, for example, removing generic or commonly used words from your search and replacing them with more specific terms, or enclosing specific words that must appear next to each other in quotation marks. If your problem is the inverse – that is, you've had too few hits – the suggestion may well be to add synonyms to broaden your search.

Not all search tools suggest the following as a way of typing in your search terms. Some suggest using standard English questions, for example. However, most tools do support the following suggestions to some extent and you may find using them improves the relevance of your hit list.

### Selecting and structuring search terms

There are two key decisions to be made when searching. The first concerns the actual words (or search terms) you use for your search. The second is related to how you organise those words. This is particularly relevant for more advanced searching where you may consider search logic, especially using the + and – signs, and Boolean Operators (see 'Search Logic', pages 129–30).

Essential to your success in locating the correct information you need on the Net is your choice of search terms – that is, the keywords or phrases you select to type into the search tool to try and reach your goal. There are also common ways of organising your search terms to make them more effective.

If you are trying to locate information about London's new big wheel attraction, for instance, you might initially key in the following: London Big Wheel. This may get good results but they are likely to be buried within a lot of material with 'London' being the only specified word in some documents, or only 'Big' or only 'Wheel'.

To refine the search further you could enter 'London "Ferris wheel"', substituting the word 'Big' for the more specific word 'Ferris' and uniting it with wheel by putting the two words in quotation marks. Even better would be to quote the proper name of the wheel: '"London Eye" "Ferris wheel"'. The phrase that you must have in your document is '"London Eye"' so you should place a + in front of this. Your search term would therefore become ' + "London Eye" "Ferris wheel"'.

The words you select should be terms or phrases that are commonly used, perhaps exclusively used, in the subject area you are searching for, like 'Ferris'. Jargon words may be particularly applicable.

Also, you could try using Boolean Operators. For example the above would read as: London AND Eye AND Ferris AND wheel or '"London Eye" AND "Ferris Wheel"'.

Some search tools are **case sensitive**, so a way of distinguishing between 'polish' and 'Polish' is to use a capital 'P'. Proper nouns should be capitalised – for example, '"Millennium Dome"' or 'Millennium AND Dome' should provide better hits than '"millennium dome"' and certainly more focused ones than 'millennium dome', '+millennium +dome' or 'millennium AND dome'. You will also target the search by adding: +London.

It sounds obvious, but check your spelling as well. '"Sydney Opera House"' will clearly give different results to 'Sidney opera house'.

Sometimes the stem of words such as 'paint' is automatically extended by the search tool to include extensions such as 'painter' and 'painting'. Similarly, wildcards can sometimes be used, where * can be appended to the end of a word so that other words using the same letters at the beginning will be included in the search – for example, 'tele*' will probably deliver references to telephones, television and telepathy.

### Search logic

Standard ways of making your search more specific include those shown on pages 130–31. They are supported by most, but not all, the search tools. The + and – signs should be placed directly in front of each word, with a space between the end of that word and the next.

| OPERATOR | EXAMPLE SEARCH | LOCATES PAGES WHICH INCLUDE |
|---|---|---|
| + | +Icon +Internet +Books | all the words, together in any order, or separately. A '+' in front of a word makes it mandatory that it is present. |
| – | +Icon –Internet +Books | 'Icon' and 'Books', together in any order, or separately, but excluding 'Internet'. |
| "..." | 'Icon Internet Books' | the whole phrase, with the words in the order indicated. |

## Boolean Logic

Most search tools support natural language searching, which basically means you can use plain English without having to resort to complex search syntax. However, a few search engines, especially for advanced searches, insist on Boolean Logic searches, while some support both. Boolean searching operators allow you to make more sophisticated advanced searches using standard operators. If you're using a search engine you're unfamiliar with and not getting the results you want it's worth checking out the search instructions to see if they include **Boolean Logic**.

| OPERATOR | EXAMPLE SEARCH | LOCATES PAGES WHICH INCLUDE |
|---|---|---|
| AND | Icon AND Books | both words – that is, both 'Icon' and 'Books', but not necessarily together. Narrows a search. |
| OR | Icon OR Books | either of the two words, or both of them, that is, pages with just 'Icon' or just 'Books' or both 'Icon' and 'Books'. Expands a search. |
| NOT | Icon NOT Books | only the first word and exclude the second – that is, pages with 'Icon' and without 'Books'. Must be used with AND. |
| NEAR | (Icon AND Books) NEAR Internet | the phrase when it appears with ten words of the word – that is, 'Internet' when it is found with ten words of the phrase 'Icon Books'. |
| (...) | Icon NOT (Internet OR Books) | the first word and excluding both of the two words in parenthesis – that is, 'Icon' where it appears without 'Internet' or 'Books'. Parentheses are used to ensure operators are combined in the right when more than one is used. |

Different search engines have different rules, for example some will insist on 'AND NOT' being used rather than just 'NOT'. Some search engines recognise the equivalent characters, as well as the Broken term, for example the characters '+' and '&' may be substituted for 'AND'. If you are interested in using more sophisticated search techniques, check out the Advanced Search instructions provided by your search engine.

### Searching using a directory

When entering a directory site you will be faced with a group of main category headings such as Arts & Entertainment, Business & Finance, Health & Fitness, Recreation & Sports, Society & Culture, and Travel. These are a bit like the sections in a library. Usually there will be between ten and twenty top level categories. Select the one that most closely matches the general area of your search.

So, to find out about plays currently showing at the London base of the Royal Shakespeare Company, you may begin with Arts & Humanities. Having entered that category you will find a series of sub-heading options to pursue. Select one of these (perhaps Performing Arts) and keep doing this logically until you can go no further. A tracking chart will appear at the top of the page, delineating each step with a forward slash (/) or an arrow (>), for example:

Arts_&_Humanities/Performing_Arts/Theatre/Theatre_Companies/Royal_Shakespeare_Company/

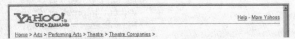

This will take you to a choice of two sites – the RSC's official site and an unofficial one. Choosing the official one at www.rsc.org.uk allows you to go to its schedules for London and find out the dates. The chart will keep track of where you are within the directory's hierarchical structure. With some search tools you will be able to begin a keyword or phrase search at any point, covering just the sites in the category you are in. Effectively, you are narrowing down the possibilities the further down the hierarchical structure you get, throwing out irrelevant sites and thus increasing your chances of finding relevant information.

## Searching using multi-search tool

On entering the homepage for some of these tools you may be asked to confirm which search engines you wish to search. You usually specify these by ticking the appropriate boxes. In others you automatically sort all the search facilities on their site.

One inconvenience in some multi-search tools is having to type the search terms into each individual search tool's box. This can be overcome using Edit Copy from the main **toolbar**. All-in-one lists all site search bars; go into them individually and return to All-in-one by pressing the backbutton. In other tools you only have to type in the search term once.

Simply enter your search terms in the same way as you would with a standard search engine. Your selection will automatically be applied across all or some of the search tools as specified. The hit list for each search engine may appear in a separate browser window, as with GoGettem. Alternatively, they may appear in groupings for each search engine within the same window as with 1blink.

As the results for each engine are shown separately, you can compare and contrast the relative performances in terms of both quantity and quality of each search tool.

## Searching using meta-search tools

As with multi-search tools, you enter your search terms as you would in a standard search engine. The main difference is how the results are presented. The hit list will consist of results from all the search engines merged and sorted together to produce a list with the most relevant at the top.

With Copernic 2000 you can open up the program directly from your **hard disk**, or from within your browser. You also have the option to make it the default search facility within your browser. Copernic 2000 allows you to determine which search tools you search within and permits you to restructure the appearance of your search results. It also provides the option to save both the search terms and the hit list for updating and reference at a later date.

## USING THE INTERNET

The **Internet** has a number of useful applications – not least of which is exploring all aspects of the retail trade and partaking in global business opportunities, as the text that follows shows.

## What can I use the Internet for?

The Internet is a giant store of information which is at your disposal. Almost every topic you can think of will have some references on the Internet. You can get at that information in various ways. For example, if you know that there is specific information on the Web that you need and you know where to find it, it is a simple process to locate it. If you know the **Website** address of an organisation you are interested in, you can key it straight into the address bar at the top of your **browser** window and you will be taken directly to its Website. The quickest way to find and retrieve general information is to use the search **tools** and key in either an enquiry subject, or a more specific word or phrase. From the resulting list of Websites you should find relevant information.

As well as finding information, you can also use the Internet for a variety of other purposes. For example, the Internet is a great way of communicating with people. You can use the Internet to send **e-mail** to other users who are connected to the Internet, and you can participate in e-mail discussion forums on subjects in which you are interested. You can communicate in real time using **chat** facilities and, if you have the right equipment, you can use the Internet to communicate by voice.

The **World Wide Web** is also a new media space where you can pick up the daily news and current affairs commentary, and find out about events that are happening all over the world, such as concerts, theatre performances and sports competitions. You can also send and receive **software**, music and video material over the Internet, and you can become an **online** publisher by establishing you own Website.

Over the past five years, the Web has developed into a vast commercial arena where you can buy, sell and market goods and services. It's virtually impossible to list all the things that the Internet can be used for.

Below is a snapshot of the activities in which the Internet can play an important part.

- Buying and selling property.
- Financial applications, including banking, insurance, stock listings and share trading.
- Shopping: from individual specialist retailers to supermarket chains and department stores, with almost every consumer item now available via the Web.
- Travel, including holiday destination information, maps and guides, booking accommodation, flights and package holidays, rail and coach timetables, and booking.
- Local information about the area in which you live, local government, town planning, health issues.
- Contacting people.
- Official and unofficial news, views and opinions.
- Culture and the arts, including Internet artworks, galleries, and information about events and performances.
- Entertainment, including information about television, and music and film releases (with the ability to watch films and listen to the radio, and see and hear concerts live).
- Research and reference materials, including dictionaries, encyclopaedias and guides.
- Educational establishments and courses.
- Communicating with e-mails and voice.

## Shopping on the Net

With the shopping applications of the **Net** has come a new
spate of terms to describe these transactions.

*e-commerce*

What is **e-commerce**? Put simply, it is making financial transactions electronically over the Web, or buying and selling over
the Internet. It's become a key phrase in recent years and has,
for many, become a principle function of the Net.

In many ways, e-commerce is in direct opposition to the
visions of the early users of the Internet. The philosophy of the
Internet was grounded in sharing – ideas, thoughts, information
and software. The Web would not exist if Tim Berners-Lee, the
originator of the concept of the Web, had not taken the option
to make the original Web software free to all by **posting** it on an
**FTP** site. There is still much on the Net that is free: much of the
information is free, **access** to the Net itself can be free, in many
instances connection calls to the Net are free, there are free
downloadable music files, and free entertainment in the form
of concerts and debates, and free novels, plays and poetry.
Web radio stations are free and there is much free software.
There are even **sites** that, however unlikely it seems, purport
to pay you a small sum per hour to **surf** the Net, and others
that pay you to listen to the radio (see www.getpaid4.com and
www.radiofreecash.com). They are a form of market research,
and you are asked to register when you hear or see an ad.

Having said that, e-commerce has become one of the stal-
wart functions of the Web. It is the linchpin of the so-called
'new economy', where information is the key to business
efficiency.

*e-tailing and retailing*

There's a clear difference between traditional established 'old
economy' retailers and the new 'e-tailers'. The older concerns

are creating a presence on the Web by using it as a billboard, posting an advertising and editorial information site for their products and services. The 'new economy' e-tailers' business is based around Web-functionality and is dependent on a revised approach to doing business that encompasses all the possibilities the Internet offers.

When retail businesses first started to take notice of the Web, most company sites were of the first type, but this is changing. Companies that are taking advantage of the new means of building a personal relationship with the customer that the Internet offers are also remoulding business models and paradigms. In response, many traditional businesses are now turning their attention to Internet start-ups, whose incursions into their customer-base are now considered a threat, by moving their big budgets into e-commerce development in an attempt to regain lost ground and beat the new kids on the block at their own game.

The retailing industry is at the leading edge of many of the most recent Internet technological developments. The Internet is changing both the way in which retailers interface with their customers and their relationship with supply chains. In many ways, the Internet electronically extends the principles of direct marketing. Companies are building closer personal relationships with their customers using **eCRM** (Electronic Customer Management). By reinforcing old relationships and establishing new ones through personalised Websites and e-mail, companies hope that customers will return again and again.

On the larger retail sites, which can carry thousands of items, finding the product you want can sometimes be a problem. Most sites of this kind now supply search facilities, as well as categorised browsing. Many sites are able to automatically create a customer profile. The more you use the site, the more the site will become tailored to your tastes. Other sites will request personal product preference information from you and customise a version of the site specifically to your tastes. There has been a proliferation of sites employing this technology, often in the form of tailorable on-screen options, prefixed with 'My ...'. As well as making your personal interface into the information provided on the site simpler, by using this option, subconsciously or otherwise, you are also interacting with the site and thus becoming more committed or loyal to it.

The Internet has been instrumental in driving down the cost of some consumer goods in the UK. The international perspective that the Net delivers has driven home the fact that UK prices for many items are significantly higher than in other similar regions, primarily the USA and some European countries. Even though this has been known for some time, the Net makes it easier to buy goods overseas and have them shipped to the UK – even with duties and shipping costs they can work out cheaper. This has led many UK-based companies to lower their prices to compete in the mass market delivered by the Net. However, it's by no means certain that prices on the Web are cheaper than elsewhere, so check carefully.

One of the main reasons people cite for using Web shopping facilities is not price benefits, however, but convenience. The Web is effectively an upgraded and extended mail-order service on a grand scale and delivery to your door is a big advantage, especially for goods that might not be available in your local high street. The other big convenience is that orders can be placed twenty-four hours a day, seven days a week.

On occasions, Web shopping can be a frustrating experience, but there's a few things you can do to lessen the prospect of problems, such as checking the goods you want are actually in stock and confirming the anticipated delivery date. It's amazing how many Web retailers, or e-tailers, don't actually tell you when there's a six-month waiting list for the product you expect to receive next week.

Check what the returns policy is. If the goods are not as described, or are damaged, you may have to send them back. Also, check what guarantee or warranty the product has. And investigate hidden costs, such as shipping. We've all heard tales of the £15 shipping charge for goods that cost £5. These should be clearly stated on the Website. Also it may be worth checking who pays returns shipping charges should it be necessary to return goods, and remember that tax and VAT charges may be imposed if you are buying goods from overseas.

If you are worried about the integrity of the company you are buying from, question whether you should do business with them. Check that address and telephone details are supplied. Above all, keep a record of all your transactions for reference should anything go wrong.

At retail sites you establish an account by providing your payment details, billing address and delivery address. The account is then password protected. Most retail sites operate a shopping basket, cart or trolley system. You roam the site marking items for inclusion in your shopping trolley, as you would in your local supermarket. By linking to the shopping basket screen you can check what items you have selected and how much they cost. You can also remove items if you change your mind or make a mistake. At the checkout, when your order is processed you may receive a confirmation e-mail. The better sites will also provide an 'order status' link, which enables you to check how your order is progressing.

## Payment security

There used to be many concerns about credit card security when people first started using the Internet to make their purchases. These fears have been pretty much allayed now by the introduction of security processes that are probably far more stringent than those in place when you give your card number to an organisation over the phone, which most of us wouldn't think twice about, or pay with it in a restaurant. Millions of transactions now take place daily without the emergence of any major scare stories.

Most Internet card transactions are now encrypted, which means they are scrambled to make it difficult for anyone coming across your details to understand them. Retails sites should employ **Internet security** systems such as **SSL** (Secure Sockets Layer) to protect the data you provide. All ordering information – including name, address and payment card numbers – should be encrypted while it is in transit, which will ensure it is virtually impossible to decipher should it find its way into the wrong hands *en route*. When giving your credit card details, look out for the on-screen closed padlock icon. This indicates that the information you are supplying is being encrypted.

Reputable e-tailers will provide a safe shopping guarantee that should cover you if anything goes wrong with your transaction. Similarly, banks and other institutions that provide credit cards will usually build-in protection. If you are concerned you should check with your card supplier what protection you have in place.

## Finding retail Websites

With millions of Websites to choose from, it's impossible to provide here anything other than a very small selection of suggested sites. Similarly there are many things that you can buy over the Web that we don't have room to suggest. Treat the sites mentioned on the next two pages as samples to investigate rather than recommendations, and if you're interested in seeing similar sites, use the Web search tools outlined in the section 'Searching the Internet' (see pages 107–34) to help you discover them. Many of the sites on pages 141–2 now have regional variations and sites in specific languages. Where these options exist they will usually be indicated on the **homepage**, and you can link to them from there.

*Shopping search engines, directories and portals*

One of the best ways to find out what the Web has to offer shopping-wise is to **browse** or search your way through shopping directory or **portal** sites. These are sites which provide links to retail sites. They employ the same techniques of listing and searching as the broad search tool mentioned earlier, applying them to the niche area of shopping. Comparison shopping **agents** try to locate the lowest prices on the Net.

You could check out the following.

    www.e-britain.co.uk
    www.edirectory.co.uk
    www.selectsurf.com
    www.shopmate.co.uk
    www.shopsmart.com
    www.shoptour.co.uk
    www.topoftheshops.co.uk
    www.zoom.uk

*Bargains*

Auctions, bucket shops, second-hand stores and classified ads, and community purchasing schemes were around before the Internet. But the Web has given new impetus to these old ideas, extending their reach, effectiveness and appeal.

Check out the following.

www.lastminute.com
The infamous lastminute.com is, in many ways, a bucket shop for the twenty-first century. It takes 'perishable' goods, such as flight and concert tickets, and sells them at the last minute at reduced prices. While this sort of business did exist before the Internet, clearly easy availability of information and the speed of transactions make it an ideal business proposition for the Internet.

www.letsbuyit.com
An electronic age version of shopping co-operatives.
Co-buyers who want the same product club together
to gain purchasing power and negotiate discounts from
retailers. Pan-European purchasing means that prices
are lower.

www.Loot.com
An online version of the popular classified ads
publication with lots of extra facilities, including online
auctions and the Lootcafe.

www.ebay.co.uk
www.qxl.com
Online **auctions** have become a popular sport for
bargain hunters, and QXL and ebay are two of the
largest dedicated online auction houses.

In Netspeak, online auction sites are sometimes referred to as
person-to-person online trading communities, reflecting the
inclusion of chat and **message board** facilities where interested parties can discuss the various items they have for sale
and exchange. Sites will usually have search options that use
general Internet search and browse facilities. You can both
browse to see if there's anything you are interested in, and
search for specific items prior to the auction. In order to place a
bid, you have to register with the site for security reasons. You
use '+' and '–' buttons to make your bids against the current
price.

Another alternative is to place a reserve highest bid, known
as the bid limit option. This confidentially states the highest
price you're prepared to pay and bids are automatically made
on your behalf until the specified amount is reached or the
auction finishes at a lower price. All bids are legally binding, so
this is a serious business.

## Books

Online booksellers are one of the great successes of **e-tailing**. A few of the big players in this arena are listed below, but there are others to choose from. Many publishers have their own sites listing back catalogues and promoting new titles. The Net is being used by suppliers as a means of improving the reach of their marketing efforts, and to improve ordering and delivery systems. However, the real possibilities of the Net in relation to distribution are yet to be explored by publishers and resellers. The distribution of books, like music and software, over the Net looks set to be an area of development and innovation in the coming years, once issues of copyright and the role of the existing distribution channels are clarified.

There are thousands of free and charged for downloadable **e-books** available on the Internet. These tend to be vanity publishing or public domain out-of-copyright texts, such as the works of Shakespeare and the Classics. Free books tend to be less attractively formatted than paid for books on demand. A kind of vanity publishing for the electronic age, POD (Publishing On Demand) enables living authors to pay to have their books formatted and distributed electronically. Many recoup their costs and a smaller number have progressed to paperback production.

Check out the following online book shops.

www.amazon.com
www.amazon.co.uk
One of the original Web retail success stories. This site still supplies a wide-ranging choice of books and CDs, but has now expanded to cover a whole range of other retail items and has become a bit of a market stall. You can locate new, used and hard-to-find items through its zShops, and take part in online auctions. On the US site goods are also available through onsite concessions,

such as sothebys.amazon.com for arts and collectibles. Other options include electronics, toys, and health and beauty products.

www.bol.com
BOL actually stands for Bertelsmann Online, not Books Online as many think. Bertelsmann is one of the world's largest media companies. It's easily navigated site has its focus firmly on books and music, and includes innovative BOL TV video-on-demand interviews with best-selling authors. Bertelsmann also has a strategic relationship with AOL, supplying content worldwide.

www.waterstones.co.uk
Online site of the popular high street bookstore, offering free post and packaging for any books for collection at your nearest store.

www.bookfinder.com
A book location service that will sort through over 15 million new, used, rare and out-of-print books to find the one you are looking for.

The following is a list of sample publisher sites.

www.cup.cam.ac.uk
www.iconbooks.co.uk
www.oup.co.uk
www.penguin.co.uk
www.plutobooks.com
www.routledge.co.uk

Downloadable and online texts.

www.1stbooks.com
www.eastgate.com
www.onlineoriginals.com
www.promo.net

## CDs and videos

There are lots of sites publicising and selling the latest CD and video releases, with Amazon and BOL proving to be significant players in this market. These sites often post a short taster of a few tracks for each CD and carry huge catalogues. You can even order your own custom CDs. At the CD exchange you can swap and trade second-hand sounds. Some US sites also sell into the UK. Online CD stores may be cheaper than the high street (sometimes), but for a more radical approach to music on the Web, check 'Music' in the following 'Broadcasting, Media & Music' section.

You may want to take a look at the following.

> www.cdhut.com
> www.cdnow.com
> www.thecdexchange.com
> www.tunes.com
> www.blackstar.co.uk
> www.videoext.co.uk

> www.evenbetter.com
> One of the best online comparison shopping services for books, music and films. Type in your selection and this service searches the Web for the cheapest prices available, delivering impressively comprehensive comparison tables indicating the cheapest option.
> A Bertelsmann subsidiary.

## Clothes

Selling clothes over the Web has a chequered history. Consumers, not surprisingly, are using the online versions of the high street shops they already use, probably because they know the likely fit of clothing that those shops supply. Speciality Websites selling items not generally available elsewhere are also doing well, as are sites specialising in one type of item, such as underwear, where sizes are more consistent across brands. There are thousands of clothes shopping sites on the Web, ranging from the department store sites to designer or brand sites. Let the **search engines** do the work for you.

Meanwhile, here are three sites that you could check out.

www.clothingconnection.co.uk
www.designersdirect.com
www.marksandspencer.co.uk

### Electrical

Not surprisingly, there are lots of e-tailers specialising in electronic goods. Many of them are like Internet department stores. They often offer substantial discounts on certain products. It's worth checking their prices against those in the high street. Only buy from reputable sources, however, since you may need to return such relatively high-cost items if they don't work. Many of these stores also offer CDs and **DVD**s (Digital Versatile Disks) as well as televisions, computers and computer games.

Below are a couple of sites that fit into the 'electrical' category.

www.jungle.com
www.tempo.co.uk

### Independent food, drink and fresh produce retailers

At the opposite end of the scale to the large supermarkets a number of small speciality food producers are making headway with sales over the Web. By marketing and selling their produce directly to the customer, and cutting out the middleman, small producers can keep prices reasonable. There are many schemes for fresh produce such as organic fruit and vegetables sold by the box, but these are sometimes limited by local delivery areas, although as these projects become popular they are widening in scope. Smoked fish, soups, flowers and plants, hampers, cheese, tea and coffee, meats and wine are just some popular home delivery options.

The following Websites give a flavour of this kind of produce.

www.crocus.co.uk
www.interflora.co.uk
www.martins-seafresh.co.uk
www.organicdelivery.co.uk
www.organicsdirect.com
www.organictrail.freeserve.co.uk
www.realmeat.co.uk
www.riverford.co.uk
www.shetlandsseafood.co.uk
www.simplyorganic.net
www.theorganicshop.co.uk
www.worldfoods.co.uk

## Supermarket chains

Most of the major supermarkets now provide online shopping and deliver direct to your door after you've placed your order over the Net. Check returns policy and whether the goods you want are in stock.

Here are three major supermarkets that are now selling online.

www.tesco.co.uk
www.sainsburys.co.uk
www.waitrose.co.uk

## Vehicles

Here are just two of the most popular Websites.

www.autotrader.co.uk
This is an upgraded version of the popular used-car sales magazine.

www.carbusters.com
Established by the consumer organisation Which? to
support the Consumers' Association's campaign for
cheaper cars. This site provides access to cars at
European prices.

## Broadcasting over the Internet

Broadcasting on the Web is a huge and potentially bewildering
subject. Part of the confusion is caused by terminology traditionally associated with broadcasting being adopted as
Webspeak, with a similar but slightly different meaning.
'Channel', for instance, is often used on the Web to refer to
groups of information about a subject, rather than a television
or radio channel in the usual sense.

There are two broad types of Websites relating to broadcasting. First are the Websites of traditional broadcast media
channels, such as terrestrial, cable, digital and satellite channels, and radio channels. These channels were established
before the Internet and exist independently of the Web. Their
content cross-references to other media. Second are those
Web- or Net-broadcasting company sites whose contents owe
their existence to the broadcasting potential of the Internet
itself. Their content is not carried by other media and is solely
Internet-based.

With the advent of developments such as 'streaming' and
video-on-demand (VOD) technologies, and with the wider
availability of faster broadband connections to the Internet,
broadcasting looks set to be an area of huge growth in the
forthcoming years.

The linkage of large media conglomerates and Internet-
centric companies, such as the merger of Time Warner and
AOL, will be instrumental in driving the development of the
Internet as a broadcast medium.

## Traditional television on the Web

Most non-Web television companies now have Websites that cross-reference to their television programmes. The main function of these sites is to promote and gain loyalty for their television channel programmes. For example, using the Internet as an interactive interface, it is often possible, after watching a programme on terrestrial television, to **logon** to that programme's Website and have a chat conversation with one of the show's celebrities or its director. The BBC's huge Website has groups of pages dedicated to its best and most popular programmes like the *EastEnders* section of BBC Online (www.bbc.co.uk/eastenders/). The pages for this widely watched soap opera contain episode updates, character biographies, a set map, interviews with actors and character biographies. BBC Online is a leading example of this type of Website.

There are huge numbers of fan sites which complement official Websites dedicated to television programmes. They contain content that is not controlled by the programme makers or broadcasters, but which is often tacitly sanctioned by the inclusion of sitelinks from the official Website, as is the case with *EastEnders*, whose official Webpages currently include links to US and newsgroup *EastEnders*' fan sites. Think of a cult television series and it is probably the subject of hundreds of fan sites. Try searching on *Red Dwarf*, *Star Trek*, *Dr Who* or *The Prisoner*, for example. As well as channel and fan sites, you can also learn about the creation of programmes by visiting television production companies' Websites.

World news and current affairs are a significant presence on the Web, and both the BBC and CNN have extensive Web news channels, complementing their twenty-four hour news coverage on television. The BBC's news site is linked to its main site, but is a separate entity (www.news.bbc.co.uk). Some video material from TV is available as **VOD** (Video-On-Demand) on this type of Website, but most of the material is text based with complementary still images. Where short video clips of content previously broadcast on terrestrial television are available on, for example, the BBC's news site, they appear to the majority of us who use slow Net connections as faltering and diminished compared to the TV version. The value of placing material of this sort on Websites is that it becomes available to a widespread Net-based audience that cannot receive the TV programmes.

Not surprisingly, television channel sites usually carry details of forthcoming programmes in the form of listings. There are also a number of independent listing services, such as Gypsy Media's downloadable DigiGuide for the UK. DigiGuide is an interactive programme guide (IPG) that is available both online and **offline**. DigiGuide also hosts a useful TV library and user feedback forum.

### Audio-visual Net-only broadcasting

The Net is set to become one of the most far-reaching broadcasting systems the world has ever seen. The limitations of geography that are inherent in all other television systems don't apply with the Net. The old channels are limited by the transmitter-receiver system, where if the transmitter or cable-feed doesn't reach your receiver you cannot get the channel. However, wherever there is any device that can receive the full services of the Internet, it will be able to receive Internet broadcasting channels, regardless of where the device is geographically located.

There are a number of fledgling Web-based channels that claim to be 'television'. At the present time these compare unfavourably with what you may see on conventional television, both in terms of content and presentation. Whatever the hype may say, unless you have an extremely fast **broadband** connection, the pictures received will vary from just about bearable to unwatchable. Some of the content is useful, although much of it can be disappointing.

The better content is often that which is unique to the Web, as there seems little point in viewing something over the Net if you can watch it with better sound and quality pictures on TV. Streaming is the technology that allows live events to be transmitted across the Internet as they are happening and it works best with high **bandwidth** connections, such as **ADSL** or cable. For the viewer using slower connections, the disappointments of hesitant reception, usually interspersed with loss of picture breaks due to buffering or Web-**congestion**, can be outweighed by the positives of being able to see an otherwise unviewable event. Some of the best unique events broadcast over the Web are live concerts by big name acts. Recent months have seen live concerts by The Cure, Paul Weller and Oasis, for instance. After transmission, these are sometimes stored for a short period and made available to viewers on demand.

Using the broad sweep of the Net, large numbers of viewers can be garnered for supposedly 'minority-interest' subjects. When all the viewers who are interested in a particular subject are added up across the whole of the Net, they have the potential to reach significant figures. For example, there might be more people interested in, say, fishing or coin collecting, across the whole of the Internet's constituency than the numbers who watch the most popular soap-operas in just one national region. This means that niche interests become viable as subjects for a Web-based television channel. If the number of viewers is high enough, advertising support and revenue will follow, making topics and themes that wouldn't warrant even a regular half-hour programme on traditional television channels viable as the subject matter for a whole Net-based television channel.

For a glimpse into the future of broadcasting on the Internet, take a look at Medium4's site. This company is leading the way in Internet-only television and currently hosts fifty-two channels over five networks, including the NicheTV network, which

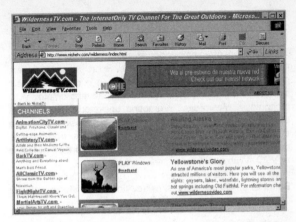

carries channels about art history, film noir, the martial arts and railways, among many others. You will need the latest versions of **RealPlayer** or Windows Media Player to view the programmes, some of which are only available across fast connections. Using higher speed broadband connections, the service comes close to traditional television quality and will not suffer from the buffering delays that will be experienced using lower speed **modem** connections. The service Medium4 provides is on-demand but uses streaming technology, which means that programmes can be watched over again instantly, but cannot be downloaded and saved on your computer.

### Video-on-Demand (VOD)

Unlike real-time streaming, VOD material is available to be watched twenty-four hours a day, as and when you want, giving viewers real-time **interactivity** and complete control over viewing times. Like conventional video, it includes fast forward and rewind facilities. VOD is increasingly being incorporated into Websites of all descriptions, and is bringing an element of true **multi-media** to environments that are still dominated by textual information.

Examples of Websites using VOD include news sites, where video clips are often embedded as an audio-visual supplement to text-based journalistic news items. Short clips and trailers promoting current film releases are found in celebrity gossip and movie marketing sites. Additionally, adverts employ VOD technology. Music sites promoting unsigned musicians are also a good place to find VOD in the form of music videos, and a number of music sites transmit concerts live from venues using streaming technology, then make the concert available as VOD via an archive.

Below and opposite is a list of traditional television broadcast channel Websites.

www.abc.go.com
Website of the ABC US entertainment channel.

www.bbc.co.uk
A multitude of different sites covering many television programmes, together with a choice of video clips from the BBC's archives.

www.bloomberg.com/tv/
Presents financial and business news with the aid of video clips. Has streaming 24/7 international language financial news channels that are also available via satellite and cable.

www.channel4.com
Contains news and updates for the UK's Channel 4.

www.cnn.com/videoselect/
Well-known US news channel with VOD reports from around the world.

www.historytelevision.ca
An educational channel from Canada.

www.news.bbc.co.uk
BBC news in text and images, and BBC television news
on video.

www.pbs.org
Schedules, news and information about programmes
broadcast by the US public broadcasting service.

Below are some Internet-only television sites.

www.medium4.com
Exciting Internet-only TV network. Channels include
foreigntv.com and medium4film.com

www.nichetv.com
A selection of Internet-only on-demand streaming
specific interest channels.

www.yestv.co.uk
New generation broadband Internet television portal that
provides television programmes, films and music VOD,
together with e-mail and a selection of Internet material
via ADSL-connected phonelines and cable.

www.zdtv.com
Technology news channel with lots of VOD features.

Below and on the following page is a selection of other audio-
visual broadcasting-related sites.

www.ananova.com
Ananova Ltd is the UK company that provides ready-for-
publication packages of news, sports, events listing and
information, and interactive services to many Websites
and news portal sites. Perhaps set to become a cult Web

figure, perhaps destined for obscurity, Ananova, the world's first **virtual** newscaster, reads out the news headlines at this Website. Find out more by reading the on-site A-files. (See screen grab opposite.)

www.broadcast.yahoo.com
Yahoo! broadcast site with links to 500 radio stations and 65 TV stations.

www.digiguide.com
TV listings guide, available both online and offline, and via **WAP** (Wireless Application Protocol) mobile phones.

www.dotmusic.com
Streaming broadcasts of live concerts and VOD archives.

www.ftv.fr
Fashion channel from Paris.

www.merseytv.com
Mersey Television is the independent television production company that developed the UK Channel 4 soaps *Brookside* and *Hollyoaks*.

www.multimedia.lycos.com
Excellent multi-media search site.

www.onlinetvuk.com
Excellent live Webcast and VOD site featuring band performances from London bars.

www.tvlibrary.co.uk
Details and links for television programmes.

www.windowsmedia.com
MSN's guide to broadcast channels on the Web.

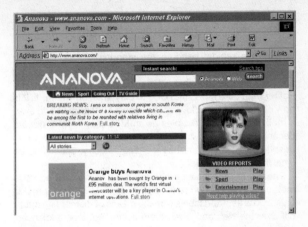

## Music

There are thousands of sites distributing music, officially and unofficially, over the Web. The music varies from sound files of well-known contemporary pop figures, through classical, folk and world music, to the music of obscure bands aspiring to break into the mainstream and those musicians who just want their music to be heard.

The music appears in a number of different formats, including audio-visual performances as **MPEG** files, and within real-time streaming broadcasts as used by Net-radio stations, or as downloadable soundfiles – the most notorious and glorious of which is the **MP3** file.

### MP3s

MP3 files are currently causing big ructions in the music industry. The high-**compression**, high-quality capabilities of MP3 files means it is now possible to download songs and play them back in near-CD quality stereo on your computer. Massively reduced download times due to the compressed nature of the **files** ensures that downloading music from the Web is a viable proposition.

MP3 has rapidly become the standard for downloading music files, and there are many **compatible** software programs and hardware devices that have quickly arrived on the market. Rather than burn MP3s into CDs to play them on your hi-fi, it is now possible to buy a low-cost portable MP3 **player**, and even a mobile phone that doubles as an MP3 player. MP3 players became available to the general public in 1998 and were, despite opposition from the recording industry, deemed to be legal the following year.

The key to MP3's success is that it is a highly cost-effective method of promotion and distribution. MP3 files provide unknown artists and labels with the means of distributing material over the Net, and gives them access to large audiences, effectively levelling the playing field as they fight it out for visibility with the big corporate players of the recording industry.

The main problem is that as well as promoting unsigned musicians' music, many of the MP3 files available on the Net contain music pirated from mainstream CDs. Technology exists to convert CDs into MP3s and upload them on to the Internet where they can be downloaded by anyone. There are huge claims being made about the loss of revenue being experienced by the recording industry due to the illegal downloading of MP3 files.

The real challenge is to a complacent record industry, which attempted to block out the issue of the Net for years. Part of the problem is that the record industry continues to rely on CD price maintenance to bring in its profits and currently offers no viable alternative to those who wish to own music files distributed over the Internet. It is only just beginning to structure a simple way to buy music by established artists legally over the Web. Rather than threatening legal action against MP3 and digital music download sites, as the recording industry is, at least in part, doing, a policy of embracing digital sound formats and working with the new technology would seem to be a more positive and potentially rewarding way ahead.

CDs are an outdated way of distributing music involving packaging, printing, pressing, road distribution and delivery. Distribution can be undertaken a lot more effectively (in terms of cost, too) over the Web. Some estimates suggest the price per track of legitimately purchased music over the Net should be around 33 pence. If a reasonable price was levied, at least the downloader would be faced with a moral choice between making a reasonable payment and piracy.

Many commentators believe that MP3 technology will be surpassed and that, while it is inevitable that legitimate mainstream music files will soon be distributed in a big way over the Net, the process will involve electronic tagging of tracks that will render them unique and traceable. Record companies do look likely to place their frontline and back catalogue acts on the Web eventually, but in secure formats, and perhaps not playable on MP3 players.

Liquid Audio, an alternative format to MP3, is being embraced by many of the big music companies in a move towards legitimately distributing music over the Net. BMG, the entertainment arm of media conglomerate Bertelsmann, is planning to make music content available through online retailers using Liquid Audio software. Liquid Audio is also working to make its audio player and digitised music catalogue compatible with WMA (Windows Media Audio) format. The same technology is employed in the half-way house digital music kiosks that have started arriving in high street stores. These in-store updateable music databases, from which tracks can be burned into CDs in the store, stop short of linking to the Web.

In a recent further clampdown on MP3 distribution, **AOL** Germany was found to be legally responsible as an **ISP** for MP3 downloads made using its service. ISPs have always maintained that they are not responsible for information that is downloaded using the facilities they provide, as they are merely providing an Internet access service, and this decision would appear to have far-reaching implications beyond the music industry.

The turning point that seems to have spurred the recording industry to its recent rear-guard action is the development of the Napster MP3 file search, location and sharing software that lets people exchange MP3 files in a direct manner. Napster is currently being demonised by the recording industry, and by some highly successful artists generally and the rock band Metallica in particular. The development of the My.MP3.com service, which allowed people to store their music online at the MP3.com Website, added further fuel to the confrontation.

Record companies are threatening to turn the Internet's technology back on those who exploit it. In an attempt to halt the distribution of MP3 files using Napster, Web maps and tracing technology are being employed to see the points from which the files are being distributed. Trying to track down individuals downloading and swapping music for their own listening pleasure may be a route adopted by the industry, although taking legal action against them is likely to cost far more than the lost revenues and could be seen as a sledge-hammer to crack a nut. In tandem, the threats of the phonographic industry's spokespeople have all the overtones of the shrieks and outcries of an industry almost wilfully alienating its customer base.

But MP3 distributors are fighting back, and new distribution software such as Gnutella and Scour continues to distribute MP3 files. As they use non-centralised distribution techniques, these systems will make it difficult to home-in on downloaders.

This debate strikes at the heart of the principles and philosophy of the Net. The Web was born of a **freeware**, **shareware** attitude, whereby information was posted freely for the use of all, even from its very inception, when the original Website formatting software was made freely available. Big business has subsequently colonised the Web, pumped millions of dollars into advancing the technology and is now attempting, in this instance in the form of the record industry, to bring hardline business principles to bear, thus giving rise to conflict.

On a broader level, the implications are interesting. Much of the music on the Web is by unsigned bands and musicians who simply want an audience for their efforts. Simultaneously, the musical diversity offered by global music is being recognised, and recording broadcast quality music is no longer as expensive it used to be. Maybe we are moving back to a period when music is once again free, as it was before the recording industry was created. Perhaps the notion of music as 'product' is being diminished. It may be that the period of recording superstars is drawing to a close, with the Web giving access to wider styles and influences, encouraging music consumers to break free from the narrow choices offered by traditional record and radio companies.

These are hot topics and the Ziff Davis technology news site is a useful place to follow developments and debates (www.zdnet.com).

Below and on the next page is a list of MP3 Websites that you might like to check out.

www.818music.com
A showcase promoting new talent with MP3 downloads.

www.mp3.com
A site with free downloadable files mainly from unheard of unsigned acts, as mainstream acts have been removed from the site under legal pressure.

www.mp3.lycos.com
This is a great search facility for MP3 files. Claims to be the world's largest MP3 site, with over a million files.

www.mp3sound.com
A large collection of MP3 files.

www.napster.com
The latest information about Napster.

www.peoplesound.com
Excellent highly accessible site which will mail sounds
directly to your e-mail. Lots of quality free downloadable
soundfiles.

www.realsounds.com
Quality site with downloadable files.

www.scour.com
Find music, films and radio sites, start your own radio
station, understand rippers and lots more.

www.zeropaid.com
The latest information about Gnutella.

## Radio stations

Although the audiences for Net radio are relatively small at
present, there are thousands of radio stations on the Net, and
listening figures are going to increase along with the numbers
of Net users. Web radio uses streaming technology and is particularly designed to play in background mode so you can
continue to surf while listening. Potentially, every radio station
is available over the Internet, from the well-known international
stations like BBC worldwide to the smallest local radio. There's
also a growing band of Internet-only stations which are reminiscent in style to some of the old maverick pirate radio
stations. You can even create your own station with radiosonic-
net using audio on demand by providing details of the type of
songs and artists you like. Some of the stations just use music,
while others have chatty IJs (Internet Jockeys).

For a sample of what to expect, try the following.

www.broadcast.com/bbc/
www.guitaradio.com
www.radio.sonicnet.com
www.spikeradio.com
www.spinner.com

## Media players

The Web offers a variety of multi-media manifestations, such as Web radio, video clips, VOD sequences and live audio-visual netcasts. In order to see and hear these, you will need to download one of the many available media players. These are at the heart of the Web's multi-media experience and **downloading** should only take a few minutes.

The media players are a good source of examples of Web media stations and networks as they have automatic links to many channels, and you can compile a Favorites link list as you find them on the Web in the same was as you can with your browser. The size of the viewing screen on these players varies according to the material you are watching. You can change the picture size by placing the cursor over the screen, clicking on the right mouse button and choosing one of the size options. Unless you are watching using a fast connection, the picture quality is better on a smaller screen.

### Choosing a media player

Media players are becoming pretty sophisticated. Choosing the right one for you is like selecting which hi-fi you prefer, forgetting things like price, delivery and availability, rather concentrating on which one sounds best and delivers the best picture. Sound, as with hi-fi systems, will be dictated primarily by what kind of speakers you are using. If you have integral speakers on your laptop, for instance, the sound will be constricted and tinny like that of a mono transistor radio. If you are using a desktop linked up to heavy-duty speakers, then the sound will be broader, deeper and with improved quality stereo. Generally, though, the sound – even the alleged near-CD quality sound of MP3 files – will be thinner and more constricted than you are used to from a quality TV or hi-fi system. Again, this is an area that looks set to improve over the next year or so.

The players are available from the sites shown on pages 165–7, but you can usually also download them from the Website hosting the sound or audio-video material you wish to access. For the casual Net music listener this is probably the best way to proceed. Simply click on the RealPlayer, or Quicktime, or other icon and follow the on-screen instructions. If you are using a later version of Windows, then you will probably already have Windows Audio Player on your computer. However, it may be worth downloading more than one media player as not all material runs on all players. Media players are frequently updated and it is worth downloading the latest version as facilities improve. Registering when you download will ensure you receive e-mail newsletters outlining the latest new features, sites and upgrades.

## Using a media player

Once you have downloaded your media player you are in a position to view multi-media files, which can take some time, depending on the size of the file. This time does not have to be wasted, though, because when downloading music or video files you don't have to wait for the download to complete before continuing to use the Net. Downloading can be put into **background** mode, simply by minimising, and you can continue surfing. You could even repeat this process a few times and download many files simultaneously, although overburdening your computer **system** may mean each file downloads slower and if too many are in operation at once problems may set in. Trial and error will indicate how much your particular computer and communications system can cope with.

You can add music and video files to your media player's Favorites list. To save the files more permanently (if permitted), you can download them to your **hard disk**. This can take some time depending on the speed of your connection. To download some files you need to buy a higher level version of the audio player. Most of the free players are fine for casual listening, but if you want to get more sophisticated and become a sound file collector with store and ordering facilities, then you may want to consider upgrading your free player. These are available from the main player Websites, but they will cost money. You can upgrade over the Web by submitting your credit card details and automatically downloading the software.

The presentation of the media player on-screen seems to be of great significance to some people. **Skins**, which changes the way your media player looks, are the latest craze – particularly for audio-only players. Skins are the graphic images that house the buttons and displays that overlay your media player. They are the interface via which you reach the content – a bit like the casing and buttons on a hi-fi or mobile phone. If these things matter to you, or you're just curious, check out WinAmp's site's skin catwalk. There are thousands of them, judged and rated – a fetishist's paradise.

Below and on the following pages is a selection of media and MP3 player Websites.

Hum (www.xaudio.com)
Play MP3s on portable devices with the latest MP3 player for **Windows CE**.

Liquid Audio (www.liquidaudio.com)
Authorised MP3 player, designed to play paid for MP3s.

Music Match Jukebox (www.musicmatch.com)
Popular MP3 player that allows you to record your own

MP3s, create custom audio CDs or MP3 CDs, organise and store music.

MTV (www.mpegtv.com)
Also known as the MpegTV Player. A video player for Linux and other UNIX platforms.

QuickTime (www.apple.com/quicktime/)
Apple's media player. Upgradable to QuickTimePro cost option.

RealPlayer (www.realplayer.com)
Ubiquitous popular media player. Free, but upgradable to RealPlayer Plus cost option.

Sonique (www.sonique.com)
Media and MP3 player supporting all the latest formats and featuring customisable skins (see picture above). From Mediascience, a Lycos company.

WinAmp (www.winamp.com)
Highly thought of high-fidelity music player for **Windows 95/98/NT** from Nullsoft. Supports MP3, CD and other audio formats, and thousands of skins.

Windows Media Player (www.microsoft.com)
Microsoft's media player provided with later versions of
Windows OS.

WPlay Pro (www.mp3rulz.com)
MP3 player shareware.

Below is another useful media application site.

Beatnik (www.beatnik.com)
An interactive audio system for adding interactive music
and sound content to Websites, such as sounds
triggered by cursor movement over a graphical image.

## Webcams

This curious Web phenomena comprises permanent cameras
that are placed at strategic sites around the world which send
their images to your computer in real-time as static pictures
updated over periods ranging from every few seconds to every
few minutes – like some global CCTV surveillance device. All
the world is here: you can see the wildlife in Africa, the traffic in
Trafalgar Square, the South Pole or into someone's bedroom.

Here are some sites to check out.

www.earthcam.com
www.gorilla.cam.za
www.steveweb.com/80clicks www.webcams.com
www.webcams.at

## MIDI

**MIDI** files turn up in all sorts of places, especially on fan sites
where budding synthesiser players have uploaded computerised versions of their musical heroes' best tracks. MIDI

stands for Musical Instrument Digital Interface and is a protocol that was developed in the early 1980s specifying how electronic musical instruments can work together. The protocol specifies both a hardware interface and a language for passing musically meaningful messages.

Digitised MIDI files take up very little room and can be downloaded in a few seconds. These frequently hilariously cheesy MIDI interpretations have to be heard to be appreciated. Check out your favourite artist's fan sites for MIDI files when you need a laugh.

## Other things you can find on the Web

As you've probably gathered by now, there's a fair chance you'll find just about anything you're looking for on the Web. The text that follows covers some subject areas that we haven't yet covered.

## Culture and the arts

Most major venues now have an information site providing venue and ticketing details, and events listings.

Look for the individual Websites of galleries, venues, theatre and dance companies.

www.tate.org.uk
The Tate is the foremost collection of galleries in the UK housing part of the national art collection. Check out the programme details of the new TateModern at Bankside.

www.thelowry.org.uk
This is the Website for Salford's answer to the Bilbao Guggenheim. It gives details about a stunning new gallery to house the national collection of local artist L.S. Lowry's paintings, plus theatre and arts facilities.

www.timeout.com
Look in the city events section to find out what's going on in counties around the world.

www.whatsonwhen.com
An invaluable and impressive resource for those interested in worldwide cultural events.

## Education

Most schools, colleges and universities have their own Web-sites where you can find information about courses, staff, syllabus, facilities, libraries and everything else you'd need to know about these seats of learning. Many sites also have application forms which can save the bother of waiting for the snail mail.

As well as a whole raft of Web-based educational tools that can help you learn anything from Spanish to the works of Shakespeare, there's also plenty of informative reference sites.

Check out the following handful of examples.

www.oed.com
The *Oxford English Dictionary* online. A great resource, but at £350 per annum for individual subscribers, not one that will be available to all.

www.britannica.com
www.encyclopedia.com
www.namss.org.uk/ssorgs.html
www.sbn.co.uk
www.thesaurus.com

## Environmental issues and world concerns

All the good (or not so good, depending on your view) causes you can think of are likely to have Websites galore. **Usenet** pages will also carry lots of views and opinions, unsavoury and otherwise, relating to these issues and concerns.

Check out the following.

www.actionaid.org
www.amnesty.org
www.corporatewatch.org
www.forumforthefuture.org.uk
www.greenpeace.org
www.mcspotlight.org

## Financial services

This is one of the biggest and busiest sectors of the Web. It's said that the world of banking has changed more in the last ten years than in the previous one hundred. And, of course, it's technology that's driven that change, with Internet banking being the latest in a series of recent developments to affect the banks and other financial institutions.

Here are a few of the Internet's financial resources.

www.economist.com
An online version of the informed journal of world politics and finance.

www.first-e.com
Europe's first Internet-only bank.

www.inlandrevenue.gov.uk
News and information about tax and national insurance in the UK.

www.moneysupermarket.com
Central financial services site providing mortgage, personal loans, conveyancing and other general advice and services.

www.mrscohen.com
Marketing-friendly money management advice service.

www.screentrade.co.uk
Search for the cheapest insurance quote from a range
of insurers.

www.smile.co.uk
The online bank designed especially for the Internet. Part
of the Co-op.

## Health

Medical self-help sites are one of the latest fashions of the
Web. These online self-diagnosis sites provide updated versions of the home doctor books of old. Sites include those
relating to health news, searchable encyclopaedia, live chats
with doctors, special features covering such topics as sex and
relationships, support groups, pregnancy and childbirth, and
interactive 'Ask the Doctor' features.

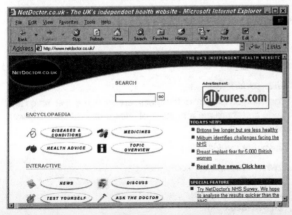

Check out the following.

www.netdoctor.com (see screen grab on page 171)
www.planetmedica.co.uk

Alternative health Websites include these two.

www.clickmango.com
www.thinknatural.com

## Hobbies, sports, collectors

Thousands of sites cater for every sport, hobby or collection that you can imagine. Type your favourite group, singer, football team, writer, television show, artist, car or anything else into one of the search tools, and the chances are you'll find something on the Net that is related to your interests.

To get you started, check out the following.

www.sportal.co.uk
As the name suggests, a portal for sports fans covering most popular sports.

## Silver surfers and kids

Age is no barrier for users of the Net.

### Silver surfers

A growing proportion of Internet users are in the over-fifties age range and there are a number of sites created especially with them in mind.

Check out the following.

www.2young2retire.com
www.idf50.co.uk
www.lifebegins.net
www.vavo.com

*Kids*

There are thousands of sites created especially for children, covering entertainment, education and advice, although many are very US-orientated.

The following search engines will help you find a selection of kid-friendly sites.

www.askjeevesforkids.com
www.surfmonkey.com
www.yahoolighans.com

## Mobile connections

WAP (Wireless Application Protocol) technology brings Web functionality to specially designed mobile phones. WAP is the world standard permitting mobile phones to access the Internet. This is one area where Europe leads the USA. Data-enabled mobile phones have a higher penetration in Europe than in the US.

These services provide only limited Internet access, covering selected channels for news, sports, share prices, weather, TV listings and an entertainment search. Phone-only e-auctions are also predicted. Banking and personal finance companies have signed-up enthusiastically to WAP technology, with Egg, First-e, Woolwich and First Direct all making launch plans for WAP services. Current **GSM** (Global Standard for Mobile Communications) technology already allows e-mail merges with SMS (Short Message Services), allowing you to send and receive e-mail text messages, faxes, and dictate e-mails to worldwide addresses and UK phone numbers.

WAP phones have bigger display screens to allow you to read the Web through a microbrowser and are fitted with special software, so you won't be able to use old mobiles to access the Net. One of the drawbacks is that WAP displays a cut-down monotone text-only version of Websites, which in some ways takes us back to the pre-graphic Internet – except, of course, there's more useful information available nowadays. It's also likely to be a fiddley experience as there's no point-and-click mouse option, rather scrolling with the up/down keys or a navigational roller bar. Larger colour displays are expected in a couple of years. The service will improve when an improved communication service, GPRS (General Packet Radio Service), is introduced over the GSM mobile phone network.

Here are a few Websites to check out.

www.btcellnet.co.uk
www.genie.co.uk
www.vodaphone.net

## Newspapers, magazines and journals

Most mainstream publications now have a Website of one sort or another. The information and services on offer vary enormously. The best are very impressive.

Check out the following.

www.guardian.co.uk
www.ft.com
www.qonline.co.uk

## Politics

Keen to demonstrate their grasp of the latest technological and media developments, most of the major political parties now have their own Websites. There are thousands of sites dealing with the issues of party and world politics, included a fair quota of **newsgroup** sites.

A selection of sites is given on page 175.

www.conservative-party.org.uk
www.labour.org.uk

www.politicsonline.com
US-orientated site, but with a worldwide element.

www.prime-minister.gov.uk
Tony proves he's a technological man of the people.

## Property

Buying and selling residential property on the Web is a booming business, with a number of nationwide Websites in the UK. In return for a no commission arrangement you have to register with the site. There are also long-term rental accommodation Websites, but these tend to operate regionally.

For buying and selling, look at the following.

www.homefreehome.co.uk
www.housenet.co.uk
www.housesearch.uk.com
www.houseweb.co.uk
www.easier.co.uk

If it's rented accommodation you're after, then the options below may help.

www.citylets.com
www.net-lettings.co.uk

## Recruitment

Many sites are dedicated to helping you find the job of your dreams. There are also a number of sites to help you construct the ultimate CV. Additionally, some companies list job opportunities on their corporate Websites.

Check out the following selection.

> www.cityjobs.com
> www.jobsite.co.uk
> www.recruitlink.co.uk
> www.stopgap.co.uk
> www.topjobs.co.uk

## Social Services and local information

The Net isn't just for matters of global importance. You can get local and regional information as well.

Here are a few sites to check.

> www.adviceguide.org.uk
> Citizens advice bureau, providing advice and information about your rights.

> www.home-repo.org
> Home ownership can sometimes go wrong. This sites offers advice to those having difficulties with lenders or those who have had their homes repossessed.

> www.lawrights.co.uk
> Legal information and services for England and Wales.

> www.multimap.com
> Provides maps of street names for London and of postcodes for the rest of UK. World maps also available.

> www.streetmap.co.uk
> Provides street maps for greater London and road atlas maps for mainland Britain.

> www.streetmap.com
> Multi-link map site.

www.upmystreet.com
Learn about the area you live in, including
information about the local government, council
tax and schools.

## Software

There is much software, free and charged for, available on the
Net. If you know the publisher of the software you want, visit
the official Website, where it is likely to be downloadable. If
you're just interested in seeing what's out there, then browse
one of the software centre Websites.

Most software that is available is fairly easy to install if you
follow the instructions, but you should be reasonably technically aware before downloading masses of software to your
computer. Be sure to organise the directories and folders on
your hard drive in such a way that you will be able to find your
way around the files.

Check out the following.

www.windowsupdate.microsoft.com
One of the most valuable sites for keeping your
systems software up to date is the Microsoft
Windows Update site. Here you will find all the
latest versions of all essential Internet Explorer
and Windows software, plus lots of interesting
and useful extensions.

cws.Internet.com
shareware.cnet.com
www.andover.net
www.download.com
www.freeprograms.com
www.softseek.com
www.tucows.com

## Stocks and shares

Another area of the Net that is gaining increasing interest is share dealing, and investing in Internet stocks seems to have become a widespread, and, for some, lucrative, pass time.

### Share dealing

The rise in interest in high technology and Internet stocks has coincided with an upsurge in personal share ownership in Western economies. This phenomenon is manifest in the huge growth in the number of companies offering advice to would-be traders and small-investors. The rise and rapid spread of investment clubs also reflects this trend.

The world of share dealing does not remain static for long in an electronic age and at the time of writing, the London and Frankfurt stock exchanges look set to merge under the title of iX (International Exchange), with the US technology exchange NASDAQ registering an interest as well, so the infrastructure of the share dealing system looks set to change. The Internet makes trading quicker and more immediate. It also brings it within reach of anyone who has a Net-connected computer. For those who are interested in dabbling on the stock exchange there are many Net-based companies waiting to offer advice and suggestions.

Check out the following.

www.fool.co.uk
Advice on personal money management from Motley Fool, including suggestions for investment clubs.

www.proshare.org.uk
The not-for-profit organisation that provides independent advice and a variety of services designed to help and encourage private investors. Heaps of advice for investment clubs.

www.hemscott.co.uk
www.sharepeople.com
www.tradingcentral.com
Share trading advice and service sites.

## Investing in Internet stocks

While there are many success stories on the Web, there have also been a number of e-tailing failures. Many companies, having started off with great expectations, are finding the reality a little harder to bear, and there are concerns about the long-term security of some Web retailers. It's well-documented that virtually none of the Web-based retailers are currently turning in healthy profits. Most are actually turning in losses and expect to do so for many years to come, so any share purchase is a quick rise-quick sell opportunity or a long-term investment.

The primary requirement for any successful e-tailer is traffic through its Website. If customers are visiting and the product is right, sales will result. If the customers aren't visiting in the first place, Web-based retailers can have the best products or services at the lowest prices but it will mean nothing. It's no accident that the dotcoms who have money in the bank are spending it establishing strong brand identities. Millions of pounds are being invested in marketing activities as companies promote their Websites with heavy advertising campaigns through conventional print and broadcast media. This is evident by the escalating number of ads on television and in the daily papers that are either for services based exclusively on the Web or for an established brand name's Website address.

The Internet share bubble burst on the UK stock exchange in April 2000. Lastminute, Freeserve and QXL all suffered heavy drops in their share prices. Until this point, Internet stocks were widely perceived as safe-bet glamour stocks. As it had only just launched with what now seems a wildly optimistic offer price and then saw its share price decline drastically in the coming weeks, Lastminute.com has the dubious honour of being symbolic of the mixed fortunes that can be the lot of an e-tailer. One minute feted by city analysts and investors, the next harangued, Lastminute had the misfortune to be at the juncture of a turning point in investor attitudes to dotcom stocks.

In many ways, it was fortunate that the bubble burst when it did. There appears to be a more sensible approach to investment in Internet companies now prevailing. Whether there is a sound business proposition in place has to be the bottom-line judgement when investing in a dotcom company. Without it, the best hype, marketing and management bravado will not help long-term survival. If the business plan doesn't add-up on paper, then there's little reason why it would do so in the long term on the Net either.

The decline in fortunes experienced by some dotcoms may make life a little tougher for Internet start-ups from now on, but that's no bad thing. Venture capitalists are likely to make more considered funding decisions in future, with investors paying more attention to the feasibility of their business plans.

Traditional old economy businesses are now coming to the Web in droves and beginning to see the Internet as integral to the way they will do business in the twenty-first century. They are beginning to interweave the Net into their business infrastructure, and it may well be a mix of 'new economy' dotcom start-ups and 'old economy' Net-aware companies that become the backbone of e-commerce.

It's worth remembering that no dotcom company has success guaranteed, and a fine balance of prudence and risk-taking usually wins the day when investing in shares. The skill or luck is in getting that balance right. While falls in stock prices affect every shareholder, it's often the smaller investor who is hit hardest. Shares can be easy to buy when they're on the up, but they are more difficult to offload when in freefall. Share dealing generally is not for the faint-hearted and Internet stocks are more of a gamble than most.

# Transport

You can make bookings for all forms of transport over the Web.

## Rail

Some of these sites offer small discounts on ticket prices for booking online.

www.eurotunnel.com
Road and freight connections to continental Europe via Dover.

www.eurostar.com
The rail service linking London's Waterloo station with Lille, Paris and Brussels.

www.londontransport.co.uk
Information about London travel, including buses, underground and river services. Promises to imminently include journeys planners. Real-time travel news useful for important journeys.

www.thetrainline.com
UK national online booking systems covering all rail networks.

# Travel

As well as booking your flights, you can find a mass of information about the places you are planning to travel to including country and city guides, and maps.

## Flights

Flights sold directly to the customer by budget airlines are one of the Web's greatest e-commerce successes. Ryan Air and Easyjet in particular set the pace with no-frills easy-to-use Websites offering quick responses and cheap prices. Ryanair's site has more than lived up to the expectations the company set when it launched it in January 2000, hitting the annual target of diverting 25 per cent of bookings through the Website in just three months.

Check out the following.

www.buzzaway.com
www.easyjet.co.uk
www.ebookers
www.go-fly.com
www.ryanair.com
www.virgin-express.com

Other travel sites include the ones listed below.

www.bargainholidays.com
The UK's biggest independent database of late availability holiday, city break and flight-only deals.

www.fco.gov.uk/
Online guide to the countries where you may be at risk.

www.h2g2.com
An idiosyncratic site that divides its categories at top level into three sections: Life, The Universe, and Everything. Yes, H2G2 stands for Hitchhikers Guide to the Galaxy.

www.lonelyplanet.com
Well-designed lively site based on the guides familiar to all independent travellers. Readily accessible information includes the interactive and useful 'Postcards' from on the road travellers and the irreverent, but occasionally informative 'Thorn Tree'.

www.mytravelguide.com
Travel planning portal for the independent traveller.

www.timeout.com
Excellently designed international city guide site,
including information about accommodation and events.

## Voice communication

Text-based e-mail and chat have been covered in some depth
earlier (see pages 74–106). However, one area where the Net
seems set to burgeon in the future is telephony. It is already
possible to communicate over the Web using voice, although
you and the person you are communicating with will require
mutually compatible telephony software and a microphone and
speaker or headset. You can use the Web to call someone on a
telephone, and you can make video calls if you have a video
camera. Some systems are also offering a voice and video
mail facility, whereby you can leave messages for contacts
to pick up. A recent development with big implications for
e-commerce is the incorporation of direct telephone calls into
Websites, whereby enquirers can dial companies direct.

With Internet phoning, your voice is broken down into
'packets' and then reassembled at the destination the same
way that other digital information is when transported over the
Net. This can result in non-synchronity during conversations.
That's a minor disadvantage. However, one of the great advantages is cost, especially for international calls. When lines that
are able simultaneously to carry voice and data become more
readily available, then Web telephony is likely to become more
widespread.

In the meantime, check out these sites.

www.icq.com/networks/InternetTelephony
www.phonefree.com
www.realcall.net
www.rockettalk.com
www.webphone.com

# PART TWO

# INTERNET DICTIONARY

Welcome to the A to Z part of the book. This section contains over 1,000 Internet-related terms, and is designed to be used either as a quick-reference guide or as a way of learning about the Internet following a multitude of routes. Underneath most entries is a list of links. These links take you to other entries in the dictionary that have some sort of connection with the entry you have just read. By moving from one link to another, a reader's knowledge can grow in a way that can't be achieved through the conventional use of a linear narrative. Paths continuously branch off one another, sometimes rejoining later. Lists of shorthand used online, error messages that users are likely to come across, emoticons, newsgroup categories and file extensions are shown separately from the main A to Z section for ease-of-use.

    With the space constraints placed on a book of this type, and the fact that the world of the Internet is expanding at a phenomenal rate, there are invariably entries that have not been included. If you would like to suggest an entry for future editions or if you have any comments, please e-mail us at internet@iconbooks.co.uk

# A

**about.com (www.about.com)**
A directory-based search tool with a network of niche vertical sites uniquely led by named expert guides based in over twenty countries.
*Links: Directory (Internet), Portal, Search engine, Vertical portal,*

**Access**
Internet access (or accessing the Internet) is the gaining of entry to the Internet in order to, for example, browse, obtain information or communicate with other people by e-mail. The three most common ways of accessing the Internet are as follows.

- Network connection: these are found in universities, schools, businesses and so on where fast access is provided through the use of dedicated lines.
- SLIP/PPP connection: Internet Service Providers offer SLIP (Serial Line Interface Protocol) or PPP (Point-to-Point Protocol) connections. This is often referred to as Dial-up networking, and allows PCs to dial into their servers and use software applications such as Explorer, Netscape Navigator and Eudora to get the most out of the Internet.
- Online services: these include America Online, CompuServe and Microsoft Network.

*Links: Dial-up networking, e-mail, Internet, ISP, OSP, SLIP/PPP*

**Access (Microsoft)**
A database program that enables users to store information. Examples include names and addresses or lists with notes,

such as all the books a person owns with synopses. Access is also used by Web developers as a format in which information is held on a server allowing users to search for information within the site.

*Links: Database, Query, Relational database*

### Access control

A security system that protects a computer (or computer network) from unauthorised access.

*Links: Accessware, Authentication, Firewall, Security*

### Access number

The telephone number used to dial into an Internet (or Online) Service Provider (ISP). ISPs often provide a list of telephone numbers that can be used to 'dial-in' to their service. It is useful to have a few numbers to dial to help avoid frustrating busy signals and/or no connections.

*Links: Access, ISP, OSP*

### Access time

The time taken from the moment a computer makes a request for data to the instant it is supplied. These could be requests made to the computer's hard disk, or the Internet for example. This time is often very short when concerning the former two but can be measured in seconds and even minutes when dealing with the Internet. The Internet is much more dependent on external factors such as the amount of traffic and the speed of the connection.

*Links: Bandwidth, Cache, Clock speed, CPU, Response time*

### Accessware

Security is very important on the Internet, and ways of improving and allowing secure access to a network are of imperative concern. Accessware describes sophisticated programs that provide this facility without the simple blocking of unwanted

access. It does this by integrating many of the things considered vital when trying to produce a secure intranet or extranet. These include access control, usernames, information management and privacy.
*Links: Access control, Authentication, Extranet, Intranet, Security, Username*

### Account

When users sign up with an Internet Service Provider (ISP), they are given a username and a password. This is their account. It allows the ISP to check whether they are an authorised user of its facilities when they dial the given access number. An account is also usually required to use computer networks, be they within the workplace, universities or schools and so on.
*Links: ISP, Password, Username*

### ACDSee

A Web design software program. It allows viewing and editing of graphic images for Windows and supports many image file formats including GIF and JPEG.
*Links: Bitmap, GIF, JPEG*

### Active/Activate

The 'active' window is the window in which the user is currently working. The 'active' program is the program currently running. It is important to remember (especially if several windows are open at one time) that when a command is entered in any program, it usually applies only to the active window. If the user is activating a window, they are choosing a window in which they want to work. This can be done by moving the mouse over the chosen window and clicking once (if using Windows, click the left mouse button).
*Links: Graphical User Interface*

### Active Matrix Display

A type of display for laptops with better resolution and contrast than traditional passive matrix displays. A separate transistor controls each screen pixel, offering a much quicker refresh rate. A TFT display is the most common example of this type of flat-panel display and the two terms are often used interchangeably.

*Links: FED, TFT screen*

### ActiveX

Microsoft technology that permits multi-media facilities to be used over the Web when using Internet Explorer. These include moving and animated objects, live audio, and interactivity that uses a computer's sound and video cards and can be viewed in real time. For example, users would be able to listen to online radio, watch video clips or listen to music samples using these controls. This is achieved by allowing a computer program to run from inside a Webpage. Internet Explorer places the ActiveX controls (effectively plug-ins) in their own folder. In Windows, this folder (called Downloaded Program Files) is located inside C:\Windows. With Macs, it is System Folder/Extensions/ActiveX Controls.

*Links: ActiveX control, ADO, Internet Explorer, Java, Multi-media, Plug-in*

### ActiveX control

An applet (small program) that permits multi-media facilities on Webpages. These are often automatically downloaded and executed by Web browsers and have full access to the Windows operating system. They are a type of plug-in and it is these that enable Internet Explorer to play ActiveX components.

*Links: ActiveX, ADO, Applet, Internet Explorer, Java, Multi-media, Plug-in, Windows*

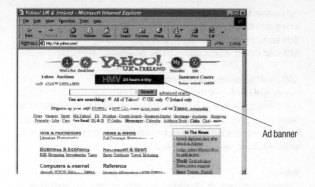

Ad banner

## Ad banner

These are so-called because they stretch across the tops of Webpages in horizontal strips and are the most common of the many ways of advertising on the Web. By placing an advertisement on a Webpage, a company can link to its own site or buffer/splash page. Using this method it is possible to generate a great number of visitors who wouldn't normally have visited the site. They can cost anything from zero to upwards of £10,000 ($16,000) per month depending, on the number of page views the Website receives and the relevance of visitor. For example, a financial institution may get fewer visitors if it advertises on another financially based site as opposed to a search engine but these visitors may prove to be more receptive to the advertiser's products.

*Links: Ad server, Auditor, Buffer page, Button, Cost per sale, Impressions, Marketing, Splash page*

## Ad server

A Website's ad banners are managed and tracked, including the collation of usage statistics, by sophisticated programs or type servers. This can prove extremely useful to the advertiser.

Ad banners can also be rotated or changed. A user who visits a site many times will consequently be exposed to many different ads as opposed to the same one again and again.
*Links: Ad banner, ASP, Auditor, DHTML, Impressions, Marketing*

### ADC (Analog-to-Digital Converter)

A piece of hardware that converts data from analogue to digital – an example being a modem, which converts digital data from a computer into analogue data for the telephone and vice versa. Another example is scanning a photo on to a computer.
*Links: Analogue, DAC, Digital, Modem*

### Add-on

Commonly used to describe a product that is designed to complement another product. An example of this would be a sound card.
*Links: Expansion board, Graphic accelerator, Sound card*

### Address (e-mail, Internet and Web)

Addresses are needed in order to find people, places and information on the Internet. These addresses can contain letters, numbers and symbols. Through the use of addresses, people can send and receive e-mail, files and documents, and look at Websites. e-mail addresses take the form username@hostname.domain. The username is a name a person has chosen to identify themselves. The hostname is the name of their e-mail provider. The symbol in the middle is the 'at' symbol (@). The e-mail address would be read aloud as 'username at hostname dot domain'. A user's e-mail address might be John.Smith@aname.co.uk

In this instance, the username is 'John.Smith', 'aname' is hosting their address, and '.co.uk' shows it is a UK commercial company. If John Smith were telling someone his e-mail address, he would say it was 'John dot Smith at aname dot co dot uk'.

A Web address is the same as a URL or Uniform Resource Locator. This address starts with http://www. followed by a domain name. Because domain names are international many companies use their country name instead of dot com (for example, Penguin Books in the UK is www.penguin.co.uk and Penguin Books Canada www.penguin.ca).
*Links: Address book, At/@, Domain name, e-mail, Internet, URL, WWW*

### Address book
The place where information is kept regarding all the individuals and groups that are likely to be sent e-mails by the user. This information includes URL addresses, house addresses, telephone numbers and so on. Also known as 'Nicknames' with earlier versions of Eudora.
*Links: Address, Eudora, Netscape Messenger, Outlook Express*

### ADN (Advanced Digital Network)
This term is typically used when talking about 56 kbps leased or dedicated lines.
*Links: bps, Dedicated line, Leased line*

### ADO (ActiveX Data Objects)
An interface for data objects. This can be used to access all manner of different types of data, including Webpages and spreadsheets as well as relational databases.
*Links: ActiveX, Relational database*

### Adobe Acrobat
A software program that can save documents with all of their formatting for uploading to the Web. This is extremely useful if a company wishes to show and allow the downloading of its brochure, or of an order form to be printed and posted. It is also one of the ways of displaying text and images in an e-book. Documents are saved as Portable Document Format (PDF) files, and can be displayed and printed from any computer

using any platform. In order to view Acrobat documents the user's computer must be equipped with the Adobe Acrobat reader, which can be obtained free of charge by downloading from the Adobe Internet site (www.adobe.com), and often from sites that hold PDF files.
*Links: ClearType, Cross-platform, Microsoft Reader, PDF, PGML*

### Adobe Photoshop
One of the most widely used professional paint programs. It is often used in Web design to render a homepage visual in the form of a jpeg image, for example.
*Links: GIF, JPEG*

### Adobe Postscript
See Postscript.

### ADSL (Asymmetric Digital Subscriber Line)
Many believe that this will be one of the more popular choices for Internet access over the next few years. This technology uses upgraded phone lines, and supports simultaneous Internet browsing and phone use. The line is asymmetric, in that it has more capacity for data received by a computer (such as graphics, video, audio and software upgrades) than for data that is sent (such as e-mail and browser commands). With ADSL data rates of up to 500k can be received (downstream) and up to 250k can be sent (upstream). ADSL requires a special ADSL modem and usage is fairly limited at the moment.
*Links: Downloading, High-speed connections, ISDN, POTS, Upload*

### Agent
Often called 'Web agents' or 'autonomous agents', these enable users to specify their interests and preferences, then set to work in the background locating relevant information for the user on the Internet.
*Links: AI, Auto-bot, Bot, Daemon, Fuzzy logic*

### AGP (Accelerated Graphics Port)
An interface specification developed by Intel that was designed with 3D graphics in mind. These deal with the greater through-put of data by allowing the graphics controller direct access to the main memory. People who use a computer for games should certainly consider getting a good AGP graphics card.
*Links: Games, Graphics accelerator, VRML*

### AI (Artificial Intelligence)
Many people believe that, one day, computers will be able to simulate human thinking with the result that they will be able to creatively solve problems. An example was the computer Blue, which defeated the chess master Garry Kasparov in 1997. Oth-erwise computers simply work through the steps of a solution as specified by the programmer.
*Links: Agent, Fuzzy logic, OCR*

### AIFF or AIF (Audio Interchange File Format)
A Macintosh sound file format, and one that a user is likely to encounter on the Internet. A suitable plug-in or player will be required in order to play a downloaded AIFF file. A Macintosh platform is not needed to play these files.
*Links: File extension, Macintosh, Media players, Platform*

### Aladdin Expander
Aka Stuffit Expander, this is a Windows program for extracting archived files.
*Links: Archive, Compression, StuffIt*

### Alias
An alternative name or identification of a file. An alias can also be a shortcut and serve as a link to a file in another location.
*Links: Device, File*

### Aliasing and anti-aliasing

Sometimes called the 'jaggies', aliasing is when a line or object that is supposed to have a smooth surface (like O, /, S) becomes jagged. Anti-aliasing is a software technique used in imaging systems (such as Adobe Photoshop) that compensates for this jagged effect, making the lines look smooth and continuous. However, this can give a fuzzy-like appearance to the line or object.

*Links: Jaggies, MIP mapping, Resolution*

### Alignment

The arrangement of text and graphics in relation to a margin.
*Links: Bleed*

### allonesearch.com (www.allonesearch.com)

An all-in-one multi-search site providing access to over 500 search tools for individual searches.
*Links: Directory (Internet), Meta-search tools, Multi-search tools, Portal, Search engine*

### alltheweb.com (www.alltheweb.com)

URL of Fast, a search tool using new technology developed in conjunction with Dell that promises to index the whole Web rather than just a portion, and claims to search 300 million Webpages in under half a second. Fast supports 31 languages and includes specific MP3, Multi-media and FTP search options.
*Links: Directory (Internet), Meta-search tools, Multi-search tools, Portal, Search engine*

### Alpha (version)

Before a piece of commercial software or hardware is released, it often goes through two pre-release versions. This is so it can be tested under various conditions and enable any problems that are encountered to be ironed out. The Alpha version is the first of these pre-releases; Beta, or Beta Testing phase, is the second.

*Links: Anomaly, Beta bugs, Beta testing, Bug, Hardware, Robust, Software*

### Alphanumeric

These are characters that consist of letters and numbers, but not punctuation found on a typical keyboard.

*Links: ASCII*

### Alt

When seen in the form alt. this refers to a type of newsgroup that discusses alternative topics – which consequently covers the widest variety of subjects. Users may have to state that they are eighteen years of age (or over) before being allowed to enter.

*Links: Newsgroups, Newsreader*

### Alt text

The text seen before an image on a Webpage loads. It is also the text that appears when a mouse is put on top of the image. This text can prove to be influential in the cataloguing of a site by a search engine, as some search engines 'read' these as keywords. Because of this potential, the written alt text might not necessarily be a description of the image and may even be a blatant advertising message, such as 'software for sale'. This is one technique that can be employed by Web developers to increase traffic to their sites.

*Links: Hit, Keyword, Marketing, Mouseover event, Search engine, Spamdexing*

### altavista.com (www.altavista.com)

One of the oldest and most comprehensive search engines that indexes World Wide Websites, newsgroup postings and a variety of other postings. It also provides access to the impressive Babel Fish which translates words, phrases and entire Websites into Spanish, French, German, Portuguese and Italian.

*Links: Portal, Search engine, Vertical portal*

### Alter ego

When playing one of the many text-based games (MUDs) on the Net, users take on alter egos acceptable within the game, much in the same way as in traditional role-playing games.

*Links: Avatar, Games, MOO, MUD*

### amazon.com / amazon.co.uk / amazon.de (www.amazon.com / www.amazon.co.uk / www.amazon.de)

Websites that offer the ability to purchase over one million book titles and CDs on the Internet. The .com site relates to the American market, the .co.uk to the British and the .de to the German, although it is possible to purchase books from these sites to be delivered anywhere in the world. As well as books and CDs, users can find new, used and hard-to-find items through its zShops, and take part in online auctions. On the US site goods are available through on-site concessions, such as sothebys.amazon.com for arts and collectibles. Other options include electronics, toys, and health and beauty products.

*Links: e-business, e-commerce, Shopping*

### Analogue

Data represented in a form other than binary bits (the form digital information is in) and that is continuous (for example, the information is carried in a wave-form).

*Links: ADC, Binary, Digital, Modem*

### Anchor
Webpages can be very long, so it is possible to add links that allow users to jump to the parts of the page they wish to read. The destination marked on the page for a certain link is called an anchor.
*Links: Alt text, HTML, Link*

### Angel
Someone who invests in computer or Internet related start-up companies.
*Links: Denizen, Digerati, Netizen, Newbie*

### Animated GIF
A single file that contains multiple images which a browser can play in succession giving the appearance of animated graphics. These can be placed on a Webpage in much the same way as a normal GIF image. One advantage of animated GIFs is that both Netscape Navigator and Microsoft Internet Explorer are able to display them without the need for additional software.
*Links: Applets, GIF, Java, Transparent GIF*

### Annotations
It is possible to add notes to Web documents which can then be stored on the user's local disk. These notes are made available every time the document is accessed. It is also a feature of some Web browsers.
*Links: Browser, Microsoft Reader*

### Anomaly
Used interchangeably with 'bug', this describes any computer or program problem for which no cause or reason can be found.
*Links: Alpha, Beta bugs, Bug*

### Anonymous

Many FTP sites allow visitors to connect and search through their contents and subsequently download any file on the site without visitors having to verify their user IDs and/or passwords. They are, in effect, acting anonymously.
*Links: Anonymous FTP, FTP, TFTP*

### Anonymous FTP

An option that allows visitors to connect and search through an FTP site's contents and subsequently download any file on the site without visitors having to verify their user IDs and/or passwords. If a user ID is requested, 'anonymous' can normally be entered; a user's e-mail address can be used for the password. Most FTP servers allow this, normally with a maximum number of anonymous users at any one time and often with access to designated files only. A list of anonymous FTP sites along with the files available at these sites can be obtained using the Archie system.
*Links: Archie, Downloading, FTP, TFTP*

### Anonymous posting

A message posted to a newsgroup whereby the identity of the sender is not known.
*Links: Cross-posting, Newsgroups*

### another.com (www.another.com)

A Webmail facility like Hotmail. However, this one allows users to choose their e-mail addresses by clicking on a 'Domain names' option and selecting a domain name for their e-mail address – for example, joebloggs@I-love-evertonfc.com or joebloggs@myway.com There are thousands to choose from.
*Links: Domain name, Hotmail, Webmail*

**ANSI (American National Standards Institute)**
The main industrial standardisation organisation in the US.
There are official ANSI standards in almost all industries, and
many of them are connected in some way to computers. Devel-
opments include the ASCII and SCSI.
*Links: ASCII, SCSI*

**Anti-aliasing**
See Aliasing.

**Anti-virus program**
A program that searches a computer's hard drive for viruses
and subsequently removes any that are found. Because new
viruses are constantly appearing, it is advisable to get an anti-
virus program that can receive updates, either from floppy disc
or downloaded straight from the manufacturer's Website, so
that they can be at their most effective. Most anti-virus programs allow users to scan for viruses either automatically or
manually.
*Links: Freeware, McAfee, Norton AntiVirus, Shareware, Trojan, Virus*

**AOL (America Online)**
Currently the largest online information service on the Net. It
offers subscribers e-mail, conferencing, software, the ability to
protect children online, computing support, interactive magazines and newspapers, online classes and Internet access. The
advantages of using AOL are that it can save the hassle of
finding a suitable ISP, it is easy to install and avoids any manual
configuration, and it does make information relatively easy to
find. A user's Internet address is their screen name (without any
spaces) followed by @aol.com It is possible to have up to five
screen names and each screen name produced has it own
mailbox. However, a word of warning: AOL users have become
the targets of a type of prejudice known as domainism as in
'Don't listen to him, he uses AOL'.

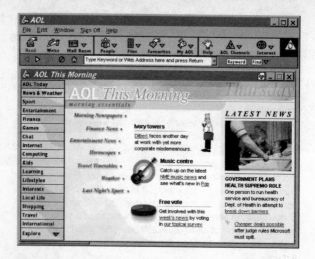

Links: *Chat, Domainism, Flash session, Instant Messenger, Interactive Web chat, ISP, OSP, Roaming service*

## AOL winsock (America Online Windows Socket)

Because AOL primarily promotes itself as an online service, its infrastructure is not ultimately designed to work with applications that require direct Internet connection. Consequently, to be able to use such applications through an AOL connection, AOL winsock is required for those users with AOL for Windows (it doesn't work with any other ISP).
*Links: WinSock*

## API (Application Program Interface)

Enables programmers to write applications that can interact with other applications by providing all the necessary building blocks. This is especially important when writing consistent applications for a particular operating system. Fortunately, most operating systems – including Windows – provide such APIs. Another example of the use of an API is with servers. With these, software developers are able to create programs that become part of the Web server itself.

*Links: Application, DLL, NSAPI*

### Aplio phone

A standalone Internet phone device that works by having the two callers possess the device both of whom are connected to the Internet. Consequently, *both* talkers are paying for the phone call, albeit at a local rate.

*Links: Internet telephony, NetMeeting*

### App

Short for application.

*Links: API, Applet, Application, Killer app*

### Apple

Apple is one of the largest manufacturers of personal computers and currently produces the Macintosh range. The first Macintosh was introduced in 1984 and was the first widely used computer with a graphical user interface (GUI), which used a mouse and icons identifying commands. Founded on 1 April 1976 by Steve Jobs and Steve Wozniak, Apples were among the first microcomputers.

*Links: Apple key, Graphical User Interface, Mac OS, Macintosh, Microprocessor, Operating system*

### Apple key

Serves as the Command key on Macintosh computers. It is identified by an apple logo.

*Links: Apple, Macintosh*

## Applet

An application so-called because it is small. It's main benefits are that it can be downloaded quickly and, providing the down-loading computer is equipped with a Java or ActiveX capable browser, it can be run on any platform. Applets carry their own software players but are designed to run from within another application. An example of an applet would be the calculator available in the accessories section of Windows. On the Web, a Java Applet could be used to flag up news in the form of a scrolling ticker tape effect for example.

*Links: ActiveX, Application, Java, Mappucino, Servlet*

## Application

A computer program that makes the computer perform useful work by providing a set of instructions. Examples include Web browser programs, databases and word processors. The other type of software is systems software.

*Links: API, Applet, Front-end, Killer app, Operating system, Program, Software*

## Application server

It is very important that visitors to a Website are able to interact with it, the most common form of which is the querying of a database. For example, it is vital that a Website selling books allows visitors to search for the books of their choice. Applica-tion servers are key to this facility. They are a program (or collection of programs) able to integrate into a Web server's environment. It is also necessary that these interact with an API that visitors can use.

*Links: API, Applet, Application, Database, Query, Server*

## Application server solution

A product that is considered (normally by the manufacturer) to be the 'answer to a need' in reference to an application server.

*Links: Application server, Server*

### Archie

The first Internet search engine. It is a tool (software) that helps people to locate material on FTP servers across the Internet. This is particularly useful for users who know the exact name of a file they would like to download but don't know where it's located. To use Archie, a user needs to connect to an Archie server and perform a search. It is effectively a search engine for files, especially program files, on anonymous FTP servers. It searches for file names or parts of file names, not content.

*Links: Anonymous FTP, FTP, Gopher, Search engine*

### Architecture

The overall design and infrastructure of the hardware and software of a computer, particularly of the former. It is also a term applied to Websites.

*Links: Scalability, Webpage, Website*

### Archive

Used both as a noun and as a verb when talking about computers and the Internet. A computer (file) or Internet host might contain an archive of files. It is also a file that contains a number of compressed files. To archive is the act of creating this file.

*Links: Back up*

### Archive site

Also known as FTP sites, these are computers whose sole purpose is to store and make available files. They are accessible through anonymous FTP and e-mail, and visitors are able to download files from them (often in compressed form). Files are usually organised by subject, enabling users to find want they want quickly.

*Links: Archive, FTP*

### ARP (Address Resolution Protocol)

This is a protocol able to convert an IP address into an Ethernet

address. It is possible to find a host's Ethernet address by broadcasting an ARP packet containing that host's Internet address. This prompts the return of the Ethernet address.
*Links: IP address, TCP/IP*

### ARPANET (Advanced Research Projects Agency Network)
The precursor to the Internet. It started in 1969 as a four-node that steadily grew. It was funded by the Pentagon and was intended to be a communications network that could withstand a nuclear attack. The network finally closed in 1990.
*Links: JANET*

### Array
In programming, arrays are series of data items that are all the same size and type – for example, an array of integers or characters.
*Links: Object-oriented programming, Program*

### Article
A newsgroup message or posting. It is possible with most newsreader programs to filter out articles that have been viewed before.
*Links: Anonymous posting, Cross-posting, Hierarchy, Newsgroups, Newsreaders, Posting, Thread*

### ASCII (American Standard Code for Information Interchange)
Pronounced 'ass-key'. A standard way of representing ordinary text as a stream of binary numbers. There are 128 characters in all, which include control codes and upper and lower case letters, numbers, punctuation marks and special characters. Each of these is represented by a seven-digit binary number: 0000000 through 1111111.
*Links: ASCII Art, BinHex, CSV, Emotags, Emoticons, MIME, UUENCODE, UUDECODE*

**ASCII Art**
An 'art form' that has been created using ASCII characters.
*Links: ASCIII*

**Ask Jeeves!**
**(www.ask.com / www.ask.co.uk / www.ajkids.com)**
An enquiry site that uses plain English questions to retrieve
data. It compares a user's questions to nearest matching questions in its database and also provides material from Web
search engines. Despite its good intentions, it can be a little hit
and miss.
*Links: Boolean Logic, Directory (Internet), Portal, Search engine*

**ASP (Active Server Pages)**
Websites sometimes have pages that change in response to
user input. These dynamic Webpages may have an .asp extension. These are similar to CGI scripts and contain either Visual
Basic or JavaScript code. An example of a use of ASP is the
ability to put up a searchable catalogue on the Web.
*Links: CGI, DHTML, HTML, JavaScript, Visual Basic*

**Aspect ratio**
Ratio that compares the width of an object to its height and is
particularly used when talking about computer graphics – for
example, a graphic with an aspect ratio of 3:1 has a width three
times as large as the height. It is also used in connection with
screens. So, if a user has a screen that is 640 x 480, the aspect
ratio is 4:3.
*Links: Bitmap, Resolution*

**Assicons**
A variation on the emoticon theme involving a particular part of
the body. One example is (_!_) – a normal ass. See appendices
for further assicons.
*Links: Emotags, Emoticons, Shorthand, Stage directions*

## Associate

The linking of each file type to the relevant application. For example, all Microsoft Word files are specified by the extension .doc and if such a file is selected, then Word itself will automatically open and load the selected file.
*Links: File extension*

## Asynchronous

The transference of data in a way that isn't timed or synchronised.
*Links: ADSL*

## AT commands

AT commands programme a number of modem hardware settings and were originally used by modem manufacturers that wanted to sell their products as being Hayes-compatible. Hayes is a modem manufacturer who standardised the software commands that allow a computer to control a modem. The commands are usually hidden under a menu option in the communications software.
*Links: Communications software, Hayes compatible, Modem*

## At/@

This ubiquitous symbol has gone from being one of the least used to one of the most used characters on a keyboard. It is primarily used to separate the domain name and the username in an e-mail address. For example, internet@iconbooks.co.uk is read and pronounced as 'internet at iconbooks dot co dot uk'. It has also become prevalent in a significant way in today's marketing practice due to its connections with the Internet.
*Links: Address, e-mail, Marketing*

## ATM (Asynchronous Transfer Mode)

Multi-media files can often be extremely large, a fact that resulted in the design of this high-speed networking scheme

and communication protocol. There is another facility with the abbreviation ATM – the Automated Teller Machine, or hole-in-the-wall, from which one can obtain money.
*Links: ADSL, ISDN, Multi-media*

### Attachment
Most e-mail programs allow users to 'add' files to an e-mail. There will normally be an 'Attach' button at the top of a new e-mail message, which, once pressed, allows the user to find and select the desired file for attaching. This makes it possible to send whatever can be put in file form – for example, family photos, cvs, brochures, reports and video clips. Attachments have also resulted in a proliferation of viruses disguised as innocent files.
*Links: e-mail, Eudora, File, MAPI, Outlook Express, Trojan, Virus*

### ATX
The current standard layout of modern PC motherboards.
*Links: Motherboard*

### AU or .au Au(dio)
Standard audio file format for the Java programming language; it is also a UNIX sound file format. It is possible that a sound file downloaded from the Net will be in this form. To play this file, a media player or the correct browser plug-in are required. Two other common sound formats on Windows are WAV and MIDI.
*Links: Digital audio, Java, Media players, MIDI, UNIX, WAV*

### Auctions, online
A type of shopping on the Internet. Various items are advertised on an auction site along with a time at which the auction of a particular item closes. To place a bid, the user needs to register with the auction site. The current highest bids are displayed, and users are able to submit bids and keep raising them until the deadline if they so wish. Also, there is often the facility for

bidders to put a maximum bid as well as their initial bid so their bids will match or better the highest bid until the maximum bid is reached. When the auction's deadline is reached, it is closed and the highest bidder is sold the item at that price. Please note that all bids are legally binding. Famous auction sites include www.ebay.com and www.qxl.com
*Links: Shopping*

### Auditor
When dealing with ad banners, it is useful that a company other than those directly involved, monitors the whole exercise (the tracking, counting, verification and so on). This company is called an Auditor.
*Links: Ad banner, Ad server, Counter, Impressions*

### AUP (Acceptable Use Policy)
The set of rules established by the owner of a computer system, or by an ISP, concerning what users can write and do using their network facilities.
*Links: TOSsed out*

### Authentication
Many Websites require visitors to authenticate their identities before they are allowed to enter – although cookies can help bypass this procedure. Authentication is also necessary when users logon to a network – for example, by dialling an ISP. This is usually achieved with a password and/or username.
*Links: Account, Authorisation, Case sensitive, Cookie, ISP, Username*

### Author
As a verb, 'author' means to create or publish a script, program or document. This is often done with a computer language such as Java or HTML. As a noun, it is the person who writes the program.
*Links: Authoring tool, HTML, Java*

**Authoring tool**
A program that is used for writing hypertext or multi-media applications. There is no obvious way of distinguishing between authoring tools and programming tools, although authoring tools are considered easier to master as they don't involve someone starting from scratch.
*Links: Author, HTML*

**Authorisation**
The stage after authentication when an attempt is made to gain access to a network resource. It is at this stage that access is either granted or denied.
*Links: Account, Authentication, Username*

**Auto-bot**
A tool that can automatically perform various functions as specified by a user. An example is that it monitors Websites in which the user is interested.
*Links: Bot, Cancelbot, NetBuddy*

**Autoexec.bat (Automatically executed batch file)**
The file that is automatically executed by DOS when a computer is switched on. It provides the computer with the commands that tell it how to start up.
*Links: Boot*

**Auto-reply**
A feature of many e-mail programs that allows a standard message to be sent to everyone who sends an e-mail to a particular address. This is particularly useful for people going on holiday who need to inform anyone contacting them that they are away. This feature is called the Out of Office Assistant in Outlook.
*Links: e-mail, Mail client*

## Autosave

On many applications data files it is possibe to save at specified intervals of time. This greatly reduces the risk of losing large amounts of data should a computer crash while the user is working on it.

*Links: Crash, Frozen*


## Avatar

A graphical representation or movable icon that represents a user in a virtual world. Avatars can look like a person, animal, object or just about anything. 3D chat rooms and VRML worlds are examples of places where someone would have an avatar. Special 3D chat programs such as Microsoft V-Chat are required to connect to a 3D chat server.

*Links: Alter ego, Chat, Games, Idoru, MUD, VRML*


## AVI (Audio Video Interleave)

A file format that users might come across on the Internet containing both video and audio – that is, moving pictures with sound. However, due to the fact that these files are typically very large, they can take a particularly long time to download. Many people prefer streaming video files that can be run in real time. Other types of video files that can be found on the Internet include MOV, MPEG and ASF.

*Links: Media players, MPEG, Multi-media, Net Toob*

# B

**B Channel (Bearer Channel)**
Able to carry up to 64 kbps, this is a channel used in ISDN service. This makes it particularly useful for transferring voice, data or video when able to operate at maximum capacity.
*Links: ISDN*

**BABT Approval**
Any modem used in the UK must be approved by the British Approval Board for Telecommunications. A green circle means approval, a red triangle means it has not been approved.
*Links: Modem*

**Back up**
To copy files into another format or physical location in case those files are ever lost on the computer. It is common to hear the phrase 'back up your files regularly'. Back up is also the name of a file that serves as a spare copy for another file as in 'do you have a back up?'.
*Links: Archive*

**Backbone**
The main communication path on to which other networks are able to connect.
*Links: T-1, T-3*

**Back-end**
An application or part of an application that doesn't directly interact with a user and usually acts as the support to the front-

end application. An example might be a database on a server.
*Links: Database, Front-end*

## Background

There are certain programs that run in the background on a computer as opposed to the foreground. An example would be the printing of a document while still working on a word processing file. The printing would be happening in the background and is independent of any input from the user. The editing of the text would be a foreground process and these have a higher priority. A background is also the area on a monitor's screen not covered by graphics and text.
*Links: Daemon, Demon, Spool*

## Backplane (Active or Passive Backplane)

There are two types of backplanes: active and passive. Both are circuit boards into which other circuit boards or expansion cards can be plugged. The difference between the two is computing circuitry. Active backplanes contain logical circuitry and are able to perform computing functions; passive backplanes contain none. This actually makes the latter easier to repair and upgrade.
*Links: Motherboard*

## Backslash

The character '\'. A forward slash is '/'.
*Links: ASCII*

## Backwards compatible

Very important when using programs as it refers to a program's ability to read a file created by an earlier version of the same program. For example, Microsoft Word 2000 can read files created by Word 5.0
*Links: Program*

## Bandwidth

The rate at which data can be transmitted. The higher the bandwidth, the faster the transmission or the greater the volume of signals that can be carried. The Internet can seem a lot slower at certain peak times in the day because the same bandwidth is dealing with a higher volume of traffic.
*Links: Access time, Latency, Multi-media, Video-conferencing, VOD*

## Banking, online

Many banks now allow customers to control their accounts using the Internet. This normally requires using no more than the Web browser. It is possible to get up-to-the-minute balances on accounts, transfer funds, pay bills and set up standing orders, as well as view and print statements. There are also some banks that work exclusively over the Internet, often with the incentive of higher interest rates to customers.
*Links: Security, SET, SSL*

## Banner advertising

See Ad banner.

## Baseband

In contrast to broadband, where a single wire may carry more than one signal simultaneously, baseband is when a network uses an entire transmission to send a solitary signal.
*Links: Broadband*

## Batch (file)

The organising of a number of files into a single group for transmitting or printing, thereby increasing the efficiency of the data transmission.
*Links: Offline*

## Baud

A unit denoting the speed with which information is transferred.

The usage of 'baud rate' in the context of modems has been replaced by the easier-to-understand 'bits per second' or bps – that is, how many bits it can send or receive per second.
*Links: Baud barf, Bit, bps, Modem*

### Baud barf
Should a modem connection not have a correct protocol setting, it is likely that users will see what seems to be gibberish on their screen. This is baud barf, as is the sound heard should the connection be disrupted.
*Links: Baud, bps, Modem*

### Bay (short for drive bay)
The physical location on a laptop where devices such as floppy disk drives, CD-ROM drives and extra battery packs can be installed. So, if there are two bays on a laptop and one is being used for an extra battery, the user can have either the floppy disk drive or the CD-ROM also installed, but not both.
*Links: Expansion board, Expansion slot*

### bbc.co.uk (www.bbc.co.uk)
One of the most popular sites in the world. It makes more news available with links to useful sites for every story. It also includes radio station sites and TV programmes, movie reviews, weather, education resources and lots more.
*Links: Broadcasting, News*

### BBEdit
An HTML authoring program for the Macintosh.
*Links: Author, HTML*

### BBS (Bulletin Board System or Service)
Message boards, sometimes called newsgroups, where 'communities' of people post messages on a variety of sub-jects – for example, politics or law. There are thousands of

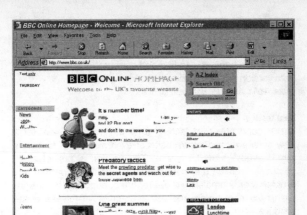

these communities on the Internet and they can vary from the very small to the very large.
*Links: Downloading, Freeware, Kermit, Newsgroups, Shareware, SIG*

### bcc (blind carbon copy)

In e-mail headers, the bcc field contains additional addresses to which copies of the message are being sent, just like the cc: (carbon copy header). However, with bcc, the recipients cannot see each other's e-mail addresses, just the one of the person sending the e-mail and their own. As a result, the main recipient does not know that copies are being distributed.
*Links: Address, cc, e-mail*

### Benchmark

A point of reference used when measuring and comparing the performance of hardware and/or software.
*Links: Clock speed*

## Beta bugs

When the beta version of a product (software, Website or hardware) is tested, any problems or anomalies that are found are termed beta bugs. It is to find and correct these bugs that the beta version is made available to certain people.

*Links: Alpha, Anomaly, Beta testing, Bug*

## Beta testing

The second phase of testing, after the alpha version, for a new software product, Website or even a piece of hardware that is almost ready for market. This version is 'pre-released' to people outside the manufacturers with the hope that any problems or anomalies will get reported, enabling the designers to fix them before the actual commercial release of the product.

*Links: Alpha, Anomaly, Beta bug, Bug, Robust*

## bigfoot.com (www.bigfoot.com)

A Webmail service that offers an e-mail address for life in the form joebloggs@bigfoot.com. Any e-mail sent to that address is forwarded to an e-mail address specified by the user (it could be at home, work or on the Web). Should users move ISP or job, they can simply alter the forwarding address on the BigFoot Website accordingly. It's the equivalent of having a PO box number.

*Links: e-mail, Hotmail, Webmail*

## Binary (numbers)

A numbering system with a base of 2 – that is, it uses only two digits, 0 and 1. Binary numbers are ideal for computers because of their exactness, and because of their electrical nature (charged versus uncharged). Building an electronic circuit that can detect the difference between two states (high current and low current, or 0 and 1) is easier and less expensive than building circuits that detect the difference among 10

states (0 through 9). The word 'bit' derives from the phrase BInary digiT.
*Links: Binary file, BinHex, Digital*

**Binary file**
A file stored in binary format and which is therefore computer-readable but not human-readable – for example, pictures or sounds.
*Links: Binary, BinHex*

**BinHex (BINary HEXadecimal)**
One way of converting non-text files (non-ASCII) into ASCII. This is needed because some e-mail programs can only handle ASCII. Most include a BinHex encoder and decoder for sending and receiving attachments.
*Links: Attachment, Binary, Decode, MIME*

**BIOS (Basic Input/Output System)**
This information is built into computers to perform the initial start up and test hardware functions, and is coded in the PC's ROM (Read Only Memory). This is directly accessed by the computer's operating system or those application programs being run. New products that are add-ons to a system some-times require their own BIOS modules that either work with or replace the existing BIOS on the system.
*Links: Hot plugging, Plug-and-Play*

**Bit**
Derived from BInary digiT, this is the basic unit of information in a binary numbering system and is the smallest unit of data in a computer. A byte is made up of eight bits.
*Links: Binary, Byte*

**Bitmap**
Bitmaps are a type of computer graphic and come in many file

formats including GIF, JPEG, TIFF and BMP. They can be read by programs such as Web browsers and edited by image software such as QuarkXpress, although they can be imported into other application programs such as word processors. A bitmap consists of rows and columns of dots. The density of the dots is known as the resolution and this determines the sharpness of the image. This can be expressed in dpi (dots per inch). Bitmapped graphics are also known as raster graphics and have the file extension .bmp
*Links: dpi, Flash, GIF, JPEG, Raster graphics, Resolution, TIFF,*
*Vector graphics*

## BITNET (Because It's Time Network)
A network that links many of the world's university computer centres and has now been combined with the Internet.
*Links: Network*

## Blatherer
Someone who types much more than is necessary, particularly in the context of newsgroups and chat rooms.
*Links: Chat, Chat room, Chatter's block, Newsgroups, Spew*

## Bleed
To run text or graphics to the very edge of the paper.
*Links: Alignment*

## Block
When used in connection with text, this means to highlight a section of text with a mouse. This 'block' of text can then be acted upon ( for example, cut and pasted).
*Links: Highlight, Tool, Word processor*

## BMP or .bmp
See Bitmap.

**Body**

In e-mail, this the actual message or body of text written by the user. This doesn't include any of the additional information contained in the e-mail message such as the header and server information. With regard to Webpages, a body is an HTML tag used to indicate the main part of the material as distinct to the header.

*Links: e-mail, Header, HTML*

**bol.com (www.bol.com) (Bertelsmann Online)**

Bertelsmann is one of the largest media companies in the world. Its easily navigated site has its focus firmly on books and music, and includes innovative BOL TV video interviews with best-selling authors.

*Links: Amazon, Shopping, Shopping cart*

**Bookmark**

Nearly all Web browsers support a bookmarking feature that

allows Web addresses to be saved so that they can easily be visited at a later time. Netscape Navigator calls these links 'Bookmarks', while Internet Explorer refers to them as 'Favorites'. Bookmarks allow users to return quickly to areas of the Web that interest them without having to spend a large amount of time searching again. Many Websites have a 'links' section (sometimes called hot lists), which are essentially just a collection of bookmarks.

*Links: Browser, Hot list, Webpage*

### Boolean Logic

Most search tools support natural language searching, which basically means a person can use plain English. However, a few search engines, especially for advanced searches, insist on Boolean Logic searches, while some support both. Boolean searching operators, when used in conjunction with the user's keywords (for example: Chess AND White AND Rook NOT Bird) allow users to make more sophisticated advanced searches (producing information on White Rook chess moves and excluding anything about the bird).

*Links: Search engine*

### Boot

To start up a computer, although 're-boot' is more commonly used. When a system is shut down, then restarted, it is being re-booted. This process helps to get rid of any bugs that may be preventing the computer from running smoothly.

*Links: Autoexec.bat, Bootable disk*

### Bootable disk

This can be used to boot a computer when its hard disk (from which a computer is normally booted) is damaged. It contains a back-up copy of the hard disk's master boot record (MBR).

*Links: Autoexec.bat, Boot*

**Bot (Robot)**
Many search engines use bots to explore the Web by retrieving
a document and following all the hyperlinks in it, then generate
catalogues that can be accessed by the search engine.
*Links: Agent, Auto-bot, Search engine*

**Bounce**
The return of an e-mail message that cannot reach its specified
destination.
*Links: Address, e-mail*

**Bozo filter**
A program that screens out e-mail and newsgroup postings
from those who are on a user's b-list (bozo list).
*Links: e-mail, Newsgroups, Newsreader*

**bps (bits/bytes per second)**
A measure of the rate of transmission of data. For example,
when using Windows, an icon showing two screens joined
appears in the bottom right-hand corner of the screen if the
computer is 'online'. When clicked on, this gives the rate of
transfer of the connection being used in bps.
*Links: Bandwidth, Baud, Bit, Modem*

**britannica.com / britannica.co.uk
(www.britannica.com / www.britannica.co.uk)**
A search engine based around *Encyclopaedia Britannica*. As
well as searching Websites and the encyclopaedia itself, this
site also trawls magazine and book lists. It is framed within a
standard-style portal offering news, sports and weather
reports.
*Links: Portal, Search engine*

**Broadband**
A transmission channel capable of carrying a large volume of

data and that can be used to send different types of signals (or channels) simultaneously. Using a broadband connection when viewing major multi-media material, such as films and streaming concerts (available over the Net) will result in improved sound and picture quality.
*Links: Baseband*

## Broadcast (e-mail)

Often, an e-mail may be a general message announcing something that needs to be sent to every necessary person – for example, a company newsletter might be sent by e-mail to everyone in the company. This e-mail is broadcast, which is different to multi-casting where a message is sent to a select list of people.
*Links: e-mail, Mailing list, MultiCast*

## Broadcasting

Broadcasting is one of the areas well served by the Internet. There are Websites dedicated to particular channels, even to particular programmes. The Net is also set to become one of the most far-reaching broadcasting systems the world has ever seen in its own right. Audio-visual material on the Web is best viewed with broadband connections such as ADSL or cable. It can be viewed at lower speed connections, but the experience is much diminished.
*Links: Channel, Webcasting*

## Broken link, or Broken graphic

One of things most infuriating to users of the Web is when a hypertext link on a Webpage doesn't work. When the user clicks on a link, either an error or misdirection occurs. A variation is a graphic that doesn't load. There are a number of reasons why this might be so. It is possible that the Web server hosting the intended destination is down, the site is hosted at

another server, the file no longer exists or the actual HTML code for the link is incorrect.
*Links: HTML, Webpage*

## Broken pipe
Error messages in certain programs that are downloading or uploading information, such as Netscape Navigator, some-times contain this term if the connection is lost mid-way through transfer. This can happen when a network or access provider is dealing with a lot of traffic.
*Links: Downloading, Error messages, Upload*

## Brokers, online
These allow trading on the financial markets. They can prove to be a lot cheaper than using traditional full-service brokers and would seem the natural next step towards share ownership and trading for those who do their financial reading and research on the Internet.
*Links: e-business*

## Browse
This word is often used when someone using the Web is essen-tially 'just looking', much in the same way that a person browses through a book or shop. A Web browser is needed to facilitate this ability.
*Links: Browser, Navigate, Surf*

## Browser
An application program that allows users to enter and find their way around the Internet, and provides a framework within which users can work. It can retrieve and display Webpages, save locations for future reference, link to search facilities, save information from the Web permanently and look at and interact with all the information on the Web. Browsers can be text-

based, meaning they do not show graphics or images, although most are text and graphics based. Browsers can also be used to access e-mail, chat, newsgroups and multi-media facilities. They can be used even when a user isn't connected to the Internet, and are useful for opening image files such as GIFs and JPEGs. Browsers read 'marked up' or coded pages (usually HTML, but not always) that reside on servers and translate the coding into what is seen as a Webpage. The most popular Web browsers are Netscape Navigator and Internet Explorer, and one of these is usually supplied on new computers.

*Links: ActiveX control, Browse, Internet Explorer, Mosaic, Multi-media, Netscape Navigator, NeoPlanet, Opera, Plug-in, Surf monkey, WWW*

### Browser compatibility

Webpages do not necessarily look identical when viewed through different browsers. Neither is it necessarily the case that a Webpage looks the same when displayed on different operating systems.

*Links: Browser, Internet Explorer, Netscape Navigator*

### Buddy lists

A service offered by some portals and by ICQ. These lists enable users to know when their friends are logged on and available to chat. AOL, for example, provides a list of AOL members online.

*Links: AOL, Chat, Facilitated chat, ICQ, Instant Messenger*

### Buffer

A memory area that holds information before sending it on to a device – for example, when printing, a print buffer holds and then supplies data as fast as it can be processed. A media player also buffers a video image before playing it.

*Links: Cache, Media players, Spool*

**Buffer page**

An Webpage used primarily for marketing purposes. Instead of going directly to the advertiser's homepage after clicking on an ad banner, a user might be sent to a buffer page. This page will also highlight and promote the special offer mentioned in the ad banner, albeit in greater detail. Buffer pages can increase a Website's ranking on search engines.

*Links: Ad banner, Homepage, Marketing, Microsite, Splash page*

**Bug**

This is a programming error that results in a program or system not working correctly. Later versions of a program may contain corrections or bug fixes. A bug should not be confused with a glitch, used when describing problems with hardware.

*Links: Alpha, Anomaly, Beta bugs, Beta testing, Glitch*

**Bullet**

A small graphic that is used to emphasise various points in a document. It works by separating listed items. The most common form of a bullet is a dot (•). This appears on the left side of the point being made.

*Links: Word processor*

**Bundled software**

Software sold with a computer or other hardware component as part of a package.

*Links: Software*

**Bus**

The transmission paths (wires) along which data is sent from one part of a computer to another.

*Links: Clock speed, Microprocessor, Motherboard*

**Button**

A graphic that can be 'clicked on', prompting an action, such

as the downloading of a program or the jumping to another Webpage. It also refers to a small ad banner.
*Links: Ad banner, Link*

## Byte (Binary term)

A unit of storage that can represent a single character such as a number, letter or symbol (for example, 1, a, !). A byte is the equivalent of eight bits.
*Links: Binary, Bit, bps*

# C

### C++
The programming language considered to be the best for creating large-scale applications, it is a superset of the C language. Java is based on C++. Both languages involve a great deal of study although many people say Java is a little easier.
*Links: Java, Object-oriented programming*

### C shell
Also known as a 'shell account', this is a UNIX-based connection with the Internet using command-line instructions.
*Links: Shell account, UNIX*

### Cable modem
A modem able to use cable TV lines and which enables PCs to receive data at up to 1.5 mbps. This is much faster than a typical computer modem that sends signals over telephone lines. Most cable modems come as part of the cable access service.
*Links: WebTV*

### Cache
Pronounced 'cash'. A cache stores information for quick access. The two most significant types of cache are the Web browser cache and disk caching. With the former, a Webpage's HTML code is stored along with any embedded features such as graphics and animation, so that if the page is accessed again, the whole page doesn't need re-downloading.

This saves a lot of time when revisiting Webpages. A user can specify how many files are allowed in the cache memory and even clear the cache. It is important to remember that when visiting a page again, the browser might only be showing the cached version of the page. Sometimes it is worth refreshing the page to make sure the most recent version is being retrieved. Disk caching is slightly different. Here information from the hard disk that the computer's processor might need to access repeatedly is stored and can be accessed much more quickly.

*Links: Access time, Level 1 cache, Level 2 cache, Load, Pentium, SDRAM, Using a previously cached copy instead, Webpage*

## CAD (Computer Aided/Assisted Design)

One area where computers have made a huge impact is in design, particularly concerning architects and engineers. Programs have been created where models of objects and the spatial environment they exist in can be pictured and controlled, whether it be in two or three dimensions. This provides an immense flexibility to designers who can now produce and manipulate virtual models of their designs in a much quicker time than traditional methods allow.

*Links: Trackball, Vector graphics, Workstation*

## Café

See Cybercafé.

## Calculators, online

These have become a popular feature on the Internet. They allow users to input various details and calculate the answer to all types of questions – for example, which mobile phone service is the best for me? How much a month would I have to pay if I got a mortgage? How much should I be saving for my pension? They can also be as basic as a currency converter.

*Links: Shopping*

### Cancelbot
A type of auto-bot program that a system administrator can use to look for, and delete, any inappropriate messages on a news-group or such like. This can prove particularly useful in the control of mail received from known spammers.
*Links: Auto-bot, Newsgroups, Spam*

### Cancelbunny
A person who deletes posted newsgroup messages, normally because they are inappropriate or are from known spammers.
*Links: Cancelbot, Spam*

### Cancelmoose
A person who does their best to eliminate spamming.
*Links: Cancelbot, Spam*

### Capture
Refers to the saving of information currently visible on a display screen and the capturing of a screen to a printer or a file.
*Links: Screen capture/dump*

### CardBus
A 32-bit version of the PCMCIA PC card standard, which can operate at speeds up to 33 MHz.
*Links: PC card, PCMCIA*

### Cascade
A list of replies to a posted message.
*Links: BBS*

### Cascading Style Sheets
These have introduced a much greater degree of flexibility for Web designers by allowing them to change the appearance of text and other objects throughout a Website without editing all the pages. A designer can create a style sheet that dictates

how the different elements, such as the text body, of any Webpage it is applied to, appear. Cascading refers to the fact that more than one style sheet can be applied to the same Webpage. It can save a lot of time and effort for a designer, as well as providing greater control over the look-and-feel of Web-pages.

*Links: HTML, Style sheets, Webpage*

### Case sensitive

Letters can either be typed in upper case (that is, ABC) or lower case (that is, abc). Some computer programs and network services are case sensitive – that is, 'ABC' is considered different data to 'abc'. Passwords and e-mail addresses can also be case sensitive. With e-mail addresses, the same case lettering should always be used to avoid any potential failures of delivery. If there's any doubt, lower case letters should always be used.

*Links: Account, Authentication, e-mail*

### cc (carbon copy)

Most e-mail programs provide an option allowing users to send more than one copy of the same e-mail message – or, to put it another way, to send the e-mail to more than one person. 'cc' is one way of doing this and allows everyone to see who else the message went to – as opposed to bcc (blind carbon copy).

*Links: bcc, e-mail, Eudora, MultiCast, Outlook Express*

### CD-R (Compact Disc-Recordable)

A CD that can be written on to create a CD-ROM or audio CD. It is also possible to keep adding data to the disk over time, so can be useful for backing up files.

*Links: CD-ROM, CD-RW, DVD, MP3, Ripping*

### CD-ROM (Compact Disc–Read Only Memory)

A compact disc used to store data that can be read by a

computer. These have proved immensely popular in computing by facilitating a large amount of storage. CDs are able to hold around 650 megabytes. As a consequence, they have become the preferred medium for the installation of programs, and have proved useful for electronic encyclopaedias and dictionaries which are now able to contain multi-media data.
*Links: CD-R, CD-RW, DVD, Multi-media, ROM*

### CD-RW (Compact Disc-Rewritable)
A CD that allows a user to write on to it a number of times so that the disc can be treated in the same way as a floppy disk. However, one drawback is that disks created using CD-RW can only be read by a CD-RW drive.
*Links: CD-ROM, CD-R, DVD, MP3*

### Celeron
The cheapest type of microprocessor from Intel. It is based on the same architecture as its Pentium II but lacks some high-performance features of the Pentium II line. The main difference between the Celeron chips and the Pentium II is a smaller Level 2 cache. With clock speeds up to 466 MHz, Celeron processors can look rather attractive at first glance in terms of power, but should really be compared to the Pentium II.
*Links: Cyrix, Intel, Microprocessor, Pentium*

### Censoring Web material
Both Internet Explorer and Netscape allow use of the PICS system whereby it is possible to exclude access from certain types of sites by setting ratings for language, nudity, sex and violence. AOL has similar features.
*Links: AOL, Censorware, Internet Explorer, Netscape Navigator, NetWatch, PICS*

### Censorware
The collective name for programs that filter or block material

from the Internet according to criteria set by the user. Popular programs include NetNanny and CyberSitter.
*Links: Censoring Web material, cyberangels.org, CyberPatrol, CyberSitter 2000, NetNanny*

### CERN (Conseil European pour la Récherché Nucléaire)
A European high-energy physics laboratory which became the largest Internet site in Europe in 1990 and was hugely influential in the spread of Internet techniques worldwide. It was at CERN in 1989 that an English researcher, Dr Tim Berners-Lee, developed the concept of the World Wide Web. He conceived a system that would make the distribution and retrieval of networked GUI hypertext documents much simpler. Working with a small team, he developed the Hypertext Transfer Protocol (HTTP) on which the Web is based.
*Links: HTTP, WWW*

### CFML (Cold Fusion Markup Language)
An extension of HTML and a markup language designed to be used with Allaire's Cold Fusion Application Server. Webpages employing Cold Fusion can be recognised by the extension .cfm
*Links: Cold Fusion, HTML*

### CGI (Common Gateway Interface)
Part of the Web's HTTP protocol, this is a method for passing data backwards and forwards between a server and an application program. For example, the submission of a form (say, a feedback form) on a Webpage requires that it is passed by the server on to an application program for processing. The application program may then return data to the server which is subsequently made available to the person who submitted the form, such as an acknowledgement of receipt message. A drawback of CGI is that a new process needs to be started every time one is performed.

*Links: ASP, cgi-bin, Counter, FastCGI, JavaScript, NSAPI, Perl, Script,*
*Server script, Servlet*

### cgi-bin (CGI binary)
Often seen as part of a Webpage's URL when a CGI program is
running or about to be run. This is because these programs are
located on a server in a directory called the cgi-bin.
*Links: CGI, Server, URL*

### Channel
There are several uses for the word 'channel' on the Internet.
Channels are the Internet Relay Chat (IRC) equivalent of chat
rooms and can be permanent. Each channel has a name,
usually starting with a # (hash) sign. Conversations within chats
are text-based with users typing in their message line by line.
As the lines are being typed, others on the channel are able to
see the message. Consequently, anyone on the channel can
respond to the message as it is revealed just by typing in their
own response, line by line. Anyone can create a channel and
call it anything that isn't already being used, but most of
the time people tend to visit channels that are more popular.
Internet phones also use channels in much the same way.
Additionally, channels are Websites designed to deliver
constantly updated information. Some online services like AOL
call their subject sections channels, as in the Technology
channel. Finally, the Internet is home to TV and radio channels.
*Links: AOL, Channel virtual area, Chat, IRC, Internet telephony*

### Channel virtual area
The places where users of IRC (Internet Relay Chat) can 'talk' to
each other. There are thousands of these on the Internet.
*Links: Channel, Chat, IRC*

### Chat
Carrying out real-time typed conversations between two or

more people using their computers. There are two main types of chat: Internet Relay Chat (IRC) and Web-chat. Most real-time chat is carried out with IRC channels, although Web-chat is fast becoming the preferred choice. IRC requires a piece of software such as mIRC to be downloaded. Once this is downloaded, it offers users the choice of chat channels. It may seem obvious but users can't chat to someone who isn't online. Chatting probably isn't the best way to keep in touch with friends unless NetBuddy lists are used or both parties are using ICQ (again this can provide limitations). Web-chat takes place in special chat rooms and chat sites, although special software isn't always needed. An example is the chat rooms in online services like AOL, but there are thousands of other chat rooms on the Internet catering for all needs and interests. Many interviews with famous people, for example, are performed in this way, invariably involving a chat facilitator.

*Links: AOL, Buddy lists, Channel, Chat history, Chat room, Facilitated chat, Ghost, Handle, ICQ, Interactive Web chat, IRC, mIRC*

### Chat history
The transcript of a chat session.
*Links: Chat*

### Chat room
See Interactive Web chat.

### Chatter's block
A type of mental block that can affect come people in chat rooms. The chatter feels that their message needs to be perfect and will often keep editing and rewording, perhaps without ever sending it. When afflicted by chatter's block, the secret is to relax and to treat online chats in the same way as a normal conversation.
*Links: Blatherer, Jabber*

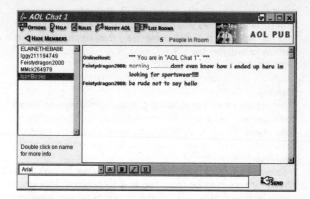

## Checkbox

A box or boxes that can be clicked on to turn an option on or off. When an option is on, either a tick or a cross appears in the box.

*Links: CGI, Drop-down menu / Droplist, GUI*

## Checksum

It is possible to check that the transmission of data happened without any error by using this mathematical calculation (this is done by the actual transmitter – for example, a modem). It is performed on the contents of a packet before and after it is sent. If the 'before' calculation does not match the 'after' calculation, this indicates errors in the transmission.

*Links: Fast packet, Modem*

## Chernobyl packet

A network packet that seriously disrupts a network, perhaps even causing it to stop functioning.

*Links: Meltdown, Network, Packet*

## Churn

Often used to describe the turnover of users on a particular ISP or online service, particularly when a free trial has been running and has recently ended.
*Links: ISP, OSP*

## Churning

When a computer is processing data but appears to be doing nothing at all.
*Links: Frozen*

## ClearType

A software font technology that makes it easier for text on a computer screen to be read. The new technology comprises software that makes use of the space between pixels to smooth and redefine the edges and appearance of displayed fonts, making them sharper and easier to see. ClearType can reportedly improve the quality of displayed text by up to 300 per cent on LCD monitors using digital interfaces and by 20 to 40 per cent on those with analogue interfaces. It can be implemented at the operating system level or within applications. The technology is expected to play a major role in the publishing of electronic books and many publishers like Penguin Books have already signed up with Microsoft to produce e-books using this technology.
*Links: Adobe Acrobat, e-books, Microsoft Reader, PGML*

## Click

The act of pressing down a mouse button, typically with the intention of activating something, such as a hyperlink or button.
*Links: Click here, Hyperlink, Right click*

## Click here

Any person who spends a significant amount of time on the Internet will come across this much used (and some might say

unnecessary) hyperlinked phrase. The idea behind it is to make it as obvious as possible where the people who created the page would like the visitor to go next.
*Links: Hyperlink*

## Click rate

A Web marketing term that describes the number of clicks on a Web ad against the number of views or downloads of the ad. It is normally expressed as a percentage. For example, if one hundred people are exposed to an ad but only five of them actually click on it, the click rate would be one in twenty, or 5 per cent.
*Links: Ad banner, Ad server, Auditor, Click, Clickstreams, Close rate, Cost per sale, Marketing*

## Clickable graphic

A graphic with 'active' areas that can be clicked on. There can be many areas that are hyperlinked and these can take a user to different sections of a Website or to other Websites. For example, an image of a city might be designed to allow users to click on a district or building that will then bring up information or another Webpage about that place.
*Links: Hot spots, Hyperlink*

## Clickly

A contraction of clicking quickly.
*Links: Prolly*

## Clicks

An online marketing term that refers to the number of times users click on an ad. This term is also used to describe the number of Webpages that must be loaded in order to reach a particuear destination, for example 'It's four clicks in'.
*Links: Ad banner, Ad server, Auditor, Click rate, Clickstreams, Close rate, Cost per sale, Marketing*

## Clickstreams

The paths users take as they surf the Web. Software is available that can track users' clickstreams. This can help owners of sites identify visitors' preferences and interests, helping them to plan future developments. (For example, if the majority of visitors look at a certain product in blue, the manufacturer might be forewarned of a potentially high demand in this version. It is effectively a form of market research, but without the consumer knowing it.)

*Links: Ad banner, Ad server, Auditor, Clicks, Close rate, Cost per sale, Marketing*

## Client

Used either when describing an actual computer or the software running on it. A remote computer, such as a PC, connected to a host or server computer is a client of that server. Client software programs are those that run on a personal computer but rely on a server to perform their operations – for example, e-mail software.

*Links: Client/Server Network, Host, Mail client, POP3, Server, Software*

## Client/Server Network or Relationship

A network in which client computers (individual PCs) connect with a central server computer that holds resources (for example, e-mail) the client computers can share. An online service such as AOL and its members is an example of this.

*Links: AOL, Client, Network, Server*

## Clock speed

The speed at which a microprocessor executes instructions. It is expressed in megahertz (MHz) – one MHz is equal to one million cycles per second. The higher the better, although it must be remembered that these processors are also reliant on the abilities of the computer's other components.

*Links: CPU, Microprocessor, Overclocking*

**Part Two: Internet Dictionary** | 241

**Close rate**
The rate of purchases as set against the number of views of a product. For example, if one person buys a product for every one hundred that view it, then the close rate is one in a hundred. This can help better evaluation of, say, an advertising campaign than by merely looking at the click rate.
*Links: Ad banners, Ad server, Auditor, Click rate, Cost per sale, Marketing*

**Cluster**
A group of two or more sectors on a computer disk, also known as an allocation unit.
*Links: Sector*

**cnet.com (www.cnet.com) (The Computer Network)**
The definitive Website on the Internet concerning computer technology. Among its services are Auctions, Downloads, Free Newsletters, Games, Help and How-Tos, News, Stock Quotes and Tech Jobs. It is the home of:

shareware.com
download.com
news.com
computers.com (and others).

It is directory based with keyword searches.
*Links: Auctions, Freeware, Shareware*

**Cobweb site**
A Website that hasn't been updated for a while.
*Links: Broken link, Ghost site, Website*

**Code**
As a verb, this is to write a computer program or macro.
*Links: Macro, Macro virus, Program*

## Codec (Coder-decoder)

A generic term for a program that converts audio or video data into and out of digital form. An example would be RealAudio.
*Links: Media players*

## Cold Fusion

A Web application development tool that enables the creation of dynamic-page applications and interactive Websites. These applications can integrate with server technologies such as relational databases. Developers using this technology don't need to use complex programming languages like Visual Basic, Java or C++. This is because the functionality that is provided by these languages is also provided by Cold Fusion and in a much easier-to-understand manner of server-side tags that look like HTML tags. Cold Fusion can be used to put up a searchable catalogue, for example.
*Links: ASP, CFML, Dynamic content*

## Colour depth

The number of different colours a single pixel in an image file can contain. For example, GIF files have a colour depth of 256 colours and JPEGs of 16.7 million colours.
*Links: GIF, JPEG, Resolution*

## .com (Commercial)

A top-level domain name. It usually denotes the owner of the domain name as being a commercial organisation.
*Links: Companies, Domain name*

## COM

Often associated with a number (COM1, COM2 and so on) this is used to denote the plug-in sockets (or serial ports) in the back of a computer for attaching devices such as a modem or a printer. COM is a contraction of communications.
*Links: Modem, Serial port*

**Command line**
The location on a screen where a command is expected.
*Links: Shell account, UNIX*

**Commerce server**
A server that enables secure transactions to occur online, usually with a credit card, by employing a secured socket layer (SSL).
*Links: Security, SET, SSL*

**Communications protocol**
Any standard that specifies how (that is, in what format), devices communicate. The collection of rules defining any format is called a protocol.
*Links: MacTCP, Protocol, TCP/IP*

**Communications software**
Needed to permit computers to access and communicate with other computers using telephone lines. The software works with the computer's modem, instructing which procedures to carry out – including making the actual connection in the first instance. The software is typically built into the operating system on the computer and needs to be configured correctly before it can successfully be used. ISP software often does this automatically. One example of communications software is Windows Dial-up Networking.
*Links: Dial-up networking*

**Companies, online**
If a company has a Website, it can usually be found by typing www.companyname.com or .co.uk or .com.au or whatever the regional country suffix is. For example, Icon Books's Website is www.iconbooks.co.uk
*Links: Addresses, .com, Country codes, e-business, e-commerce, URL*

**Compatible**
Used to illustrate the ability of one device or program to work with another.
*Links: Add-on, Cross-platform*

**Compile**
When a computer translates code written in a computer language into an executable form.
*Links: Code, Program*

**Compression**
This process of making computer data smaller is undertaken in order to minimise downloading time and storage space on a computer. For example, someone who wants to send a photo to a friend might compress it first to speed up its transmission and receipt. Compressed files are made by removing unnecessary information and spaces. Files that contain large amounts of data (such as multi-media files) are usually compressed before being made accessible over the Internet, as are a lot of shareware or freeware programs. Compressed files can be recognised by their file extensions. The most common are .zip, .sit, .bin and the self-extracting .exe. The two most popular compression programmes are WinZip for PCs and StuffIt for Macs. These are also able to decompress files.
*Links: File extension, Lossless compression, Lossy compression, MP3, Self-extracting files, WinZip*

**CompuServe Information Service**
A popular online service (now owned by AOL) geared towards business users. e-mail addresses come in the form username@compuserve.com
*Links: AOL, OSP*

**Configuration**
This word has a number of similar meanings. It is used to

describe how a computer's operating system is set up. It is also used to describe the component make-up of a computer system – that is, the hardware units such as the processor, the modem and the monitor. It can also be used to describe how the software and hardware communicate with one another.
*Links: Configure*

### Configure
To alter software or hardware actions by modifying their settings.
*Links: Configuration*

### Congestion
When traffic on the Internet is so heavy that it slows down the network's response time.
*Links: Access time, Bandwidth, Latency*

### Connect
The establishment of Internet access so that all the features of the Net can be used – for example, browsing, downloading and e-mailing.
*Links: Access, Access account, Network*

### Connect time
The amount of time that a user is connected to the Internet. Many ISPs and online services (such as AOL) charge users per unit of connection time, while others offer free unlimited connection. (However, a user may still need to be wary of phone charges and help-line premium-rate calls.)
*Links: Access, Access time, Connect, Connectivity*

### Connectivity
Used to describe a program or device's ability to work with other programs or devices. It can also be used to describe the state of being connected to the Internet or some other type of

computer network. If connectivity is lost on the Internet, the user is no longer online and must try to reconnect to their ISP or Online Service Provider. Connectivity can be troublesome if there are a lot of people using the same connection.
*Links: Access, Access time, Connect, Connect time, ISP, OSP*

## Content
The information available on a Website and how it is presented. What is important is not how much information is available, but the quality and general ease with which it can be navigated. Many people judge a Website purely on its content. Online service providers, for example, aim to satisfy all their users' needs through their own content and promote Web browsing as an option rather than purpose.
*Links: Cold Fusion, Content provider, DHTML, OSP, Website*

## Content provider
Applies to anyone who supplies content for a Website. It is also used to describe Websites themselves whose whole basis is the content they contain – rather than, say, a retail site whose main purpose is to sell goods. It is normally expected that the content constantly changes and doesn't remain static. One obvious example of this would be a news provider. Some people charge for access to their content, relying on it being of a must-have nature. Others offer it for free, hoping to generate Web traffic income through advertising. Brittanica.com is one example of an excellent content provider. There are newly established companies whose role is purely to provide content for portals and so on – for example, Ananova.
*Links: Content, Portal, Vertical portal*

## Contextual commerce
When online editorial content is used to help sell a product.
*Links: Buffer page, Splash page*

**Control panel**
An area in Windows that can be used to change Windows and hardware settings. For example, there is a modem icon in the control panel that can be clicked on, allowing the computer's modem settings to be altered.
*Links: Windows*

**Conversation view**
An option available on the bulletin boards of the Microsoft Network. It helps visitors quickly identify conversations of interest by showing the first message of each thread. These can then be expanded.
*Links: BBS, MSN, Newsgroups, Thread*

**Cookie**
A small file (typically no more than 5 k) kept on a user's computer that has been placed there by a Web server allowing the server to remember the user's visit at a later time. Cookies allow Web servers to personalise Webpages by storing any information a user may have told the server during any previous visits of its site – for example, username and password. A cookie can just contain an ID number with the user's stored details actually residing on the Website's server. A server accesses this information when the user connects to a Website that wants to know this information. For example, any user who has bought something from Amazon and returned to its site at a later date is often 'personally' greeted; this has been done using cookie technology. It is through the use of cookies that 'shopping cart' technology works. Cookies can become a privacy problem when others know who a visitor is and collect information about their Net use, interests and preferences. It is possible to exercise control over cookies with programmes such as Cookie Muncher. Netscape versions 3.0 upwards and Internet Explorer 4.0 upwards also provide cookie controls.
*Links: Authentication, Marketing, Security, Shopping*

## CoolTalk

A real-time Internet telephone tool similar in type to NetMeeting. It can help avoid long-distance phone charges by using the local-rate connection of the Internet (although both users may be paying for the call as they are both attached to the Net).
*Links: Internet telephony, NetMeeting*

## Copernic 2000 (www.copernic2000.com)

One of the best meta-search tools, which is likely to save time and effort and deliver results. It can be downloaded from the Web and resides on the user's hard disk.
*Links: Multi-search tools, Search engine*

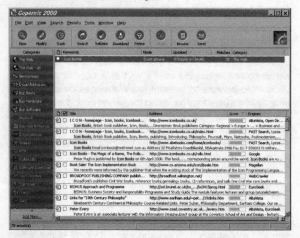

## Cost per sale

Another way of measuring the effectiveness of online advertising. It is a calculation of the actual advertising cost for each resulting sale. Ad banners' costs are normally determined on clickthrough rate, but if very few of these people clicking

through make a purchase then the benefits are low. Equally, another banner may result in a low clickthrough rate but with a higher percentage of sale. Many factors have to be considered when advertising on the Web.
*Links: Ad banner, Click rate, Marketing*

### Counter
A program that provides a Website with an indication of how many visitors it is getting. The counts themselves are usually only visible on sites that want to demonstrate how popular they are. They work by counting the number of people who visit a particular page, most commonly the homepage. It can also work by being part of any CGI application and therefore linked to user input. Additionally, there are monitoring services available that provide a much more detailed analysis.
*Links: Auditor, CGI, Marketing*

### Country codes
In a URL or e-mail address, instead of, or as well as, seeing the 'usual' .com (.net, .org, .edu, or .gov), a two-letter abbreviation may be seen, particularly when the Website is from a country other than the USA. This signifies the country in which the Website originates from. Examples of these codes include:

| | |
|---|---|
| .ad | – Andorra |
| .ar | – Argentina |
| .at | – Austria |
| .au | – Australia |
| .br | – Brazil |
| .ca | – Canada |
| .ch | – Switzerland |
| .de | – Germany |
| .fi | – Finland |
| .it | – Italy |
| .mx | – Mexico |

.nl   – Netherlands
.nz   – New Zealand
.pt   – Portugal
.th   – Thailand
.tw   – Taiwan.

There are a number of people who are using these country codes to create interesting Website address. An example could be www.b.ad
*Links: Address, Companies, Domain name, URL*

## Coupons, online

Some retailers now place money-off coupons online allowing users to print them out. It might be that the site asks the user for the post or zip code before presenting a list of relevant coupons. These can often then be used in high-street shops.
*Links: e-tailing, Marketing*

## CPT (Cost Per Thousand)

A term often used in Web marketing that refers to the cost associated with a particular amount of Webpage views, typically through the use of an ad banner. For example, an ad banner might cost an advertiser £50 every thousand times an ad is downloaded by a viewer.
*Links: Ad banner, Click rate, Cost per sale*

## CPU (Central Processing Unit)

Often referred to as the processor or microprocessor. It is where most calculations take place. Examples include the Intel Pentium and Motorola 68040 chips which can be found in a PC and Mac respectively. The speeds of these units are expressed in MHz and it can be hard to keep up with the increases in speed in new chips. An example would be a 500 MHz Pentium III chip.
*Links: Celeron, Cyrix, Hardware, Intel, Microprocessor, Pentium*

# Cracker
Someone who deliberately breaks into a computer system, breaching its security. The term itself should not be confused with 'hacker'. Hackers generally deplore cracking. The term 'cracker' was coined in 1985 by hackers in defence against journalistic misuse of hacker, although many forms of news media still use hacker when talking about crackers.
*Links: Access control, Hacker, Security, Warez*

# Crapplet
A poorly written or worthless Java applet.
*Links: Applet, Java, Servlet*

# Crash
If a computer crashes it means it has stopped working or that a program has aborted without being told to. If this happens repeatedly it can signify a serious problem with either the computer hardware or software.
*Links: Frozen, ScanDisk*

# Crawler
A program that roams the Net looking for new and updated Webpages – one of the ways a search engine collects its data.
*Links: Agent, AltaVista, Auto-bot, Search engine, Spider, WebCrawler*

# CRC (Cyclical Redundancy Check)
A technique for checking errors when transmitting data. It can prompt the transmission to keep trying until successful.
*Links: Checksum*

# Cross-platform
Used to describe the ability of software or hardware to run in the same way whatever the platform – for example, a program that can work identically on both Windows and Macintosh .
*Links: Macintosh, Platform, Windows*

## Cross-posting
Considered rude, this is the posting of a message across a number of newsgroups, message boards or e-mail distribution lists.
*Links: Anonymous posting, Newsgroups, Posting*

## Crunch
The efficient processing of large amounts of information. An example of a tool to do this is a number cruncher, a device or program designed for processing numbers.
*Links: Calculators*

## CSP (Commerce Server Provider)
A company that provides an individual or business with the ability to perform online transactions, almost always a lot cheaper in the short term than owning a dedicated server. The CSP will either charge a commission, rent per item for sale, or even both.
*Links: e-business, e-commerce, e-tailing*

## CSV (Comma Separated Values)
People don't all use the same table-oriented applications (such as, for example, Microsoft Excel). To ensure that any data requiring this sort of application works on another person's system, people often supply a CSV file. This contains tabular data as a series of ASCII text files with each column value separated by a comma and with each row starting on a new line. For example:

Smith,John, Managing Director, 1234-5678
Jones,Paul, IT Director, 2345-6789
Davies,Lisa, Marketing Director, 3456-7890
… and so on.

*Links: Cross-platform, Database, Flat file*

**CTS (Clear To Send)**
One of the wires in a serial port used in modem communications, this allows the modem to inform the computer that it is ready for instructions.
*Links: Modem*

**CU-SeeME**
Pronounced 'see you see me'. A free conferencing application that enables people to conduct voice and video conferencing sessions. It can be used over the Internet or any TCP/IP network, and runs on both Windows and Macintosh computers. It is able to offer full-colour video, audio, chat window and white-board communications. An enhanced version allows real-time person-to-person or group conferencing.
*Links: Internet telephony, NetMeeting, TCP/IP, Video-conferencing*

**CuteFTP (www.cuteftp.com)**
An FTP client that can be used to transfer files and which also has an MP3 search engine.
*Links: FTP, MP3, WS_FTP*

**Cyber**
A prefix typically used to describe the appended word as belonging to the world of computer technology, such as the Internet.
*Links: Cybercafé, Cybercide, Cybernetics, Cyberspace, Cybersquatter, Cybrarian*

**cyberangels.org**
Website of an organisation that provides help concerning most aspects of online safety, including a kids' safety section and a parents' guide to the Internet.
*Links: Censoring Web material, Net Filtering Program, PICS, Pornography*

## Cybercafé (aka Internet café)

A place where people can go to access the Internet. These are often traditional cafés with computers whose Internet time can be rented. Cybercafés prove useful for people travelling who want to keep in touch with friends and family using a Webmail address, such as Hotmail. A cybercafé can be used by people who don't have access to the Net at work, home or college. It is also a term describing a virtual place where Net users meet online to chat.
*Links: Roaming service, Webmail*

## Cybercide

The killing or ending of a virtual character or avatar. It is often used in connection with VR games.
*Links: Avatar, MOO, MUD, Virtual, VRML*

## Cybernetics

The science or study of control or regulation mechanisms in human and machine systems, including computers. From the Greek 'kybernetes', meaning steersman or governor.
*Links: AI, Fuzzy logic*

## CyberPatrol

A Net filtering program designed to monitor someone's use of the Internet and prevent unsuitable sites being viewed. It contains two lists of Websites called CyberNOT and CyberYES. The former contains a list of known sites with adult content. These are blocked should a child try to access one of them. The CyberYES list provides sites that are likely to be of interest to children. The program also filters IRC, FTP sites, newsgroups, games and other applications. There is currently a subscription charge and updates of the two lists can be downloaded.
*Links: Censoring Web material, Censorware, Pornography, IRC, Net Filtering Program, Newsgroups*

### CyberSitter 2000

A Net filtering program whereby the user chooses what to have blocked – for example, e-mail, newsgroups and FTP sites. Filters can be further tailored so that online auctions, or sites selling weapons, for instance are blocked. Any attempts to access blocked sites are recorded and it is possible for a parent to define a list of banned words and phrases as well as a list of sites that can always be accessed.

*Links: Censoring Web material, Censorware, Net Filtering Program, Pornography, Security*

### Cyberspace

Term first coined by William Gibson in his science fantasy novel *Neuromancer* published in 1984 in which the hero connects a computer directly into his brain. These days, the term has generated a variety of definitions and meanings – perhaps the best being the network of computer networks and all the information held on it about everything, everywhere.

*Links: Cyber*

### Cybersquatter

Someone who registers a domain name which should really belong to someone else. The most famous example so far has been the www.princess-of-wales.co.uk Website owned by someone with no connection to the Royal Family. Cybersquatting is invariably done with the intention of making money, whether it be through the creation of a popular Website or through the auctioning of the domain name itself.

*Links: Cyber, Domain name*

### Cybrarian

Someone who makes a living researching and retrieving information online.

*Links: Infosurfing, Lynx*

## Cyrix

A company that produces microprocessors that are typically cheaper than those of its competitor Intel.

*Links: CPU, Intel, Microprocessor*

# D

**DAC (Digital-to-Analogue Converter)**
See ADC.

**Daemon**
A UNIX term for a type of program that runs in the background handling periodic service requests that the computer will expect to receive from time to time. Operating systems other than UNIX provide support for daemons, though they're often given other names. Windows, for example, refers to daemons as system agents and services. The send mail daemon, for example, runs continuously but becomes active only when e-mail is sent or received.
*Links: Demon, UNIX*

**DARPA (Defense Advanced Research Projects Agency)**
See ARPANET.

**Data**
Plural of the word datum, although many people treat data as a singular form. It has a variety of similar yet distinct meanings. Data can be information entered into a computer or, even more specifically, information that is converted into binary or digital form and which is thus much more convenient to process or transmit.
*Links: Binary, Data traffic, Digital*

**Data traffic**
The number of TCP/IP packets crossing a network.
*Links: Bandwidth, TCP/IP, Traffic*

## Database

A collection of information organised so that it can be easily accessed and maintained. The most common type of database is the relational form; this type is said to be tabular. Here, the data is defined so that it can be reorganised and accessed in a number of different ways.
*Links: Access, Application server, Cold Fusion, Database Front-end, Dynamic content, Field, Keyword, Query, Relational database, Schema, Servlet, Spider, SQL*

## Database front-end

An interface that integrates Web applications with database programs on the Internet. For example, the look-and-feel of an online bookshop's Website is the front-end of its database of books.
*Links: Back-end, Database, Front-end*

## Datagram

See Packet.

## DDN (Defense Data Network)

A section of the Internet used for unsecured communications between US military bases and their contractors.
*Links: Network*

## debriefing.com (www.debriefing.com)

A meta-search tool that uses Yahoo!, AltaVista and Excite search engines among others. It merges and removes duplicates, and ranks results. It is also available in French.
*Links: Meta-search tools, Portal, Search engine*

## Debug

To find and fix errors in a program.
*Links: Anomaly, Bug, Code, Program*

**Decode**
The act of converting encoded data back to its original form.
*Links: Decryption, Encryption, Public Key Cryptography, Wallet*

**Decryption**
The process of converting encrypted data (content masked from unauthorised people) into its original form. This is vital for transferring important information such as credit card details and is necessary to minimise fraud.
*Links: Decode, Public Key Cryptography, Wallet*

**Dedicated line**
A telecommunications line that enables a computer to have a permanent connection to the Internet so that the user need not 'dial-up' every time Internet access is required.
*Links: Access, Leased line*

**Dedicated server**
A server that performs no activities other than its server tasks. It may be established for example, when the volume of traffic through a site is expected to be sufficient that the site needs to be hosted on a machine of its own.
*Links: Server*

**Default**
A default setting is chosen by the user to be implemented automatically in the event that another preference is *not* specified. For example, a computer might have a default setting that opens the e-mail In box whenever the e-mail program is opened. The Webpage that a browser views every time it opens is its default page.
*Links: Default browser*

**Default browser**
This is the browser that is automatically launched when a user

clicks on a HTML file. Both Netscape and Internet Explorer may be installed, but only one may be the default browser.
*Links: Default, Internet Explorer, Netscape Navigator*

### deja.com (www.deja.com)
Website for searching and displaying newsgroups. It can make finding specific information in Usenet a lot easier than hunting for it using a newsreader, as it gives access to some 35,000 Usenet newsgroups and 18,000 discussion forums.
*Links: CNET, Newsgroups, Usenet*

### Delivery receipt
An optional e-mail feature that notifies users when their e-mail messages have been delivered to their recipients.
*Links: e-mail*

### Dell Computers
The world's largest mail order computer seller and a leading light in e-commerce. The company very much utilises the Web's one-to-one marketing capabilities, cutting out the middle man and selling direct to the consumer.
*Links: e-commerce, e-tailing, Marketing*

### Delurk
To participate actively in a online discussion after a period of just watching or lurking.
*Links: Chat, Lurk, Newsgroups*

### Demon
As opposed to a 'daemon', this is part of a program that is not invoked explicitly (as, say, the smtp daemon is when mail needs to be sent), but that lies dormant waiting for some condition(s) to occur – for example, an unprompted help box. Some people use 'demon' when describing part of a program and 'daemon' for an operating system process.

*Links: Daemon*

## Denizen
A pejorative term for a person on the Internet.
*Links: Angel, Net God, Netizen, Newbie, Web guru*

## Desktop
The computer screen consisting of those objects frequently used such as software icons, pull-down menus or the toolbar. It is also an abbreviated form of desktop computer, a personal computer that sits on top of a desk, and is added on to terms to intimate their existence on PCs – for example, desktop publishing.
*Links: Desktop publishing, Desktop video*

## Desktop publishing
The creation of publications that integrate text and graphics – for example, brochures, posters/flyers and newsletters. Desktop publication applications include Microsoft Publisher, QuarkXPress and Adobe PageMaker.
*Links: Desktop*

## Desktop video
The integration of the camcorder and the home computer with the result that sophisticated editing techniques can now easily be performed.
*Links: Desktop*

## Device
Any piece of hardware that can be *attached* to a computer – for example, keyboards, scanners, CD-ROMS and printers. Motherboards, Processors and RAM are not considered to be devices, as these are all essential to a computer.
*Links: COM, Device driver, Flow control, Hot plugging, Jabber, Modem, Mouse, PC card, Peripheral device, Plug-and-Play, Port, SCSI, USB*

### Device driver

Program that allows a particular device, such as a printer or mouse, to work with a computer. This is achieved by converting the more general input/output instructions of the operating system to messages that the device type can understand. When an operating system is bought, many device drivers are already built in, but often when newer versions of devices, or even a totally new device, are bought, the correct device driver will need to be installed. The computer should request the installation of a new driver if necessary.

*Links: Hot plugging, Modem, Mouse, PC card, Peripheral device, Plug-and-Play*

### DHTML (Dynamic HTML)

A more recent type of HTML, Dynamic HTML provides Web designers and developers with much greater control over the look and feel of Web pages, and the ability to create Webpages more responsive to user interaction.

*Links: ASP, Cold Fusion, Dynamic content, Dynamic fonts, JavaScript, On the fly, SSI*

### Dial-up account

A type of Internet account that allows a user to dial up an Internet Service Provider (ISP) or Online Service using a modem.

*Links: Access, Access account, ISP, OSP*

### Dial-up connection/networking

The typical form of Internet connection for home users; it involves dialling-up an Internet Service Provider's (ISP) computer using a modem and traditional telephone system. Dial-up networking is also a feature of Windows, enabling users to store connection information for dialling a particular network or ISP.

*Links: Access, Communications software, Dedicated line, ISP, Logon script*

**Digerati**
Derived from 'literati', this word is used to describe the digitally informed.
*Links: Net God, Web guru*

**DigiCash**
See e-cash.

**Digital**
In digital electronic computers, two electrical states (positive and non-positive) correspond to the 1s (positive) and the 0s (non-positive) of binary numbers, with the data transmitted or stored as a string of 0s and 1s. Each of these digits is referred to as a bit and these make up a byte. A modem is used to convert the digital information in a computer to analogue signals for a phone line and vice versa.
*Links: ADC, ADSL, Analogue, Digital audio, DSS, ISDN, Modem*

**Digital audio**
Sound stored in a binary form (0s and 1s). Examples of digital audio files include .au and .wav. These can be played by players such as RealAudio and MediaCast. The MP3 file with reputedly near-CD quality is also an example of digital audio; it can be played on players such as WinAmp and Sonique.
*Links: .au, MP3, RealAudio, WinAmp*

**Digital camera**
Records and stores photographic images in a digital form that can then be transferred to a computer and manipulated if so desired. Most of the major camera manufacturers produce digital cameras.
*Links: Desktop video*

**Digital cash**
See e-cash.

## Digital certificates

These concern e-mail security and are used as a form of protection for information sent. They attach a secure signature that acts a bit like a passport by authenticating the sender's identity. This way the receiver is able to know for certain that senders are who they say they are. These can be obtained from certificated authorities – for example, VeriSign.

*Links: e-business, e-mail security, PGP, Public Key Cryptography, SET, Wallet*

## Digital Versatile Disk (DVD)

An optical disk technology that is expected to replace the CD-ROM disk in the coming years. One of the many reasons for this is the amount of information a DVD can hold; just one side is capable of 4.7 gigabytes as opposed to 600 megabytes on a CD-ROM. Additionally, a DVD can use two layers on each side of the disk, allowing storage of up to 17 gigabytes on a single disc. The DVD can also play regular CD-ROM disks. A DVD can store video, music or a mixture of the two.

*Links: CD-ROM*

## Digizine

A digital magazine available on a CD-ROM.

*Links: e-journal, e-zine, Magazines, Zine*

## DIMM (Dual Inline Memory Module)

Memory modules that hold RAM and are the equivalent of double SIMMs.

*Links: RAM, SIMM*

## Direct connection

A permanent connection between a computer system and the Internet. Also referred to as a leased line because it is leased from a telephone company.

*Links: Dial-up networking, Dedicated line, Leased line*

**Directory (on a computer)**
Also called a folder, this is a table of contents of all files contained on, or in a specific section of, a computer disk. A directory can show file name, file size, date and time created, file type and author.
*Links: Archive, File, Mailbox*

**Directory (on the Internet)**
One type of tool available on the Internet designed to help a user find information relating to specific areas of interest. The information within directories is more structured than it is within search engines. They are usually formatted hierarchically into vertical Internet directories or category listings, under general headings such as Business and Commerce, Entertainment, Leisure and Recreation, and Science. These headings are shown in the directory's homepage. Sub-headings are reached by clicking on one of the general headings, further dividing the contents into smaller, more manageable portions about evermore specific topics. Users can usually search for a specific keyword or phrase during this subdivision process, when they feel they are getting near their target. The most famous directories on the Internet are Hotbot and Yahoo!
*Links: cnet, dmoz, go, gogettem, looksmart, MSN, Multi-search tools, Portal, Specialist search sites*

**DirectX**
An application program interface (API) that enhances multi-media capabilities on a computer. It provides improved playback of different types of multi-media (for example, with games or active Webpages) and manages 3D graphics better than many console computers.
*Links: API, Multi-media*

**Dirty connection**
An unusually slow Internet connection. One reason for this can

be heavy traffic between a computer's connection and the ISP being used.
*Links: Bandwidth, Latency*

### Discussion board

Also called a bulletin board, this is where a person can leave and expect to see responses to messages. A lot of people just like to read these boards. As well as being created for this purpose, bulletin board services were also designed to allow the exchange of files. Chat groups are essentially bulletin boards operating in real time.
*Links: BBS, Chat, Discussion group, Mailing list, Newsgroups, SIG*

### Discussion group

Often associated with newsgroups, this is a group of people who exchange messages about particular topics. Discussion groups are a bit like guestbooks, but have the advantage of threading messages – that is, displaying messages and their replies together. Discussion groups vary widely in their variety and format, from swapping recipes to debating politics.
*Links: BBS, Chat, Discussion board, Mailing list, Newsgroups, SIG*

### Dithering

Sometimes the colour specified by a file can't actually be supported by the program opening the file. The program attempts to approximate the colour, possibly by using a mixture of colours that are available. This is called dithering. It becomes a factor with Webpages when a colour specified can't be supported by the browser being used. The quality of the approximation varies from appearing to be identical to being really rather different.

*Links: Browser, Browser compatibility, Netscape colour palette*

**DLL (Dynamic Link Library)**

A collection or library of small programs, any of which can be called into operation when needed by a larger program. These can be used when the larger program needs to communicate with a specific device such as a printer – the small program being packaged as a DLL program or file usually with a .dll, .exe, .drv or .fon extension. The main advantage of doing this is that the DLL files don't get loaded into the RAM together with the main program until needed and therefore space is saved in RAM. For example, when using Microsoft Word, the printer DLL file is only loaded and run when a print request is made.
*Links: API, RAM*

**dmoz.org (www.dmoz.org)**

Aims to be the biggest hand-built open directory on the Net, compiled by thousands of voluntary online editors. It is an interesting alternative to the mainstream.
*Links: Directory (Internet), Multi-search tools, Search engine*

**DNS (Domain Name System/Service/Server)**

A system housed on a number of servers on the Internet that converts the domain names to a unique number known as an IP (Internet Protocol) address. Users will often see the IP address displayed by their Web browsers when they are connecting to a particular computer. For example, iconbooks.co.uk is converted into 194.130.58.202 This IP address is actually what allows the wanted site to be located but it is obviously much easier for people to remember the name of a site.
*Links: Daemon, IP, IP address, TCP/IP*

**.doc**

A Microsoft Word document that can also normally be opened using Wordpad. Double-clicking a word file will normally result in Word being opened along with the file.
*Links: Associate, File extension, Microsoft Word*

## Docking station
A piece of hardware that allows a portable computer (for example, a laptop) also to be able to act as a desktop computer. The portable computer is inserted into the docking station, which will allow for greater connectivity – for example, to Monitors, full-size keyboards, printers and expansion slots. Docking stations are often specific to their particular makes of portable computer.
*Links: Device*

## Document
On the Web, this is any file that contains text, media or hyperlinks that can be transferred from one computer to another.
*Links: Downloading, Server*

## Document info
A feature of Netscape Navigator that provides a large quantity of information about the Webpage being viewed, including the URLs of images within the document, source, content length, encryption and certification. This menu item can be selected by pulling down the 'View' menu and highlighting 'Document Info'.
*Links: Document source, Netscape Navigator*

## Document source
Another feature of Netscape Navigator, which opens a window that displays the source code (for example, HTML, JavaScript) of whatever Webpage is being viewed.
*Links: Document source, Internet Explorer, Netscape Navigator*

## dogpile.com (www.dogpile.com)
Part of the Go2Net group; provides an excellent meta-search of Web engines using Metacrawler, Usenet sources and FTP archives.
*Links: Meta-search tools*

**Domain name**

The unique name that identifies a Website and is the 'address' or URL of that site. This is also how you describe the name that is at the right of the @ sign in an e-mail address. For example, iconbooks.co.uk is the domain name of the Website for the publisher of this book. The 'co' part of the domain name reflects the purpose of the organisation or entity (in this case, 'commercial') and is called the top-level domain name. The 'iconbooks' part of the domain name defines the organisation or entity and, together with the top-level, is called the second-level domain name. This second-level domain name maps, and is effectively the readable version of, the Internet address. There are organisations that register domain names for a small fee and prevent others from registering the same name. Current suffixes for domain names include:

.com — for commercial organisations
.edu — for educational institutions
.gov — for government
.int — for international organisation
.mil — for military
.net — for Internet or networking organisation
.org — for non-profit organisation.

New suffixes now mean that more domain names are available. Examples might be:

.arts — for arts and cultural entities
.firm — for business
.info — for information services
.non — for individuals
.rec — for recreation and entertainment
.store — for merchants
.web — for Web services.

There are also country codes such as:

| | |
|---|---|
| .au | – for Australia |
| .ca | – for Canada |
| .nz | – for New Zealand |

*Links: Address, Country codes, Cybersquatter, DNS, Domainism, Hostname, InterNIC, IP address, Meta tag, NIC, PING, Registering a domain name, Server, URL, Website, Whois*

## Domainism

A form of prejudice against people based purely on their Internet address. For example, some users adopt a dismissive attitude towards anyone who posts from a commercial online service. 'Why should anyone listen to you, you're posting from aol.com!'
*Links: AOL, Domain name, Flame, Netiquette, Newsgroups*

## Dongle

A connecting cable that allows a PC card modem to connect to a phone line. It is also a security measure to prevent the copying of software.
*Links: Modem, PC card, PCMCIA*

## DOS (Disk Operating System)

The first widely used operating system in PCs. The first Windows operating system sat on top of DOS and the latest Windows systems are able to emulate it. DOS is command driven and is non-graphically line-oriented. Its prompt to enter a command looks like this:

C:\>

*Links: Autoexec.bat, .exe, IP address, ScanDisk, Wildcard \*.\**

## DOT address

See IP address.

### Down
Any Website that (for any reason) can't be accessed for a period of time is said to be down, as in 'their Website was down this afternoon'.
*Links: Broken link, Broken pipe, Downtime*

### Downtime
The length of time a Website is down.
*Links: Down*

### Downloading
The process of receiving a file through transmission from one computer to another.
*Links: Bandwidth, FTP*

### dpi (dots per inch)
A way of quantifying the resolution of something (often graphics, but can also be text). The higher the dpi, the greater the resolution.
*Links: Bitmap, Resolution*

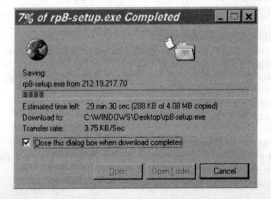

## Dreamweaver

A range of software products or tools by Macromedia used in Website development. It can work with JavaScript and HTML, and uses a What You See Is What You Get (WYSIWYG – see the Appendices for more acronyms) editor. It can also support Cascading Style Sheets and XML and is popular with professional Website designers.

*Links: Cascading Style Sheets, HTML, JavaScript, XML*

## Driver

See Device driver.

## Drop-down menu / Droplist

A list of options that drops down when a down arrow button is clicked.

*Links: Graphical User Interface, Menu bar, Pop-up*

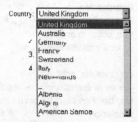

## Dropout

Occurs when connection to the Internet is lost.

*Links: Connectivity*

## DSS (Digital Satellite System)

Allows a user to receive information at a high speed from a satellite using an antenna, coaxial cable, PC adapter card and the relevant software. Unfortunately, it is not currently possible to send data using this method; a dial-up connection and an ISP are still required.

*Links: ADSL, Dial-up connection / networking, ISDN*

## DSS (Digital Signature Standard)

A technology used to confirm that any electronic information received has not been altered.

*Links: Digital certificates, e-mail security, Packet sniffer, Security*

**DSVD (Digital Simultaneous Voice and Data)**
When a modem is able to carry voice and data at the same time so that a person can talk to someone while transferring files.
*Links: ADSL, Modem*

**Dumb terminal**
A monitor without any internal microprocessor but able to respond to simple commands.
*Links: Remote terminal, Telnet, Terminal, Terminal emulation*

**DVD (Digital Versatile Disk)**
See Digital Versatile Disk.

**Dynamic content**
Refers to a Website or page whose content often changes. When a user's browser makes a request for one of these pages, the Web server creates an HTML page from the content on a database and returns it to the requesting browser. This is what allows the pages to be dynamic rather than static. Dynamic content can also be applied to search engines. Every query made with a search engine creates a dynamic page – the content returned is based on the user's request. Web applications such as ASP or Cold Fusion are typically the driving force behind dynamic content.
*Links: ASP, Cold Fusion, Content, Dynamic content, Dynamic fonts, JavaScript, On the fly, SSI*

**Dynamic fonts**
It is possible for Web designers to create new fonts for Web-pages. To be able to view the font, a special file describing how to display that particular set of font images is downloaded as a plug-in from the Web server along with the first page that uses it.
*Links: DHTML, Font, Plug-in*

**Dynamic Link Library**
See DLL.

**Dynamic rotation**
The ability to rotate or change ad banners. A user who visits a site several times will consequently be exposed to many ads as opposed to the same one again and again – the latter being a static banner. Using ad servers allows visitors to a Website to be targeted by ads more specific to them. For example, if the user is visiting a newspaper's Website and looks at the financial pages of the paper, it makes sense for a financially related ad to be displayed. The whole process allows a much greater tailoring of ad deliveries, unthinkable with traditional media.
*Links: Ad banner, Ad server, ASP, Auditor, DHTML, Hardwired, Impressions, Marketing*

# E

**e-1**
The European equivalent of the T-1 leased-line connection. e-1 transmits data at around 2 megabits per second.
*Links: Backbone, Leased line, T-1, T-3*

**EARN (European Academic and Research Network)**
The European equivalent of BITNET.
*Links: BITNET*

**Easter egg**
A hidden message or screen in an application or on a Website. It can be a special feature that is not otherwise made obvious but when 'discovered' or 'clicked on' offers something special. This could be hidden tricks, games or even just the names of the programmers who created the product. The gauntlet is thrown down to users by programmers to find any buried Easter eggs.
*Links: Program, Software*

**e-books (electronic books)**
Any book that can be downloaded and read on a computer or special reader. The publishing world is in a state of flux at the moment concerning the future of books, although there is an almost universal agreement that the future of books involves the electronic format in one way or another. Penguin Books, for example, has given its backing to Microsoft Reader and is planning to supply 1,000 classics of literature in this format. Examples of special software that make the whole experience

as authentic as possible are Adobe Acrobat and Microsoft Reader.

*Links: Adobe Acrobat, ClearType, PDF, PGML, Microsoft Reader*

## e-business (electronic business)

Any business that is performed on the Internet can be said to be e-business. Almost every type of conceivable business is now conducted on the Web, from business-to-business (such as buying parts and supplies from one company to another), to business-to-consumer (such as selling books to customers, making travel bookings, buying and selling stocks and shares … the list is endless). Security is often someone's biggest concern when using the Web for business. This has prompted the latest versions of Web browsers to include inbuilt security. Additionally, digital certificates can now be issued to companies and individuals.

*Links: Auctions, e-commerce, e-tailing, EDI, Security, SET, Shopping, Travel*

## e-cash

A way of paying for goods bought over the Internet. It is possible to buy digital cash from an e-cash company – for example, DigiCash – and this can be used with retailers who accept e-cash. This is a way of avoiding sending credit card numbers over the Internet.

*Links: e-business, e-commerce, e-tailing*

## e-commerce (electronic commerce)

Put simply, e-commerce is the making of financial transactions electronically over the Web. Examples of e-commerce might include the business-to-business exchange of data as well as the more traditional way of selling products using credit cards. The latter is made possible by the use of software programs that can run the main functions of an e-commerce Website, such as product display, online ordering and inventory

management. The software works in conjunction with online payment systems to process payments and resides on a com- merce server. Perhaps the greatest assets of e-commerce is that it is global and available for business twenty-four hours a day, seven days a week. e-commerce has become a key phrase in recent years and, for many, is the principle function of the Net.
*Links: Amazon, SET, Security, Security zones, Shopping*

### eCRM (Electronic Customer Management)
Concerns the way in which companies are building closer per- sonal relationships with their customers. By reinforcing old relationships and establishing new ones through personalised Websites and push technologies, the Internet electronically extends the principles of direct marketing by being able to provide one-to-one selling to anyone in the world.
*Links: e-business, Marketing, Push*

### e-cruiting
The recruiting of people online.
*Links: e-business*

### EDI (Electronic Data Interchange)
A standard used by businesses to transmit documents such as invoices and purchase orders to each other electronically. The parties who exchange EDI messages (which can be encrypted and decrypted) are referred to as trading partners.
*Links: e-business*

### Editor (HTML)
A program used to write and edit HTML code. For Windows there is HTMLed. For Macintosh users there is BBEdit.
*Links: BBEdit, FrontPage, HTML*

### .edu

A top-level domain name (standing for education) assigned to URLs for universities or other educational institutions in the United States (for example, www.columbia.edu). The British equivalent is ac.uk; the New Zealand is ac.nz and so on – 'ac' being an abbreviation of 'academic'.
*Links: Domain name*

### e-form (electronic form)

The electronic version of a paper form. The advantages are the elimination of printing costs, distributing pre-printed forms and storage. It removes the calculation of how many forms to print and avoids any wastage. e-forms also ease changing mistakes and automatic formatting, calculation and validation.
*Links: Adobe Acrobat, CGI, PDF*

### EgoSurfers

People who search the Web with the intention of checking the number of places their names appear. It can also be applied more specifically to authors of books who constantly check their sales ranking on Amazon.
*Links: Denizen, Netizen, Newbie*

### e-journal (electronic journal)

A regularly published journal, typically academic, located on the Web. It might also be published in the traditional manner.
*Links: Zine*

### Electronic publishing

Whenever users display, present or 'post' any written, auditory or visual media on to the World Wide Web, it can be said they are 'publishing' electronic content. Most traditional newspapers and magazines now 'electronically publish' in an electronic form on the Web where access is typically 'free' or available through a free membership. Some sites charge a sub-

scription price. Publishing electronically is a lot easier and much less expensive than 'print' publishing.
*Links: Content, Content provider, e-journal, Webpage, Website, Zine*

### e-mail (electronic mail)

One of the original functions of the Internet; quite simply, it is electronically transmitted mail on a computer. It is one of the main reasons why people become Internet users. As opposed to the traditional way of sending something through the post (aka 'snail mail'), e-mail sends messages instantaneously (well, almost) anywhere in the world. It is the most popular use of the Internet because of the capability to send messages at any time, to anyone, for less money than it would cost to mail a letter or call someone by telephone. It is non-intrusive, and correspondents can read and answer their e-mail when they want to. Two of the more popular e-mail programs are Eudora and Outlook Express. Communicating via e-mail has taken on a new form. Because the messages are quick and instant, and it is easy to send many messages at once, over time, distribution lists have evolved among users that send around jokes, news or photos for example. In addition, a whole new language has developed based on acronyms; BFN (bye for now), is a famous one (an extensive list can be found in the Appendices).
*Links: Address, Address book, Assicons, e-mail filtering, e-mail forwarding, e-mail never-neverland, e-mail reflector, e-mail security, e-mail shorthand, Emotags, Emoticons, IMAP, Mailing list, Packet sniffer, POP3, Push*

### e-mail filtering

It is possible to filter incoming mail into designated mailboxes either as it arrives or afterwards, depending on preference. This can be done in Outlook Express by using the Message Rules option in the Tools menu and in Netscape Messenger using Message Filters in the Edit menu.
*Links: e-mail, Mailbox, Mailing list*

## e-mail forwarding

The ability to share an e-mail with someone other than the original sender. This is much the same as forwarding traditional mail.

*Links: Address, e-mail*

## e-mail never-neverland

An imaginary place where lost e-mail is said to end up.

*Links: Address, e-mail*

## e-mail reflector

A program that broadcasts e-mail forwarded to it to addresses on a distribution list. One member of the distribution list composes an e-mail message or replies to one. The user then sends the message to the e-mail reflector. This then forwards a copy to each person on the list. The list can be managed so that everyone always has the most recent version.

*Links: ListServ, Mailing list, MajorDomo, Re-mailer*

## e-mail security

The safety of any information sent and the reliability of any information received. Security is an issue with e-mail because of packet sniffers and (in the case of Webmail), crackers. One way of reducing any risk is by using Public Key Cryptography, one popular method of which uses a digital certificate to protect information sent by attaching a secure signature. These are issued by certificate authorities such as VeriSign.

*Links: Digital certificates, Encryption, Public Key Cryptography, Security*

## e-mail shorthand

Commonly used phrases reduced to the acronymic form. They are designed to make e-mails quicker to write. For example IMO is In My Humble Opinion. An extensive list of these can be found in the Appendices.

*Links: Assicons, Chat, e-mail, Emotags, Emoticons, e-mail*

**Embedded hyperlink**

A hyperlink that lies within a line of text.

*Links: Hyperlink*

**Emblaze**

A set of products from Geo Interactive that uses Java applets to play specially formatted media files. When a visiting browser downloads the applet, the file can be told to automatically play once loaded.

*Links: Applet*

**Emotags**

Mock HTML tags, such as <hug> or <ironic>, used in e-mail and chat groups to introduce a human quality to messages.

*Links: Assicons, Emoticons, Stage directions*

**Emoticons (Emotion icon)**

A sequence of ASCII characters originally meant to represent emotion in electronic mail or news (which some still do, although there are new 'emoticons' that represent things other than emotions). An example would be :-) These icons follow after the punctuation (or in place of the punctuation) at the end of a sentence. They can be 'seen' better if the head is tilted to the left. A colon represents eyes, a dash represents the nose and the right parenthesis represents the mouth. It should also be pointed out that they look best in the Times New Roman font.

*Links: Assicons, e-mail shorthand, Emotags, Stage directions*

**Encryption**

The most effective way of achieving data security by making transmitted information unreadable to everyone except the receiver. It has proved particularly useful – indeed necessary – in the establishment of the acceptance of sending credit card details over the Internet and all that this implies to e-commerce.

*Links: Decryption, Digital certificates, e-mail security, Public Key Cryptography, Security*

**End user**
The final or ultimate user of a computer system.
*Links: Client*

**.eps (encapsulated postscript)**
A graphics file written in the PostScript language. It usually implies that the file contains a bitmapped representation of the graphics for display purposes. These files can be imported into programs such as Adobe PageMaker and Quark.
*Links: Bitmap, PostScript*

**ERP (Enterprise Resource Planning)**
A business management system that integrates all the facets of a business, including the planning, manufacturing, sales and marketing. It has become a popular methodology and, as a result, software applications have been written to help implement it.
*Links: e-business, eCRM*

**Error messages**
A comprehensive list of these can be found in the Appendices.

**e-tailing (electronic retailing)**
One aspect (probably the main one) of e-commerce. There is still a clear difference between traditional established 'old economy' retailers creating a Web presence by using the Web as a billboard, posting an advertising and editorial information site for their products and services, and 'new economy' e-tailers whose business is based around Web-functionality and is dependent on a revised approach to doing business that encompasses all the possibilities that the Internet offers. The e-tailing industry is at the leading edge of many of the most

recent Internet technological developments. And the Internet has been instrumental in driving down the cost of some consumer goods in the UK, particularly as one of the latest trends is the price comparison site that can quickly compare costs from a number of different e-tailers and link a potential customer to them.
*Links: Companies, e-business, e-commerce*

### e-text
A text document in electronic form; it could be anything from a Readme file to a short note.
*Links: e-form, Readme*

### Ethernet
A LAN (Local Area Network) protocol that supports data transfer rates of up to 10 mbs (megabits per second). It is probably the most popular type of LAN within the workplace, and is used primarily for linking computers and peripheral devices, such as printers, together.
*Links: ARP, LAN, Network*

### Eudora
One of the most popular and best e-mail applications on the Internet, designed for use with SLIP or PPP Internet accounts. Eudora programs are available for both Windows and Macintosh. Eudora also provides Webmail.
*Links: Address book, Attachment, e-mail, Liteware, Mail client, Webmail*

### euroseek.com (www.euroseek.com)
A refreshingly Euro-centric portal and search engine offering searches in thirty-nine different European languages. It offers a blended global and national outlook. Searches can be delimited by national boundaries (for example, Slovenia or Turkey), international regions (for example, Scandinavia) and special domains, such as 'military' or 'government'. The site

also covers the USA and Asia.
*Links: Directory (Internet), Portal, Search engine, Vertical portal*

### excite.com / excite.co.uk / excite.com.au
### (www.excite.com / www.excite.co.uk / www.excite.com.au)

One of the most popular search engines. In addition to a comprehensive subject directory, Excite scans Webpages and Usenet groups for keyword matches and creates summaries of each match. The site also includes directory channels. Many international versions, including Australia, Canada, France, Germany and Sweden, are available.
*Links: Directory (Internet), Portal, Search engine*

### .exe

A self-executing Windows or DOS program.
*Links: DOS, Extension, File extension, Self-extracting files, Windows*

### Expansion board

A printed circuit board that can be inserted into a computer to increase its capabilities. Examples include graphics accelerators, sound cards and internal modems.
*Links: Add-on, Backplane, Bay, Docking station, Expansion slot, Slot, Sound card*

### Expansion slot

A socket in a computer into which an expansion device can be inserted, adding new capabilities to the computer.
*Links: Add-on, Expansion board, Slot, Sound card*

### Export

Describes data that has been formatted so that another application can understand and use it. The application being exported to is importing the data.
*Links: Cross-platform, Import, Portability*

### Extension

The letters after the dot in a file's name. This enables users quickly to understand the type of file something is without having to 'open' or try to use it by describing its format. For example, a file named iconbooks.html means that the file is coded in HTML and therefore must be viewed with a compatible program such as a Web browser in order to see it properly. For details on what can correctly open various files, refer to the Appendices.

*Links: File extension*

### External viewer

See Helper application.

### Extranet

The connecting of two or more intranets, or an intranet that is partially accessible to authorised outsiders. An example of use might be for two or more companies to connect their intranets, allowing them to communicate and do business over the Internet within their own virtual area.

*Links: Intranet, Network*

### Eyeballs

The viewing audience of a Website.

*Links: Marketing, Portal, Vertical portal*

### e-zine (electronic magazine)

See Zine.

# F

## Facilitated chat

When a host or facilitator controls the messages that appear on the chat screen, usually found when there is a guest speaker or online interview. This ensures that there isn't an overwhelming amount of questions all being asked at once and some sort of structure to the discussion can be provided.

*Links: Buddy lists, Channel, Chat, Chat history, Chat room, ICQ, IRC, mIRC, Moderated mailing list*

## FAQ (frequently asked question)

When users visit a Website, newsgroup or whatever, they may see a link labelled FAQ. This is a list of commonly asked questions with answers that relate to the site being visited. The aim is to assist users as much as possible without the need for them to contact the site's administrators.

*Links: Readme*

## FastCGI

A programming interface for CGI that speeds up performance by using a single process to handle multiple requests.

*Links: ASP, CGI, cgi-bin, Counter, JavaScript, NSAPI, Perl, Script, Server script, Servlet*

## Fast packet

A packet that arrives at its destination without it ever having been checked for errors. Made possible due to the new high bandwidth transmission technologies and the rare occurrence of data loss associated with these.

*Links: Packet, Packet sniffer*

### FAT (File Allocation Table)
A table that operating systems use to locate files on a disk. For instance, due to fragmentation, a file may be divided into many sections that are scattered around a disk. The FAT keeps a track of all of these.
*Links: File, Operating system*

### Favicon (favourite icon)
It is possible for users to add favourite Webpages to their Links bar, which is located next to the address bar on Internet Explorer 5.0 and above. Pages can be added to the Links bar in a variety of ways: the icon for a page can be dragged from the Address bar to the Links bar. A link from a Webpage can be dragged to the Links bar, and a link can be dragged to the Links folder in the user's Favorites list. If the Links bar does not appear on the toolbar, the View menu can be clicked, followed by pointing to Toolbars, then clicking Links. It is also possible to organise links by dragging them to a different location on the Links bar. The favicon is a customised image of the link and uses the name favicon.ico
*Links: Bookmark, Favorites, Internet Explorer, Toolbar*

### Favorites
See Bookmark.

### Fax modem
A type of modem that enables a computer to transmit and receive electronic documents as faxes.
*Links: Modem*

### fcc (forward carbon copy)
The same as 'cc' or carbon copy.
*Links: bcc, cc, e-mail*

## FED (Field Emission Display)

The popularity of the laptop computer, among other things, has necessitated improvements in the screens of these computers. FED is the technology that has made possible the thin panel of today's LCD screens.
*Links: Active Matrix Display, Screen saver, TFT screen*

## Ferret

A program that can search chosen files, databases or search engine indices for specified information.
*Links: Database, Program, Search engine*

## Fetch

A program for the Macintosh that offers different ways to connect to an FTP site. It allows users manually to type in a site's address and their login details or even choose a site from a list that the program knows about. It can also use FTP (file transfer protocol) to transfer files from a computer on to a server. This allows files to be written on a local computer, which can then be placed on the server when finished.
*Links: Anonymous FTP, FTP*

## Fibre optics

Light beams can be transmitted along optical fibres. A light beam, for example a laser, can be controlled to carry information and allows communications to be much more effective.
*Links: Digital*

## Field

An individual container or location where data is entered. It is most commonly used when talking about databases. For example, someone might be keeping a list of all the people they wish to send a Christmas card to and each entry (person) is called a record. The various parts of the record are called fields

(for example, a line where the name is entered, another for the post code and so on). However, field has come to signify much more with the advent of the Web. The subject box in an e-mail is a field, and if a form on a Webpage needed filling in, each box would be a text entry field.
*Links: CGI, Database, e-form, Query*

### File
A collection of records, data or information (like in a physical office) that, depending on the operating system, is contained within catalogues, directories or folders. A file is also an entity of data that can be transferred, such as a Word file (which takes the form name.doc) or a sound file (one form of which is sound.wav). These can be moved from one file directory to another or even attached to e-mails and transferred over the Internet.
*Links: Associate, Extension, File extension*

### File compression
See Compression.

### File extension
See Extension.

### findwhat.com (www.findwhat.com)
One of a new breed of search engines that charges for entries. This naturally results in searches dominated by commercial enterprises trying to sell you something, which is fine if that's what a user is looking for. Organisations pay for a guaranteed appearance of their site under certain subject categories.
*Links: Directory (Internet), Search engine*

### Finger
One of the first Internet services; allows users to find out more information about another Internet user, such as if they

are currently logged on. It is also available on the Web.
*Links: Internet, Whois*

**Fire off**
To send out an e-mail.
*Links: e-mail*

**Firewall**
A security system designed to prevent unauthorised users from accessing a private network. Companies often set up firewalls around their networks to prevent crackers from breaking in. Hardware, software and specified procedures provide access control. Firewalls allow only clearly intended and authorised data to reach its destination. Firewalls can limit Internet access to e-mail only, control who can telnet into the intranet and limit what other kinds of traffic can pass between an intranet and Internet. All messages passing through a firewall are examined and checked against the security criteria specified by the company.
*Links: Access control, Cracker, Gateway, Intranet, Proxy server, Security, SOCKS*

**Firmware**
Software stored in the ROM.
*Links: Hardware, ROM, Software*

**Flame**
To write uninhibited, angry and aggressive messages – a taboo on the Internet. Flaming is not to be advised, particularly as e-mails are so forwardable and posted messages so visible. It tends to be the aggressor who looks worst in these situations.
*Links: Discussion group, Domainism, e-mail, Flame war, Netiquette, Newsgroups*

**Flame bait**
When someone deliberately writes in a flaming manner in order to provoke others and perhaps begin a flame war.
*Links: Discussion group, Domainism, e-mail, Flame war, Netiquette, Newsgroups*

**Flame war**
Should flaming messages start to be exchanged between parties, it can be said that a flame war has begun.
*Links: Discussion group, Domainism, e-mail, Flame bait, Netiquette, Newsgroups*

**Flash**
A software product that allows users to produce Websites with vector and bitmap graphics, MP3 audio, form input and inter-activity. It is possible to have streaming Flash files that play while they download, and the files are extremely small. A Flash player (plug-in) is needed to view Websites using Flash; these plug-ins can be quickly and freely downloaded.
*Links: Bitmap, MP3, Plug-in, Vector graphics*

**Flash session**
A feature of AOL that automatically performs online tasks at a designated time. These are mostly used to send/receive e-mail and download large files.
*Links: AOL*

**Flat file**
Used to describe files that contain text that has had all markup or formatting removed. CSV is one type of flat file. It contains a series of records that can be said to have no structured relationship.
*Links: CSV*

### Flat file system
No connection with the previous term, this is where every file in a system of files must have a different name. There is obviously no way of distinguishing two different files if they have the same name.
*Links: Directory (computer), File*

### Floating
An application element that can be moved to different places on a screen is said to be floating and allows for the customisation of the screen. For example, it is possible to set up floating toolbars in Microsoft Word.
*Links: Floating toolbar*

### Floating Point Unit (FPU)
Also known as a numeric coprocessor, this is special circuitry in a standard microprocessor that enables numbers to be more quickly manipulated.
*Links: Microprocessor*

### Floating toolbar

Floating Toolbar

A toolbar is a collection of tools that are normally placed along the edge of a screen. For example, in Word, Bold, Italicise and Underline are just some of the tools that can be found at the top of the window. A floating toolbar is when the toolbar can be moved around the screen by using the mouse.
*Links: Floating, Menu bar, Toolbar*

### FLOPS (Floating Point Operations)
A common benchmark measurement for judging the speed of microprocessors.
*Links: Benchmark*

### Flow control
The method by which the transfer of data between two devices is managed. Examples of the types of transfer could be between a computer and a modem or between nodes on a network. This control is vital as devices can only handle a maximum of data. Too much could create an overflow resulting in lost data.
*Links: Device, Parallel port, Serial port*

### Follow-up
A reply to a Usenet (newsgroup) posting.
*Links: Newsgroups, Posting, Thread, Usenet*

### Font
The type and style of text used. Also called a 'typeface'. The type design for a set of fonts is the typeface and variations of this design form the typeface family. Thus, Helvetica is a type-face family, Helvetica italic is a typeface, and Helvetica italic 10-point is a font. In practice, font and typeface are often used without much precision, sometimes interchangeably. This book has been produced using Helvetica.
*Links: Adobe Acrobat, ClearType, Dynamic fonts, e-books, PGML*

**Footprint**

The amount of space a piece of hardware or software uses. An example could be a monitor said to have a smaller footprint than most of its competitors. This means it occupies less space on a desk.

*Links: Marketing*

**Form**

On the Web, this word is typically used to denote a part of a Webpage that involves user input – for example, an application form. The user is able to input data on to the screen and then submit these forms. A response confirming receipt is then usually returned.

*Links: CGI, e-form*

**Forward slash**

The character '/'. A backslash is '\'.

*Links: ASCII*

**Fractal**

Fractal geometry is the geometry of special types of irregular shapes. The word was coined by Benoit B. Mandelbrot from the Latin *fractus,* which describes broken stones – broken up and irregular. They are a way of measuring qualities that otherwise have no clear definition: the degree of roughness or brokenness or irregularity in an object. It is believed that fractals will play a major role in computing, particularly concerning graphics and images. They provide a way of getting immense detail on images without taking up a large amount of memory. Fractal mathematics also play a major role in the creation of special effects in films. Images of alien landscapes in the *Star Wars* films, for example, were generated on computer using fractals.

*Links: Raster graphics, Vector graphics*

**Frame source**

Relates to a particular frame on a Website and can be considered the equivalent to a document source. It is possible when printing a Webpage just to print the content of a single frame.
*Links: Document source, Frames*

**Frames**

It is quite common nowadays to come across Websites that have multiple windows but on one browser screen. These are frames (Websites will often give the choice to view either the frames or non-frames version). One of the frames can be scrolled while the other remains static. However, this is *not* the same as having two browser windows open. In frames, the pages are mutually dependent. One affects the other and so on. This can be useful when one window is a list for example,

Frames

and the other displays the information on each entry in a list. A user can scroll down a list, clicking links in which they are interested; the list stays in case they want something else, but the link clicked on comes up in the other window. It is a feature that is now supported by most browsers.

*Links: Browser, Frame source, Webpage*

### Free-mail
See Webmail.

### Freeware
Software that can be downloaded from the Internet and used without any charge. There are many sites that offer freeware downloads. Among the best are download.com (part of CNET) and shareware.com (Note: users should scan everything downloaded off the Internet using an anti-virus program.)

*Links: Liteware, Shareware, Trojan, Virus*

### Fried
Something permanently damaged or otherwise unusable – as in 'My hard drive is fried' or 'The network is totally fried'.

*Links: Robust*

### Front-end
The aspect of an application that a user sees and interacts with. As a consequence it is usually designed to be clear and easy to use.

*Links: Back-end, Database, Database front-end, Graphical User Interface*

### FrontPage/FrontPage Express
Two Web editors from Microsoft that can be used to create Webpages. FrontPage Express is available as part of Windows 98 and Internet Explorer (versions 4.0 onwards). FrontPage has more features than just HTML coding.

*Links: Editor (HTML), HTML, Internet Explorer*

**Frozen**
A computer (screen) has frozen if it is unresponsive – for example, the mouse pointer won't move or the clock has stopped.
*Links: Churning, Crash*

**FTP (File Transfer Protocol)**
A standard for moving files from one computer to another, particularly for downloading and uploading files over the Internet. A computer on the Internet that specifically stores files for users to transfer to their own computers is called an FTP site. An FTP site that doesn't require users to have their own specific user ID and password is called an anonymous FTP site. Files can be transferred using a browser or an FTP client program. On the Macintosh there is a program called Fetch, and on Windows there is WS_FTP.
*Links: Anonymous FTP, Archie, CuteFTP, Downloading, Fetch, TFTP, WS_FTP*

**FUI (Form-based User Interface)**
Where an application program presents the user with a form to complete by entering various details. Once completed, the information provided is processed and the program presents the user with another form giving its results on the previous form. An example might be a mortgage calculator.
*Links: Calculators, Form*

**Full duplex**
This refers to the transmission of data in two directions simultaneously. An example would be the telephone.
*Links: Half duplex*

**Functionality**
Functional capability.
*Links: Backwards compatible*

**Fuzzy logic**
Designed to replicate human reasoning in a better way than classical logic. In classical logic, something is simply either true or false. In fuzzy logic, there are degrees of truth. For example, a man may be tall compared to a child but not compared to a giraffe. He might be described as very tall, tall or not at all tall. With classical logic this judgement would have to be made against a standard. It might be stated that anyone above six foot is tall, so a man is tall only if he is above six foot – but this isn't how the normal human mind works. Fuzzy logic has important uses in artificial intelligence and the design of control systems. It is also used in some spellcheckers to suggest a list of probable words to replace a misspelled one.
*Links: AI, OCR*

# G

### G3
The name given by Apple Computers to the PowerPC 750 microprocessor used in their iMac and Power Macintosh personal computers.
*Links: Apple*

### galaxy.com (www.galaxy.com)
A popular and easy-to-use subject directory for finding information on the Internet. Either the subject directory can be explored or a keyword search undertaken. In 1999 Galaxy was brought under the corporate umbrella of the Fox/News Corporation.
*Links: Database, Directory (Internet), Keyword, Query,*
*Search engine*

### Gamecasts
A way of following a sports game on the Internet while it is being played. It uses a combination of text and graphics to communicate the current state of a game. It is very well developed in the US at the moment, especially for baseball.
*Links: Broadcasting, Webcasting*

### Games, online
The Internet is an obvious way for people to increase the potential of computer game playing. It enables them to play games online against other people, receive news and updates on games, download shareware games and find game guides, among other things. It can, however, be limiting in terms of

delays, depending on the connection a gamer has, but this is set to change as new and faster ways of transmitting data become available.
*Links: AGP, Avatar, Cybercide, DirectX, Graphics accelerator, MIP mapping, MUD, RSAC*

### Gatekeeping
Process by which news or information is released by those who control it.
*Links: Content provider, News*

### Gateway
An entrance to the Internet or a network. It can also be viewed as a border control between networks and as such could have other functions such as being a proxy and firewall server.
*Links: Firewall, Portal, Proxy server, Vertical portal*

### Ghost
A user session no longer occupied on an IRC channel but which the chat server continues to believe is active.
*Links: Chat, IRC, Lurk*

### Ghost site
A Website that can be viewed but which is no longer maintained. It is often very difficult to pick out as a lot of sites make no mention of their last update. This is one of the growing problems of the Internet.
*Links: Broken link, Cobweb site, Website*

### GIF (Graphic Interchange Format)
Along with JPEG, GIF is one of two most commonly used compression methods for graphic images on the Internet and, hence, can be downloaded quickly. These compression methods were developed by CompuServe to facilitate the viewing of graphic images cross-platform on different kinds of

computers (Apple Macintosh, IBM, Windows and so on). JPEGs download faster than GIFs and contain a better resolution; however, they cannot be interlaced on many Webpages. Subsequently, developers tend to opt for GIFs. This helps to achieve that 'melting' on to the screen effect that happens with interlaced images.
*Links: Adobe Photoshop, Bitmap, Colour depth, Interlaced GIF, JPEG, JPEG Optimiser, LviewPro, Paint Shop Pro, PNG, Raster graphics, Transparent GIF*

### GIF animation (Animated GIF or Multi-block GIF)
See Animated GIF.

### Gigabyte
One gigabyte is equal to 1,000 megabytes. Nowadays computers come with hard drives that are a minimum size of more than one gigabyte.
*Links: Byte, Hard drive*

### Glitch
A problem that prevents a piece of hardware from working correctly.
*Links: Anomaly, Bug*

### go.com (www.go.com)
Portal-style directory of Websites that have been reviewed.
*Links: Directory (Internet), Portal, Search engine*

### gogettem.com (www.gogettem.com)
A multi-search tool covering popular search engines with a tick option to decide which search engines are used. Brings up each search engine on-screen in an individual browser window to indicate results. Also lists 2,600 specialist directories.
*Links: Directory (Internet), Multi-search tools, Portal, Search engine*

**google.com (www.google.com)**
One of the new breed of non-portal search engines that takes into account links to other sites when ranking. This can simplify the search process and seems to deliver the results.
*Links: Directory (Internet), Multi-search tools, Portal, Search engine*

**Gopher**
An Internet server document browsing and searching system that existed before the Web and is still used today. It displays its information in the form of many menus. Items are chosen from the menus and when a wanted file is found, Gopher can display it. It can be used to scour the Internet for texts of interest and helps retrieve them. Most Web browsers include a Gopher client. Providing the server's address is known, the user can go directly to any Gopher server from their Web browser. There are also Gopher browsers – for example, Hypergopher.
*Links: Veronica*

**.gov**
A top-level domain name. It usually denotes the owner of the domain as being a branch or agency of a government.
*Links: Domain name*

**Graphic accelerator**
A chipset attached to a video board used to speed up the action of drawing lines and images on a screen, thereby enabling high-performance graphics. This power can be extended further with the use of an Accelerated Graphics Port. Most new personal computers are now sold with a graphics accelerator (often called a graphics card) already built in. Each graphics accelerator provides an application program interface (API). Some support more than one API. Among the most popular APIs are the industry standard OpenGL, Microsoft's DirectX and Direct3D. Popular 3D graphics accelerators

include 3Dfx Voodoo, and ATI 3D Rage Pro.
*Links: Add-on, AGP, CAD, Games, OpenGL*

### Graphical User Interface (GUI)

A program interface that uses a computer's ability to display graphics to make a particular program easier to use. It is akin to WYSIWYG (What You See Is What You Get). Both Windows and Macintosh use GUIs – drop-down menus are an example of the use of GUIs.
*Links: Browser, Drop-down menu / Droplist, Front-end, Mosaic*

### GSM (Global Standard for Mobile Communications)

A set of standards widely used in Europe for cellular communications.
*Links: Internet telephony, WAP, WML*

### Guestbook

One of the simplest ways for a Website to encourage feedback from its visitors. Users fill out a form. This is appended to an existing HTML file, and subsequent visitors are able to read the entries.
*Links: Discussion group, Website*

### GUI

See Graphical User Interface.

# H

## Hacker

This word is used in a variety of ways, all of which have the ultimate definition of 'clever programmer'. It can be used in a positive way but is typically meant negatively were the implication is that this cleverness is used to be deceitful – for example, by breaking into computer systems. This has resulted in the term 'cracker', on to which hackers hope to transfer these negative connotations. Judging by way the two words are used interchangeably by the media, they seem to have failed in this respect.

*Links: Cracker, Hacker jargon*

## Hacker jargon

Jargon used by hackers.

*Links: Cracker, Hacker*

## Half duplex

Processes whereby information can be transmitted in only one direction at a time.

*Links: Full duplex*

## Hand-held computer

A computer that can typically be stored in a pocket and be used while being held. 3Com, Philips, Casio and Compaq are all companies that produce hand-held computers. Windows CE is one of the most widely used operating systems for these devices.

*Links: HDML, PC card, PDA, Windows CE*

### Handle
A person's online nickname or the name they go by in a chat room. It is also known as a username.
*Links: Avatar, Chat*

### Handshake
When one computer tries to connect with another through the use of modems, they first have to establish the way in which they will transfer data. This 'communication' can be heard as crunching and other sounds immediately after dialling.
*Links: Modem*

### Hard disk
A magnetic disk on which a great deal of computer data can be stored. It is the main data *storage* unit in a computer and home computers now come with hard drives measured in gigabytes.
*Links: Byte, Sector*

### Hardware
The physical constitution of a computer (for example, the disk drive and the modem) as opposed to the programs (software) that allow a computer to do useful things.
*Links: Configuration, Device, Software*

### Hardwired
Banner ads that are set in position and delivered each time the page is downloaded. It is the opposite of dynamic rotation. This term additionally refers to anything that cannot be changed.
*Links: Ad banner, Ad server, Auditor, Dynamic rotation*

### Hayes compatible
A modem that uses the AT command set, which is the standard language for controlling modems.
*Links: AT commands, Modem*

**HDML (Hand-held Device Markup Language)**
Also know as Wireless Markup Language (WML), this is the HTML for hand-held devices, personal digital assistants (PDAs) and cellular phones.
*Links: PDA, Windows, WML*

**Header**
The part of a packet that contains various information such as the originator and destination addresses. It is also the portion of an e-mail message that is above the body of the message.
*Links: Body, e-mail, Message header, Packet*

**Helper application**
These are programs that allow a browser to deal with multi-media files such as Web radio, video clips, VOD sequences and live audio-visual netcasts. They can also work on their own without the need for a browser. TThe term is sometimes used interchangeably with media players.
*Links: Browser, Media players, Multi-media, Plug-in, Push*

**Hertz (Hz)**
The SI (international system of units of measurement) unit of frequency, equal to one cycle per second.
*Links: CPU, Microprocessor*

**Hierarchy**
A category of newsgroups or directories, or the way news-groups or directories are internally categorised. Each hierarchy contains a thread of messages.
*Links: Newsgroups, Newsreader, Thread*

**Highlight**
The act of making an object (for example, a block of text or an icon) stand out on the screen – often by selecting it.
*Links: Block, Word processor*

### High-speed connections
There are many high-speed connections to choose from but they are subject to conditions of availability. ISDN and ADSL work over phone lines but not over all phone lines, and a cable modem service requires cable TV wiring. After considering the availability of these services, cost and performance factors will then need to be considered.
*Links: ADSL, Cable, DSS, ISDN, WebTV*

### History list
An index of Internet documents that have been viewed using either the Netscape Navigator or Internet Explorer browser. They are often displayed chronologically. Internet Explorer stores the information in the form of Internet shortcuts and these are arranged into a hierarchy of folders inside the History folder. Navigator maintains a history database. Both methods enable a return to a Webpage with a single click.
*Links: Internet Explorer, Netscape Navigator*

### Hit
A request made to a server for information and often used to indicate how popular a site is. One Webpage may involve the requesting of many elements. These include any graphics and multi-media, and even the HTML file itself. Every element results in one hit so the downloading of one page might result in many hits for a Website if it is a page with lots of features. Those who want to accurately monitor visiting traffic to their Website count actual page views rather than hits.
*Links: Auditor, Counter, Impressions, Marketing, Page requests*

### Holy war
Arguments about technology that involve certain basic tenets of faith. An example could be about which is superior – for example, a Macintosh or a PC, Mac OS or Windows.
*Links: Flame bait, Flame war*

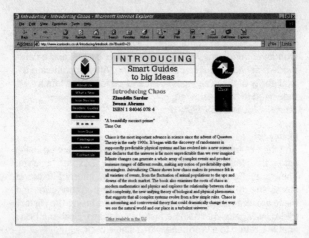

## Homepage

The entry point or first page on a Website where the site's information actually begins and from which the rest of the site can be navigated. The question 'Do you have a homepage?' commonly means 'Do you have a Website?' when dealing with individuals rather than businesses.

*Links: Address, Buffer page, Microsite, Navigate, Splash page, Webpage, Website*

## Host

A computer on the Internet that allows other computers to connect with it. In effect every computer on the Internet is a host. However, the term is usually used interchangeably with server. Host is rarely used to describe PCs unless they are acting as some sort of server.

*Links: Client, Hosting, Server*

### Hosting
The housing, serving and maintaining of files for a Website or sites.
*Links: Host, Server, Server Space Provider, Virtual hosting*

### Hostname
See Domain name.

### Hot plugging/swapping
The ability to add and remove devices, such as scanners, even while a computer is switched on with the result that the device can be used immediately. It is a feature of the Universal Serial Bus (USB) port and of PCMCIA.
*Links: Device, Device driver, PCMCIA, Plug-and-Play, Scanner, USB*

### Hot spots
Areas of an image map that are linked to different URLs. For example, a motorbike manufacturer might place hot spots on the image of one of his bikes whereby users clicking on a portion of it might be shown further information relating to that part of the bike.
*Links: Clickable graphic, Clickstreams, Image map, URL*

### hotbot.com (www.hotbot.com)
A portal-style directory and search site that is part of the Lycos Network. It contains over 110 million fully indexed Web documents on its database and is refreshed in its entirety every month. It also has sophisticated advance search features.
*Links: Directory (Internet), Lycos, Search engine*

### HotDog
HotDog Professional is a multi-featured Webpage editor. There is a more basic version called HotDog Express, which is useful for creating pages quickly.
*Links: Editor (HTML), FrontPage, HTML*

### HotJava

A Web browser that can execute programs written in the Java programming language. These programs, known as applets, can be included in HTML pages just as images are. The later versions of Netscape Navigator and Microsoft Internet Explorer are also Java-enabled browsers with the addition of many more features.

*Links: Applet, Browser, Internet Explorer, Java, Netscape Navigator*

### Hot list

A list of popular Websites usually presented as active links. Yahoo! began its life as a hot list.

*Links: Directory (Internet), Portal*

### Hotmail

A popular free Webmail system owned by Microsoft.

*Links: NetMeeting, Webmail*

### .htm

Another type of file extension used to denote an HTML file. For example, the file might be named 'file.htm' instead of 'file.html'.

*Links: Extension, HTML*

### HTML (Hypertext Markup Language)

The standard set of markup symbols used to indicate any features and links to other hypertext documents in a file intended for display on a Web browser. The individual markup codes are referred to as elements (but many people also refer to them as tags). Examples of HTML codes include:

| | |
|---|---|
| \<p\> | paragraph break |
| \<I\>...\</I\> | italics (the \<I\> marks the beginning of the italics and the \</I\> the end) |
| \<b\>...\</b\> | bold |

*Links: Broken link, Browser, Browser compatibility, CFML, DHTML, HTML*

*Reference Library, Hyperlink, Hypertext, Meta tag, SHTML, Source code, SSI, Tag, VRML, XML*

## HTML Reference Library
A Microsoft Windows program that contains a list of HTML definitions, quick reference tools and even examples of usage.
*Links: HTML*

## HTTP (Hypertext Transfer Protocol)
URLs (addresses) for Websites usually begin with 'http:'. This application protocol is the set of communication rules for the regulation of the passing of files and information around the Web.
*Links: Communications protocol, HTTPS, Protocol, TCP/IP, URL*

## HTTPS (Hypertext Transfer Protocol Secure)
A variation of http that enables 'secure' transactions to take place on the Web by using SSL encryption. Users can type in HTTPS instead of HTTP in the URL section of their browsers to enter into the 'secured mode', if applicable.
*Links: HTTP, Protocol, Security*

## Hub
A device or connection point for more than two computers to form a network, thereby allowing the transfer of data between them. It works by splitting a network cable, perhaps part of a backbone, into a set of separate cables each connecting to a distinct computer. Hubs are also grandiose Website portals that attempt to provide all the information a user needs internally, eliminating the need to search the Web.
*Links: Device, Node*

## Hyperlink (aka 'link')
This usually appears on-screen in the form of underlined text, coloured text or iconised graphics within Webpages. Once

'clicked on', a hyperlink can take a user to different locations on the Webpage, different pages within the site or to a different site altogether, as well as opening sound or audio-visual files. When the cursor (or mouse arrow) is placed over a link, it changes into the shape of a hand. Hyperlinks are created or 'coded' in HTML.
*Links: Broken link, HTML, Hypertext*

## Hypermedia
Webpage links to multi-media files.
*Links: Hyperlink, Multi-media*

## HyperTerminal
A terminal-emulation program that comes with Windows 95 and 98. It enables users to dial into a UNIX shell account from their PCs.
*Links: Telnet, Terminal emulation, UNIX*

## Hypertext
A way of writing and displaying text whose name was coined to refer to a non-linear system of information browsing and retrieval that involved links to related documents.
*Links: HTML, HTTP, Hyperlink, Surf, WWW*

# I

### iCab
The Opera browser equivalent for Macs with several of its features. Many people believe it looks and works better than Opera.
*Links: Browser, Opera*

### Icon
An image located on a computer desktop or Web browser representing a software application or file. When clicked on, the image activates the application or file. An icon can also be a non-selectable image such as a company's logo.
*Links: Associate, Button, Desktop, Extension, Shortcut*

### ICQ ('I Seek You')
A direct messaging system program able to tell users when their friends and contacts are also online (using buddy lists), thus allowing them to have real-time conversations. ICQ can be downloaded for free.
*Links: Buddy lists, Chat, IRC*

### Identity hacking
A form of deception whereby someone poses as another person.
*Links: Cracker, Security*

### Idoru
A generic term for a virtual – that is, a computer-created – media star. For example, a pop star could be created who

releases songs, conducts interviews and even grows older. One example is e-Cyas, a virtual pop singer who recently released his debut single, 'Are You Real?'. His voice was created by digitally blending those of several session musicians. e-Cyas is already receiving fan mail.
*Links: Avatar, Virtual*

### IJ (Internet Jockey)
The Internet equivalent of the traditional Disc Jockey (DJ). Some radio stations on the Internet have chatty IJs as well as playing music.
*Links: Broadcasting*

### iMac
A low-cost Macintosh computer available in a variety of colours. The iMac is Apple's attempt to reverse the dwindling numbers of people using their computers by offering a competitively priced, fun and easy-to-use computer, particularly aimed at first-time computer buyers. The Internet has resulted

in a huge explosion of interest in computing and the iMac has been designed with this in mind, the 'i' standing for Internet. Sales have exceeded expectations.
*Links: Apple, Macintosh, Mac OS*

## Image map

A graphic image allowing users to click on different areas of the image that are linked to other Webpages. Each sensitive area can be defined in terms of its X and Y co-ordinates, with each set of co-ordinates specifying a URL or Web address link.
*Links: Clickable graphic, Hot spots, URL*

## IMAP (Internet Message Access Protocol)

A method of accessing e-mail messages retained on a mail server, and considered by many to be more sophisticated than POP3. Just the heading and the sender of the letter are viewed, and a decision can be made as to whether to download the mail. One of its main advantages is that it can be accessed from any computer with Internet access so that a user is not restricted to a specific computer. As with POP, IMAP uses SMTP for communication between the e-mail client and server.
*Links: Mailbox, POP3, SMTP*

## Import

To use data produced by one application in another application. This is very important in software applications because it means that one application can work with another.
*Links: Cross-platform, Export, Portability*

## Impressions

A measure of how many times an ad on a Webpage is viewed. This is done by keeping track of the number of times the ad is downloaded. These results can be further analysed using various Web marketing programs.
*Links: Ad banner, Ad server, Auditor, Click rate*

### In box
An e-mail folder where a user receives incoming mail.
*Links: e-mail, Mailbox*

### InContext WebAnalyzer
A Windows software program for managing an Internet or intranet Website. Among its features is the ability to detect broken links on a Website and inform the manager of the site.
*Links: Auto-bot, Broken link, Intranet, Website*

### Index
A file name normally used to store the homepage of a Website. It may be set by the server for the Website as the default page. For example, a user entering http://www.iconbooks.co.uk into a browser might be presented with the page http://www.icon-books.co.uk/index.html.
*Links: Homepage, HTML*

### Indices
The plural form of index, this might be used to describe an index of indexes or a directory of directories on a Website.
*Links: Directory (Internet), Hot list*

### infind.com (www.infind.com)
Searches six engines, removes duplicates and uniquely groups results into clusters for easy understandability. There are also French and German options available.
*Links: Directory (Internet), Portal, Search engine*

### Infobahn
A synonym for the information superhighway taken from autobahn, the German word for motorway.
*Links: Information superhighway*

**Information superhighway (or I-way)**
As the Internet began to expand, the idea of an 'information superhighway' seeped into the general public consciousness when the term was coined by US vice-president Al Gore, whose High Performance Computer Act 1991 provided funds for research aimed at improving the Internet's US infrastructure. The term is widely used to mean the Internet.
*Links: Infobahn*

**infoseek.com (www.infoseek.com)**
A search engine that can scour the Web, newsgroups, FTP and Gopher sites for pages that mention a specified word or phrase.
*Links: Directory (Internet), FTP, Gopher, Newsgroups, Portal, Search engine, Usenet, Web*

**infospace.com (www.infospace.com)**
A personal directory on the Web that allows visitors to search its database in order to find an e-mail address or phone number and so on. Visitors can also add and remove their own details on the directory.
*Links: Bigfoot, WhoWhere, Yahoo!*

**Infosurfing**
The amount of time it takes to retrieve information on the Web can vary considerably. Infosurfing speeds up the whole process by browsing the Web using text only, thereby eliminating the time-consuming downloading of images, sound or video. Browsers give users the ability to turn options on and off. It is really up to users to decide whether they want information at maximum speed or would prefer to receive the full Web experience.
*Links: Cybrarian, Lynx, Surf*

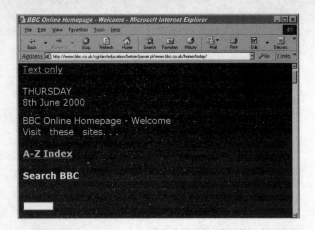

**Initialisation string**

A row of characters that prompts a modem into action – usually 'AT' for 'attention.' Most ISPs come with their own software that automatically sets the initialisation string on a user's computer.

*Links: AT commands, Modem*

**Inline image**

HTML documents sometimes contain built-in graphics which are also retrieved when the document is requested. These are then viewed by the requesting browser.

*Links: Hit, HTML, Webpage*

**InstallShield**

A product that enables users to install software with ease and safety. It can also be used to uninstall software.

*Links: Software*

### Instant Messenger (AOL)
A program that allows instant chat between users who are online. It can work with a buddy list to allow users to know when their friends are online at the same time so that they can 'buzz' them and start communicating.
*Links: AOL, Buddy lists, Chat*

### Intel
The world's largest manufacturer of computer chips whose success has been primarily influenced by a close alliance with Microsoft. Windows operating systems are designed for the architecture that Intel's chips use.
*Links: CPU, Cyrix, Microprocessor, MMX, Pentium, Wintel*

### Intelligent agent
See Agent.

### IntelliSense
A feature of Internet Explorer 5 that allows various tasks to be acted on automatically – including the correcting of address typos, filling in forms, remembering passwords, installing upgrades and completing addresses.
*Links: Internet Explorer, URL*

### Interactive Web chat
The ability to converse directly with other Web users in much the same way as IRC and sites of this nature are often called chat rooms. One example is the AOL chat rooms, although these can only be used by AOL members. Most chat rooms can be accessed by anyone with the right software.
*Links: AOL, Chat, ICQ, IRC*

### Interactivity
Used in the context of multi-media that involves responses to user input.

*Links: Flash, JavaBeans, Multi-media, Plug-in, Shockwave, VRML*

**Interlaced GIF**
A useful type of GIF that can be displayed on a Webpage faster
because it can be displayed in a rough form before all the information has been received. It quickly appears and then seems
gradually to come into focus, in a kind of melting effect.
*Links: Downloading, GIF*

**Internet**
Also known as 'the Net', this is essentially an international
system of linked computer networks that allows a variety of
data communication services to operate. These include e-mail,
the World Wide Web, newsgroups and FTP. Historically, each
of these areas was a clearly defined entity in its own right but in
recent years they have started to merge, with the Web coming
to dominate. Taken in a much more general sense, the Internet
can be seen as a great business opportunity, a means of
expanding business beyond the limitations of geography but,
perhaps most of all, it is a means of publishing and presenting
information about anything and everything.
*Links: e-mail, FTP, Network, Newsgroups, WWW*

**Internet account**
See Account.

**Internet backbone**
See Backbone.

**Internet Connection Wizard**
Comes with Windows 98 and can also be downloaded from the
Internet. It helps users sign up for a new Internet account or
even configure their computers for an existing account.
*Links: Access, Account, Dial-up connection / networking, ISP, OSP*

**Internet Explorer (Microsoft)**
Microsoft's Web browser available for Mac and Windows operating systems. It contains all the standard browser facilities, such as the ability to read HTML, so that Webpages can be viewed along with extra features like IntelliSense, which can save a user time completing routine Web tasks (for instance, automatically completing Web addresses and forms for them, and automatically detecting their network and connection status).
*Links: Browser, IntelliSense, Security zones, Status bar*

**Internet security**
See Security.

**Internet Society (ISOC)**
An organisation committed to supporting the growth and development of the Internet.
*Links: ANSI*

**Internet telephony**
The use of the Internet rather than the traditional telephone to exchange spoken or other telephone information. This is an area with great potential, especially with regard to long distance calls, as it allows all phone calls to be either free or charged at the local rate (whatever the phone charge for Internet access is). The only potential drawback is that both communicators may need to be online (depending on whether the call from a computer can be picked up on a conventional phone).
*Links: Aplio phone, Channel, CoolTalk, CU-SeeME, GSM, NetMeeting*

**InterNIC (Internet Network Information Center)**
An organisation that manages the registration of domain names. One of the companies involved is Network Solutions.
*Links: Domain name, NIC, Registering a domain name*

**Intranet**
A network confined to a single organisation, although the organisation can be spread over a number of sites. It can often appear to users exactly as the Internet does, the only difference being that it isn't accessible to those outside the organisation.
*Links: Ethernet, Extranet, LAN, Network, WAN*

**IP (Internet Protocol)**
The method by which information is transferred from one computer to another using the Internet.
*Links: Protocol, TCP/IP*

**IP address (Internet Protocol address)**
Every host computer on the Internet has a unique number, called its IP address. These numbers come in the form xxx.xxx.xxx.xxx – where each xxx is a number from 0 to 255. A Server's IP address is translated into a domain name by a Domain Name Server (DNS). An IP address can be static in which case it is the same every time a user logs on or it can be assigned based on what's available when the user logs on. Most Internet users prefer the former because it easily allows the use of software such as Internet Phone or Cu-SeeME.
*Links: CU-SeeME, DNS, ISP, PING, TCP/IP*

**iPass**
iPass provides a service between ISPs around the world to enable their customers to be authenticated when dialling into each other's services. For example, a user in London whose ISP is signed up to iPass can have local call access to the Internet in New York by dialling into a local ISP also signed up to the iPass network. This is a cost-effective solution for travellers who wish to access the Internet while travelling abroad. Special iPass software is needed and can be downloaded from ISPs offering the service.
*Links: Roaming service*

### IR (Infrared Radiation)

The same technology as that used to control a TV set with a remote control. Infrared data communication is currently playing an important role in wireless data communication due to the popularity of laptop computers, personal digital assistants (PDAs), digital cameras, mobile telephones, pagers and other devices.

*Links: Digital camera, Mouse, PDA*

### IRC (Internet Relay Chat)

A multi-user chat system allowing users to meet in channels. It was written in 1988 and came to prominence during the 1991 Gulf War and the attempted *coup* against Boris Yeltsin in 1993. Each channel begins with a # and is dedicated to a different area of interest. IRC is considered another part of the technology of the Internet in the same way that FTP, Telnet, Gopher and the Web are. Because IRC requires special software and a knowledge of relevant commands, many people tend to chat in the easier-to-use chat rooms found on the Web. All those who connect to IRC choose their own nicknames; these can be anything so long as there are no spaces between the characters that make up the name. IRC requires a piece of software such as mIRC to be downloaded. Once this is downloaded, the user is offered a choice of chat channels.

*Links: Avatar, Chat, Ghost, Interactive Web chat, Ircii, Ircle, Lag, mIRC, Netsplits*

### Ircii

A UNIX chat program. It is considered to be the best chat program available with UNIX shell accounts and is text based. There are no menus or toolbars.

*Links: Chat, Shell account, UNIX*

### Ircle

A Mac IRC program.

*Links: IRC*

## ISDN (Integrated Services Digital Network)

A set of communications standards allowing a single wire or optical fibre to carry voice, digital network services and video. The capacity of an ISDN line is 64 kbps with most telephone companies supplying two lines at once. It is currently much more widely available than ADSL and Cable modem (which are the other high-speed connection methods).

*Links: ADSL, ATM, B Channel, DSS, High-speed connections, NT-1, POTS, QoS, RNIS*

## ISP (Internet Service Provider)

A company that provides its customers with access to the Internet, typically through dial-up networking. A user's computer connects to the ISP's server, which supplies a high-speed link to the Internet. In addition to providing Internet access, ISPs often offer a number of e-mail addresses and Webspace in which users can house their own Webpages. As ISPs are a user's main means of accessing the Internet, they are highly significant and the one selected can influence the whole Internet experience.

*Links: Access, Account, Dial-up networking, e-mail, OSP, Portal*

## IT (Information Technology)

A commonly used term to describe anything related to computers and electronic communication or anything concerned with managing and processing information.

*Links: e-business*

# J

### Jabber
Talking a lot of nonsense when communicating in chat.
*Links: Blatherer, Chat, Device, Lurk*

### Jack in
A term derived from cyberfiction meaning to login to a machine or connect to a network.
*Links: Connect, Cyberspace, Login*

### Jaggies
Stairstep lines that appear where there should be smooth curves (for example, in an 'S' or '/'). This most commonly occurs because there is not enough resolution available, be it on a printer or screen. It can also occur when a bitmapped image's resolution is altered.
*Links: Aliasing, Bitmap, MIP mapping, Resolution*

### JANET (Joint Academic Network)
A network introduced by the British government in 1984 to link UK universities.
*Links: ARPANET*

### Java
A programming language that is designed for writing programs that can be easily downloaded to a computer and run immediately using a Java-compatible Web browser. Small Java applications are called applets. Java is designed for object-oriented programming. Its special features include its ability to

be able to run under any windowed operating system, programs produce similar screen displays no matter where they are run, and that they are restricted in their access to computer's file and operating system.
*Links: Applet, Browser, JavaBeans, JavaScript, JDK, Mappucino, Object-oriented programming, Servlet*

### JavaBeans
Like Java applets, JavaBean components (or 'Beans') can be used to give Webpages (or other applications) interactive capabilities such as calculating interest rates or varying page content based on user or browser characteristics.
*Links: Applet, Calculators, Java*

### JavaScript
Not to be confused with Java. JavaScript is interpreted at a higher level and is easier to learn but lacks some of Java's portability. JavaScript makes it easy to respond to user-initiated events (such as form input). Some effects that are now possible with JavaScript were once only possible with CGI. JavaScript also gives a developer the ability to provide sites with dynamic content. An example of JavaScripting is when a dialogue box appears when a mouse pointer is placed over certain parts of a site (for example, a link or a graphic).
*Links: CGI, Dynamic content, HTML, Java*

### JDK (Java Developer Kit)
A set of tools and specifications that allows Internet programmers to write Java applications.
*Links: Application, Java*

### JPEG (Joint Photographic Experts Group)
One of the two most prevalent image formats on the Internet, identified by the file suffix '.jpg'. JPEG handles only still images,

but there is another standard called MPEG for motion pictures. When a JPEG is created or an image from another format is converted to a JPEG, the quality of image required needs to be specified. The higher the quality, the larger the file, so careful choices have to be made, particularly if the Internet is involved. Images are sometimes displayed as thumbnails. This allows a lot of images to be displayed at once on the same page without taking a great deal of time to download. Visitors can decide which images they would like to look at in more detail and, by clicking on the image, they are taken to another page displaying the full image.

*Links: Adobe Photoshop, Bitmap, Colour depth, GIF, Lossy compression, MPEG, Paint Shop Pro, Raster graphics*

### JPEG Optimiser

A program that makes JPEG files smaller by compressing them. This is particularly useful for the Internet, because anything that can make page download time quicker is of benefit to the user. There are also GIF optimisers that perform the same job with GIFs.

*Links: Access time, Downloading, GIF, JPEG*

# K

### kbps
1,000 bits per second. A measurement often regarding the transmission speeds for Internet connections.
*Links: bps*

### Kermit
A protocol, and the name of program that employs this protocol, for transferring files from one computer to another. It is commonly used on BBS systems.
*Links: BBS, Protocol*

### Key pal
The electronic messaging equivalent of a pen pal.
*Links: Chat, e-mail*

### Keyword
The word or words that are entered into the search box of a search engine or any facility that employs a searchable database (for example, online bookshops). Websites also provide what they consider to be their keywords as meta tags; these are used by search engines to aid correct indexing of sites.
*Links: Database, Directory (Internet), Meta tag, Portal, Query, Search engine, Spamdexing*

### Kill file
Some newsreaders allow users to create kill files. These files are stored on users' systems, and specify types of article they

never want to read and those they always want to read. These kill files can either apply to all newsgroups or only to specific ones.
*Links: Article, Newsgroups, Newsreader*

### Killer app
Most people buy a computer so that they can run application programs. A killer app is an application program that convinces a person to make the decision to buy the system on which the application runs. For example, the spreadsheet program prompted many companies to provide desktop computers for their employees. When a new kind of computer hardware product is made available, such as a hand-held computer, manufacturers hope to entice others to develop what they believe will be the killer app that will motivate potential customers to buy the new computer. The Web browser is also an example of a killer app, and many believe the MP3 file is the killer app for broadband transmission.
*Links: App, Application, Broadband, Browser, MP3*

### Kilobyte
A measure of computer memory or storage, approximately a 1,000 bytes.
*Links: Byte*

# L

### Lag

A period of time in which it seems a computer is not connecting to a requested Website. It is also a term used in connection with IRC. The lag is the time it takes for a message to travel from the user's server to the Net. If there is a bad lag, it may be very hard for a user to keep up with a conversation.

*Links: Access time, Bandwidth, IRC*

### LAN (Local Area Network)

A network that connects computers that are within close proximity – for example, in the same room or building. This allows them to share facilities, whether this be the use of a printer, the exchange of files or even access to the Internet through a single connection. Each computer connected to a LAN is called a node.

*Links: Ethernet, Intranet, LAN server, Node, WAN*

### LAN server

A program or computer that serves other computers in a LAN. This might be, for example, where files are stored or via which the Internet is accessed.

*Links: LAN, Server*

### lastminute.com (www.lastminute.com)

This infamous site is, in many ways, a bucket shop for the twenty-first century. It takes 'perishable' goods, such as flight and concert tickets, and sells them at the last minute at reduced prices. While this sort of business did exist in various

forms before the Internet, clearly the speed of transaction and the availability of information makes it a viable proposition on the Internet.
*Links: e-commerce, Shopping*

**Latency**
Closely connected with bandwidth, this deals with the time it takes for a packet to arrive at its destination.
*Links: Bandwidth, Packet*

**Launch**
To launch a computer program or application is to start or open it. Launch is also used when referring to the day on which a Website goes 'live' on the Net – as in 'its "launch date" is next Friday'.
*Links: Application, Live, Open, Website*

**Leased line**
Also called a dedicated line, this refers to a phone line (connection) that is rented for constant access to the Internet or from one computer to another.
*Links: Dedicated line*

**Level 1 cache**
Cache memory that is part of the processor itself – fast and expensive.
*Links: Cache, Microprocessor, Pentium*

**Level 2 cache**
Cache memory that is mounted on the motherboard – slower than Level 1 cache.
*Links: Cache, Microprocessor, Motherboard, Pentium*

**Link**
See Hyperlink.

**Linux**
A UNIX-compatible operating system.
*Links: Macintosh, Operating system, UNIX, Windows*

**List server**
A program that manages a mailing list. One example of this is
LISTSERV.
*Links: LISTSERV, MajorDomo*

**LISTSERV**
An automated mailing list manager or, to put it another way, a
mail server software program. It was originally developed to
manage mail on BITNET, but the vast majority of its mailing lists
reside on the Internet. It automates the administrative side of
mailing lists using e-mail requests. Users send their requests
as an e-mail to a LISTSERV server, whether it's to be added
or removed from a mailing list. LISTSERV sites can handle
thousands of different mailing lists, serving thousands of
communities of interest – from chess players to cacti growers.
*Links: Broadcast (e-mail), e-mail reflector, List server, Mailing list,
MajorDomo, Moderated mailing list, MultiCast*

**Liteware**
A cross between freeware and shareware, one of the best
examples being Eudora Light. The software can be freely
downloaded like freeware but isn't the full-scale version. It is, in
effect, the basic model of a program. The incentive is therefore
there to purchase the 'deluxe' version.
*Links: CNET, Eudora, Freeware, Shareware*

**Live**
Commonly used to denote when a new Website will become
accessible – as in, 'Our Website will be going "live" next
month'.
*Links: Launch, Website*

**Live3D**
A plug-in that enables Navigator to view pages written in VRML (Virtual Reality Modelling Language), which is the Web's 3D language.
*Links: Avatar, Netscape Navigator, Plug-in, VRML*

**Load**
Any information that is placed into a computer or which the computer is making active. For example, a program required for use is first loaded on to the computer's RAM and a Webpage is loaded into a browser whenever accessed.
*Links: Browser, Cache, Downloading, Program, RAM, Upload*

**Log**
A record of incidents or events. For example, every time a server or Website is accessed, it may be recorded onto a log, which can later be analysed.
*Links: Auditor, Counter, Server*

**Login**
When users identify themselves as authorised to use a particular computer or Website. This normally involves an account name (username or userID) and/or password being used to gain this access. Used as a verb, the term 'to login' means the act of identification in this process.
*Links: Account, Authentication, Logout, Username*

**Logoff**
See Logout.

**Logon**
See Login.

**Logon script**
A text file that contains a small program that tells Dial-up Net-

334 | **Part Two: Internet Dictionary**

working what prompts to wait for and what to type in response.
*Links: Dial-up connection / networking, Script*


## Logout

When users exit from an application or Website. If they want to regain access, they have to login again. The term can also mean to end a session at a computer.
*Links: Login*


## Look-and-feel

The overall visual appearance and user interface of a computer program or Website. It can have implications on copyright if a company believes that the look and feel of any of its products has been copied.
*Links: Content, Graphical User Interface*


## looksmart.com (www.looksmart.com)

A widely used directory of 1.5 million Websites indexed into more than 100,000 categories. It also provides additional services, such as hosting LookSmart Live!! – an interactive self-help search community monitored by editors.
*Links: Directory (Internet), Portal, Search engine*


## Lossless compression

Data compression techniques in which no data is lost. This is vital when compressing programs.
*Links: Compression, Lossy compression*


## Lossy compression

Data compression techniques in which some data is lost, although the information lost is typically unimportant. MP3 sound files, for example, involve lossy compression.
*Links: Compression, GIF, JPEG, MP3*

**Lower case**
See Case sensitive.

**Lurk**
Watching of active newsgroups without taking part or sub-scribing. Statistics suggest this is what most people do when using newsgroups. It might even be considered the thing to do for a while, allowing users to wait until they have something interesting to say or decide if the newsgroup is of interest. It can also be applied to chat were a user acts merely as a spec-tator of others' conversations.
*Links: Blatherer, Chat, Delurk, Ghost, Jabber, Lurker, Newsgroup*

**Lurker**
A visitor to a newsgroup or chat room who simply views activity without taking part or subscribing, and therefore remains anonymous.
*Links: Blatherer, Chat, Ghost, Jabber, Lurk, Newsgroup*

**LviewPro**
A shareware graphics viewer/editor program for Microsoft Windows that can read most Image file formats and is also able to create transparent GIFs.
*Links: Adobe Photoshop, Paint Shop Pro, Transparent GIF*

**lycos.com**
A self-styled 'hub' site providing controlled searches such as Lycos Pro, MP3, Multi-media, FTP and Listening Room. It also offers links to a comprehensive network of associated sites. It is part of the CMGI network, as is AltaVista.
*Links: Hotbot, MP3*

**Lynx**
A text-based World Wide Web browser that pre-dates Naviga-tor, Explorer and Mosaic. Unlike Netscape Navigator or

Internet Explorer, it cannot display images or handle Java, but it is much faster as a result. This is useful for people who just require information. However, both Netscape and Explorer can also be set up to just text only. For users with UNIX shell accounts, Lynx may well be their only browser option.

*Links: Browser, Infosurfing, Internet Explorer, Netscape Navigator, UNIX*

# M

**Mac OS**
The operating system for Apple Computer's Macintosh line of personal computers including the iMac and Power Macintosh range. An example version is the Mac OS 8.5.
*Links: Apple, iMac, Macintosh, Operating system*

**Macintosh**
A family of personal computers introduced in 1984; the first widely used computers with Graphical User Interface, windowing and a mouse. Many people believe that Macs are easier to use than PCs, and they are extremely popular in professions that involve design work.
*Links: Apple, G3, Holy war, Operating system, QuickDraw*

**Macro**
A symbol, name or key that stands for a sequence of simpler instructions – in effect a custom command. For example, in Microsoft Word a macro can be defined which, when prompted, produces all the keyboard strokes needed to begin a letter – name, address and the insertion of the current date.
*Links: Macro virus, Virus*

**Macro virus**
A virus written in the macro language of a particular application. It is usually particularly cunning because it can hide in word processing or spreadsheet documents that use macros.
*Links: Anti-virus program, Macro, Trojan, Virus*

## MacTCP

A TCP/IP driver for the Macintosh that was essential for accessing the Internet. It has been superseded by OpenTransport.
*Links: Access, Macintosh, OpenTransport, TCP/IP*

## Magazines, online

Most magazines have Websites, and many publish every word that is in their print versions. There are even some that provide more information on their Websites than in their print versions, particularly those that offer daily updates. Magazine Websites also often contain back issues that can be looked at.
*Links: e-journal, e-zine, Zine*

## magellan.com (www.magellan.com)

A search engine that not only searches for the words or phrases entered, but also looks for ideas related to the query. Additionally, it has a search Voyeur link which shows a list of randomly selected searches undertaken by other people – so a user can see what others are looking for on the Web.
*Links: Portal, Search engine*

## Mail bomb

The sending of huge amounts of e-mail, or even a piece of e-mail of a huge size, with the express intent of crashing the recipient's mail server or mail client. They invariably affect everyone using the recipient mail server.
*Links: Chernobyl packet, Mail client, Netiquette*

## Mail client

An e-mail application, such as Outlook Express or Eudora. These client applications work in conjunction with a mail server. It is the mail server that collects the e-mail and the mail client that allows users to read it.
*Links: Client, e-mail, Eudora, Mailbox, Mail server, Outlook Express, Server*

**Mail filter**
Allows users to sort e-mail messages using the information contained in the headers, for example by sendee or date.
*Links: e-mail, Eudora, Mail client, Outlook Express*

**Mail server**
This handles incoming and outgoing mail. POP3 servers store incoming mail and SMTP servers relay outgoing mail. Mail clients (such as Eudora) retrieve and send messages to the mail server.
*Links: e-mail, IMAP, Mail client, POP3, SMTP*

**Mailbox**
The directory on a user's computer where their e-mail is stored. With the POP3 protocol, every time this mailbox is accessed by the user, any messages are downloaded onto their computer. With the IMAP protocol, a user can decide to keep any messages on the server with the result that it is accessible from any computer.
*Links: Directory (Computer), e-mail, IMAP, Mail server, POP3, Server*

**Mailing list**
Subscriber-supported discussion groups that evolved in the early days of the Internet. Because they work using e-mail, there is no special sequence to go through, as there is with newsgroups. For every mailing list there are two addresses: the mailing address, which uses a mail reflector to forward mail to sets of other addresses (that is, to the people on the list); and the administrative address. This handles the general management and maintenance of the list. Anyone can start a mailing list and, as a result, there are all sorts available. It may be that anyone can subscribe (called an open list) or subscribers may have to be approved (called a closed list). It may be that anyone can post messages, even non-subscribers (called open posting) or only subscribers (closed posting).

There are moderated lists where a moderator reviews all messages before posting them. Some subscribers request that they receive messages in a collated form, were a day's or week's (or any period of time) messages are received in one big message. Messages may be archived, too. It might also be that the reply-to header contains the list address so that when a subscriber replies everyone on the list sees the reply. Additionally, personal mailing lists can be established using e-mail address directories.

*Links: Broadcast (e-mail), LISTSERV, MajorDomo, Moderated mailing list, MultiCast, Re-mailer*

### MajorDomo

A free automatic mailing list management program.

*Links: LISTSERV, Mailing list*

### mamma.com (www.mamma.com)

'The mother of all search engines', this uses ten engines to make searches. It claims to be the largest independent meta-search tool.

*Links: Meta-search tools, Multi-search tools, Portal, Search engine*

### MAPI (Messaging/Mail Application Programming Interface)

A feature of windows that allows an e-mail to be sent from within an application (with the e-mail containing what is being worked on) or attaching the document being worked on to an e-mail. For example, somebody might be writing a report in Microsoft Word and require a colleague to look at what they've done so far. Instead of saving the document, opening Outlook Express, opening new mail, then attaching the document after sifting for it through the folder, the author can simply go to File at the top of the Word document, select 'Send to', then 'Mail Recipient' (as attachment). This is obviously much quicker and the author can continue working.

*Links: Application, Attachment, e-mail, Microsoft Word*

**Mappucino**

A Java applet (small program) that is able to show a site map of a Website.

*Links: Applet, Java, Navigate*

**Marketing**

This has taken on a whole new form as compared with traditional marketing techniques. Many people believe that the Internet's greatest asset to commercial organisations is through marketing. Anyone in the world can view or download a company's brochure, or ask for further information for example. Perhaps even more importantly, there is the great potential to make many more people than was previously possible aware of a company's products. This can have huge benefits particularly for small- to medium-sized companies whose commercial reach was limited beforehand. Another advantage with the Internet is the ability to market on a one-to-one level, something Dell, the computer manufacturer, has exploited to the full.

*Links: Ad banner, Ad server, Alt text, At, Buffer page, Click rate, Click, Clickstreams, Coupons, CPT, CSV, Dell Computers, Dynamic rotation, eCRM, Eyeballs, Footprint, Hit, Impressions, Microsite, Online, Page requests, Spam, Spamdexing, Subscribe*

**Markup language**

Any language that provides ways to indicate underlining, italics, paragraph breaks, section headings and so on in text.

*Links: ClearType, HTML, PGML, WML, XML*

**mbps**

Million bits per second.

*Links: bps, Bytes*

**McAfee VirusScan**

One of the best virus scanners available. It uses a graphical

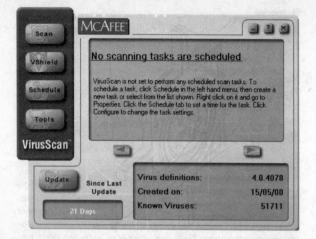

interface that can be launched and which provides access to the program components. These include VirusScan (which can scan any set of files on a local or network drive), Vshield (which automatically scans any file acted on by the user without prompting), VirusScan Schedular (which can be specified to scan drives automatically at certain times) and the ability to update its virus definition files from the Internet.
*Links: Anti-virus program, Macro virus, Norton AntiVirus, Trojan, Virus*

### MediaCast
Live and archived music can be heard over the Internet using this application.
*Links: Media players*

### Media players
To listen to Web radio and view video clips, users have to download one of the many available media players to their

computer. These are available from the manufacturers' sites but can usually also be downloaded the first time they are needed from the Websites hosting the audio-video material. A sound card is required to use a media player
*Links: AU, Helper application, Player, Plug-in, Shockwave*

## Meg
Short for megabyte.

## Megabyte
1,000 kilobytes, and a measure of computer storage and memory.
*Links: bps, Byte*

## Megaflop
A measure of a computer's speed; it can be expressed as a million floating point operations per second.
*Links: Benchmark, CPU, Microprocessor*

## Meltdown
Can be the result of a Chernobyl packet (or just misrouted packets) and is an event that causes saturation, or near saturation, on a network. It typically lasts only a short period of time.
*Links: Chernobyl packet, Network*

## Memory
The 'area' within a computer where information is stored while it is being actively worked on. When a computer is in normal operation, its memory usually contains the main parts of the operating system, plus some or all of the application programs and related data that are being used. Memory is often used as a shorter synonym for random access memory (RAM).
*Links: Cache, RAM, Operating system, SRAM*

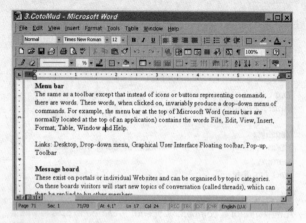

## Menu bar

The same as a toolbar except that instead of icons or buttons representing commands, there are words. These words, when clicked on, invariably produce a drop-down menu of commands. For example, the menu bar at the top of Microsoft Word (menu bars are normally located at the top of an application) contains the words File, Edit, View, Insert, Format, Table, Window and Help.

*Links: Desktop, Drop-down menu / Droplist, Floating toolbar, Graphical User Interface, Pop-up, Toolbar*

## Message board

These exist on portals or individual Websites and can be organised by topic categories. On these boards visitors will start new topics of conversation (called threads), which can then be replied to by other members.

*Links: Guestbook, Hierarchy, Newsgroups, Thread, Usenet*

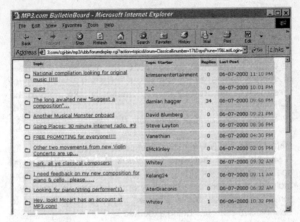

#### Message header

The information at the beginning of an e-mail or bulletin board message. Message headers contain the identities of the author and recipients, the subject of the message and the date the message was sent.

*Links: BBS, Body, e-mail, Header, Message board*

#### Meta

A prefix used in many areas of life. Usually denotes something of a higher or second order. This is best demonstrated by examples. A meta language is a language that describes other languages. Meta mathematics is the study of the structure and formal properties of mathematics as a formal system. On the Internet, there are meta tags.

*Links: Meta tag, Meta-search tools*

#### Meta tag

HTML tag used to describe the contents by displaying the key-words of a Webpage; can prove highly influential in the correct indexing of a site by a search engine. However, these tags don't actually affect the appearance of a Webpage. They also have other uses in that they can specify a page jump (that is, to a new URL address) after a certain amount of time. This might be useful, for example, for someone who registered a number of domain names, all for one site. If someone types in any of these URLs, the browser can automatically take them to the definitive address.

*Links: HTML, Keyword, Meta, Spamdexing, URL*

### metacrawler.com (www.metacrawler.com)

A search engine that uses databases of various Web-based search engines, including AltaVista, LookSmart and Lycos. Includes the interesting MetaSpy and MetaSpy Exposed features, which allow those who are voyeuristically inclined to observe live searches being executed.

*Links: AltaVista, LookSmart, Lycos, Portal, Search engine*

### Meta-search tools

These sit on top of standard search tools, simultaneously searching two or more. Which search engines and how many are simultaneously searched is usually definable by the user within the limitations of the tool. What makes meta-search tools different to multi-search sites is that the results are merged and purged, to avoid getting the same locations delivered by two or more different search engines.

*Links: Copernic 2000, Directory (Internet), Meta, Multi-search tools, Portal, Search engine*

### Microprocessor

This is where most calculations on a computer take place. The speed of the calculations are measured in MHz with faster chips constantly coming on to the market. An example of a microprocessor would be a 500 MHz Pentium III chip.

*Links: Bus, Celeron, Clock speed, CPU, Cyrix, Floating Point Unit, FLOPS,*

INTRODUCING
smart guides to big ideas

If you're a student you need *introducing*, illustrated guides to the ideas and thinkers that have shaped our world. Designed to make your life easier. Icon's *Introducing* books will help you through exams, coursework and they might even make you think.

*G3, Hertz, Intel, Level 1 cache, Level 2 cache, MIPS, MMX, Moore's Law, Motherboard, Overclocking, Pentium, Platform, Xeon*

## Microsite

Sometimes companies have what appears to be a site within a larger site, neither of which is its main site. This is often for marketing reasons. The small site serves as an introduction to the company to the people visiting the larger site. They can then proceed to the company's main site. For example, a publisher of books for students might have a microsite within a site belonging to a company that specialises in services to students. Any visitors are introduced to the publisher and can then proceed to the publisher's main Website.

*Links: Buffer page, Marketing, Splash page, Website*

## Microsoft Reader

Reading software available for PC, laptops and e-book readers designed to make onscreen reading much easier on the eye through the use of ClearType display technology. It is designed to recreate aspects of the traditional print book along with various digital benefits. These include highlighting, bookmarks, notes and drawings. Annotations can be viewed, renamed and erased. There is also the ability to use tools that use the power of the computer – for example, searching, a built-in dictionary and instant large print editions. This software is set to play a major role in whether onscreen e-books as an industry can succeed.

*Links: Adobe Acrobat, ClearType, e-books, PGML*

## MIDI (Musical Instrument Digital Interface)

A protocol developed in the early 1980s specifying how electronic musical instruments can work together (including computers). The protocol specifies both a hardware interface and a language for transmitting musical messages. Digitised MIDI files take up very little room and can be downloaded in a few seconds because the files themselves are like a form of digital sheet music, where the notes and instruments are represented – the sound itself isn't actually stored. MIDI sound files usually have an extension of .mid

*Links: Media players, Protocol*

## MIME (Multipurpose Internet Mail Extensions)

A standard for including material other than ASCII text in e-mail message. Examples are graphics, audio, video and other binary types of files. When non-text files are sent using the MIME standard they are converted (encoded) into text – although the resulting text looks like gibberish. It is then decoded at the receiving end. The MIME standard is also used by Web servers to identify the files that are being sent.

*Links: ASCII, Binary, Binary file*

## MIP mapping

In 3D animation on computers, whether dealing with games or design, this technique is often needed when images that are in high resolution in close up subsequently move away from the

viewer, perhaps ultimately disappearing from view. This technique works by combining low and high resolution versions of the same texture to reduce the jagged effect otherwise seen.
*Links: Avatar, CAD, DirectX, Games, Graphic accelerator, Live3D, OpenGL, Pentium, Pentium III, QuickTime VR, VRML, VRWeb*

## MIPS (Millions of Instructions Per Second)
A measure of the capability of a computer as they work by processing instructions.
*Links: FLOPS, Microprocessor*

## mIRC
One of the best of the many IRC programs. It automates most IRC commands and is available for all Windows operating systems.
*Links: IRC*

## Mirror site
The exact duplicate of an original Website. Despite the almost instantaneous nature of the Internet and its global feel, users in the UK can almost always download something (even as small as a single page) hosted in the UK faster than they could download the same page if it were hosted in the US. This becomes even more apparent the more popular a Website is. One reason for mirror sites is that a user wanting to download a large file (such as a freeware program) is sometimes offered a variety of sites from which to perform the download. Another is that traffic to a site can be spread around.
*Links: Bandwidth, Downloading, Website*

## MLM programs (Mailing List Management programs)
Responds to all messages that get addressed to it.
*Links: LISTSERV, Mailing list, MajorDomo, Moderated mailing list*

## MMX (Multi Media eXtensions)

A type of Intel Pentium microprocessor designed to process multi-media faster than a non-MMX processor of the same given speed. This is because the processor has been designed with multi-media in mind. To benefit from MMX, the application running usually needs to have been written to take advantage of MMX technology.

*Links: Intel, Microprocessor, Multi-media, Pentium, Wintel*

## Modem (MOdulator, DEModulator)

A device that allows a computer to connect with and use a traditional phone line with the result that it can communicate with other computers that also have the same ability. This is crucial for the Internet. The device effectively converts digital data from a computer into analogue data that a phone line can understand and vice versa. Typically there are three varieties of modems: external (which is located separate from a computer), internal (which resides inside a computer's case) and PC card (a credit card-sized modem used predominantly for small machines such as laptops).

*Links: ADC, ADSL, Analogue, AT commands, BABT Approval, Baud, Baud barf, Cable modem, Checksum, COM, Communications software, CTS, Device, Dial-up account, Dial-up connection / networking, Digital, DSVD, Fax modem, Handshake, Hayes compatible, Initialisation string, MR, OH, PC card, Serial port, USB, WinGate, WinProxy*

## Moderated mailing list

Using one of these, sent messages are received by a list administrator who then forwards it to all of the subscribers on the list. This provides a kind of quality control for a mailing list.

*Links: Broadcast (e-mail), LISTSERV, Mailing list, MajorDomo, MultiCast*

## monstercrawler.com (www.monstercrawler.com)

A multi-search tool that simultaneously searches Yahoo!, Excite, AltaVista, GoTo.com, WebCrawler and 7Search.

*Links: Directory (Internet), Portal, Search engine*

### MOO (Mud, Object Oriented)
A multi-user role-playing environment found on the Internet.
*Links: Games, MUD*

### Moore's law
Used to describe the rate at which technology is increasing the amount of data that can be stored on a microchip. It is currently doubling every year, or at least every eighteen months.
*Links: CPU, Microprocessor, RAM*

### Morphing
The animated transformation of one image into another.
*Links: CAD, Games*

### Mosaic
The first GUI Web browser available for the Macintosh, Windows and UNIX – all with the same interface. Its introduction in 1993 resulted in the Internet's userbase expanding considerably. Today's browsers have been greatly influenced by the original features of Mosaic, particularly its simple installation and use, along with its graphical capabilities.
*Links: Browser, Cross-platform, Graphical User Interface*

### Motherboard
Holds everything inside a computer together and makes it all work in tandem – for example, the RAM, CD-ROM or modem. All information that needs to be sorted out goes through the motherboard and is processed there before being sent on.
*Links: ATX, CPU, Hardware, Microprocessor, RAM*

### Motion-JPEG
Each frame in a video of this form is stored as a JPEG.
*Links: Desktop video, JPEG, MPEG*

## Mouse
A device that allows a user to move a cursor or pointer around a display screen simply by moving the device along a flat surface. It also incorporates buttons that allows items on the screen to be selected.
*Links: Bus, Device, Right click, Serial port, Trackball*

## Mouseover event (aka Rollover)
When the mouse cursor is moved over an object on a Webpage, the property of the object changes. For example, moving a mouse cursor over an image may change the image content. This is achieved by using a scripting language such as JavaScript.
*Links: JavaScript, Rollover, Webpage*

## .MOV
A Macintosh multi-media file. It is playable on the Windows operating system if the QuickTime Movie Player application is installed.
*Links: Multi-media, Net Toob, QuickTime*

**Mozilla**

The original name for Netscape Navigator, still used by some people.

*Links: Netscape Navigator*

**MP3 (MPEG-1, audio layer 3)**

One of the most used Internet search engine requests and a standard for audio compression, especially music. It is presently forcing a whole rethink for the music industry, especially concerning the issue of copyright. MP3 has been described by some as a killer app for the broadband Internet market. For example, figures in the US suggest that downloading music accounted for over 50 per cent of university traffic – a concern so large that many US universities have banned access to certain MP3 sites. Files of this type have the extension .mp3 and are capable of 10:1 compression with virtually no loss in quality. A disadvantage to this format is that an MP3 file needs to be decoded while it is being played back. This is done on a PC with a player such as WinAmp or Sonique. Alternatively, one of the many portable MP3 players on the market can be used. To create an MP3 file, 'ripping' software is required. This converts an audio sequence from a CD (for example, a song or album) on to a computer's hard drive as a wave file, which is translated to an MP3 file using another program called an 'encoder'. Both the ripping software and the encoder often come in the same package. One of the best known is MusicMatch.

*Links: CD-R, Compression, CuteFTP, Digital audio, Flash, Killer app, Lossy compression, Lycos, MusicMatch, Player, SDMI, WinAmp*

**MPEG (Motion Picture Experts Group)**

An industry research group responsible for establishing standards for compression, decompression, processing and coded representations of moving pictures and audio. It is also a type of multi-media file found on the Internet. A plug-in needs to be

installed to be able to play an MPEG movie. (Incidentally, MPEG shouldn't be confused with Motion-JPEG.)
*Links: Motion-JPEG, Multi-media, Net Toob, Plug-in*

## MR (Modem Ready)

A light on a modem that shows the unit is on.
*Links: Modem*

## MSN (Microsoft Network)

The Microsoft Network portal directory and search facility, which can be used from within the Internet Explorer browser. It can also be useful for quick searches. However, to get a broader perspective, it's best to use other search facilities as well.
*Links: Conversation view, OSP, Portal, Search engine*

## MUD (Multi-User Dungeon or Dimension)

A type of real-time Internet conference in which users can take on an identity, perhaps in the form of an avatar, and interact with one another by moving around and manipulating objects in an imaginary world. It was originally conceived as a multi-user adventure game, but the term has taken on a much more general meaning, such as chat or 3D worlds.
*Links: Alter ego, Avatar, Interactive web chat, Cybercide, Games, MOO, MUD client, Talker*

## MUD client

Enables users to connect to a MUD. It provides many useful benefits to a player including line wrap and better formatting of messages, the ability to highlight designated phrases in bold or colour, and even the ability to connect to more than one MUD at a time.
*Links: Client, MUD*

**MultiCast**

The transmission of a message to a select group of recipients. This could be an e-mail to a mailing list, although it could also include tele-conferencing and video-conferencing.
*Links: Broadcast (e-mail), Broadcasting, Mailing list,*
*Moderated mailing list*

**Multi-homing**

When an ISP has more than one link to the Internet's backbone. This means that when a user of that ISP submits a request, the fastest connection can be chosen rather than the request being restricted to one route.
*Links: Backbone, ISP*

**Multi-media**

A combination of any of the following: text, sound, still or animated graphics and video images. The term is typically used in reference to electronic media, such as the Internet and CD-ROMs
*Links: ActiveX, ActiveX control, ATM, Bandwidth, Browser, CD-ROM, Compression, Helper application, Hit, Hypermedia, Interactivity, MMX, Qos, Shockwave, Webpage*

**Multi-search tools**

Provide access to a number of different search engines and directories from one site, but deliver the results for each separately. This is a way of carrying out multiple searches using different search tools one after the other from one convenient location. The results are presented separately. This enables comparisons to be made between the different search tools, which may suggest that certain tools are more appropriate for specific research tasks than others.
*Links: Meta-search tools, Portal, Search engine*

## MusicMatch

A piece of software that can be downloaded, enabling the conversion of music from an audio CD into an MP3 file. This is achieved by combining a ripper and encoder.

*Links: MP3, Ripping*

# N

### Nav bar (navigation bar)
These are designed to help users who visit a Website and comprise of directional tools. These are listed and hyperlinked on a Webpage. They are typically determined by the names of the sections of the site.
*Links: Homepage, Mappucino, Navigate, Toolbar*

### Navigate
The directing of a route or course through the Internet as opposed to surfing (which is following where mood or chance takes someone) or browsing (just looking). However, the three terms are often used interchangeably.
*Links: Browse, Clickstreams, Content, Mappucino, Toolbar*

### NeoPlanet
A trendy and image-conscious Web browser. It has many features, including the ability to change the 'skin' or looks of the program, and is becoming an increasingly popular alternative to Netscape and Internet Explorer. It is also a lot quicker to download.
*Links: Browser, Browser compatibility*

### .net
A top-level domain name. It usually denotes a company involved in networking. However, like most top-level domain names these definitions are becoming superfluous.
*Links: Domain name*

**Net**
See Internet.

**Net Filtering Program**
See Censorware.

**Net God**
Someone who has an immense knowledge of the Internet.
*Links: Digerati, Net Personality, Web guru*

**Net Personality**
A person who regularly posts messages in many different
USENET newsgroups, and whose presence is therefore widely
known.
*Links: Newsgroups, USENET, Web guru*

**Net Police**
A pejorative term relating to those who wish to enforce their
ideas and beliefs on how the Net should function.
*Links: Net Personality*

**Net Toob**
A Windows multi-media player that is able to play most
standards found on the Internet, including MPEG, Video for
Windows (AVI) and QuickTime for Windows (MOV).
*Links: AVI, Media players, .MOV, MPEG, Multi-media, Player*

**NetBuddy**
Monitors a list of Internet Web locations specified by the user. It
then automatically checks these sites once a minute, every
hour and so on (or whatever other time period a user wishes to
specify). If any of the sites have been updated, NetBuddy lights
up the site in its list, thereby informing the user.
*Links: Auto-bot, Bot, URL-minder, Website*

**NetCenter**
Netscape's Website, which contains all the latest news and downloads for its products.
*Links: Netscape Communicator*

**Netiquette**
The acceptable ways of acting on the Internet. For example, it is considered rude to write in CAPITAL letters when communicating with someone.
*Links: Domainism, Flame, Mail bomb, SHOUTING*

**Netizen**
Someone who is involved in the Internet. It has also been used to describe people who use the Net for political purposes.
*Links: Denizen, Digerati*

**NetLoad**
An FTP program designed to transfer entire folders from one computer to another. One way of uploading Webpages.
*Links: FTP, Upload*

**NetMeeting**
An Internet telephony tool produced by Microsoft, widely considered to be the best available. It has excellent audio clarity and includes a simple interface and 'whiteboard' on which ideas can be shared.
*Links: Channel, CoolTalk, CU-SeeME, Internet telephony*

**NetNanny**
Intended for parents, guardians and teachers who wish to stop children from accessing pornographic and other undesirable material, and at the same time prevent the children's personal information – names, addresses, telephone numbers and so on – from being circulated on the Internet.
*Links: Censoring Web material, Net Filtering Program, Pornography*

**Netscape colour palette**

Netscape Navigator and Internet Explorer are able to show approximately 253 colours, no matter what computer is used. This is because the colours reside inside the browsers.

*Links: Browser, Browser compatibility, Internet Explorer,*
*Netscape Navigator*

**Netscape Communicator**

Netscape's suite of Internet programs. These include Netscape Navigator, Messenger (e-mail client), Newsgroup, Composer (HTML composing program), Conference, Netcaster (receiver for pushed channels) and Calendar.

*Links: e-mail, Internet, Netscape Messenger, Netscape Navigator*

**Netscape Messenger**

A computer-based e-mail management tool provided with the Navigator browser. It offers a high degree of integration.

*Links: e-mail*

**Netscape Navigator**

One of two the most popular Web browsers. It is produced by Netscape Communications, now owned by AOL. It was co-founded by the browser developers of Mosaic, and was faster and easier to use. When launched, the Navigator browser was given away free, which resulted not only in it taking the market by storm, but also in its acquiring a huge share of the market. At the time, Netscape Communicator was the fastest growing software company in history. Currently, almost all Internet users use either Netscape's browser or Microsoft's Internet Explorer (MSIE) browser, and many users use both. The program also allows for Gopher, FTP and Telnet access as well as e-mail, newsgroup retrieval and management.

*Links: Browse, Browser, Infosurfing, Navigate, Netscape Communicator,*
*NetWatch, Status bar, Surf*

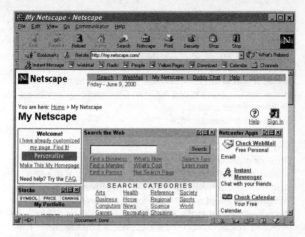

### Netscape Netcaster

Provides users with the ability to view channels, customise channel choices and subscribe to Websites.
*Links: Broadcast, Channel, Netscape Communicator, Push*

### Netscape Newsgroup

A newsreader with all the features needed to download, read and reply to newsgroup messages.
*Links: Netscape Communicator, Newsgroups*

### Netsplits

A common problem when using IRC. It occurs when one or more servers split off from the rest of the Net. The servers that split are still able to communicate with each other but not with the rest. It normally occurs as the result of an overload of users. This often doesn't last very long and can be recognised when a group of people on a channel appear to leave simultaneously.
*Links: IRC, Latency, Server*

## NetWatch

A component of Netscape Navigator that enables the browser to read a site's PICS label. This is a label that is issued to a Website and provides a standard of acceptability (important especially with children). Netwatch allows users to set their own acceptable ratings levels and will consequently block Web sites whose ratings exceed this. The page can only be viewed if the correct password is given.

*Links: Netscape Navigator, PICS*

## Network

If two or more computers are connected, they are said to be networked. The Internet itself is a network but of the term is often used more specifically. Two types of network most commonly talked about are LANs (Local Area Network), where the computers can be in the same building, or WANs (Wide Area Network), where computers are connected by telephone lines because they are situated in different geographical locations. It is also possible to interconnect networks and have subnetworks.

*Links: Internet, LAN, WAN*

## Newbie

Someone who is new to the Internet.

*Links: Denizen, Digerati, Netizen*

## News, online

The easiest place for Internet users to view current headlines and connected stories is from the portals they use. Most of these portals get their news from the same places – usually Reuters and the Associated Press. Another excellent source of news is the BBC's Website (www.bbc.co.uk). With some Websites it is possible for users to customise news by specifying their areas of interest.

*Links: Portal*

## Newsgroups

Also sometimes referred to as discussion forums or Usenet. However, not all newsgroups are Usenet newsgroups. Newsgroups are groups of people getting together on the Internet to discuss a particular subject. They consist of messages, and users are able to 'post' and 'reply to' messages from other users. Newsgroups are divided into topic areas by category name or hierarchy, indicating the very broad subject matter they cover. Category names appear at the beginning of the newsgroup's name, and include, for example, alt. biz. rec. and sci. In order to access a newsgroup, users need a news server address and a newsreader program. A news server address can be supplied by the user's ISP.

*Links: Alt, Anonymous posting, Article, BBS, Blatherer, Bozo filter, Cancelbot, Cross-posting, Discussion board, Discussion group, Domainism, Emotags, FAQ, Follow-up, Hierarchy, Kill file, Lurk, Mailing list, Net Filtering Program, Netscape Navigator, Netscape Newsgroup, Net Personality, Newsreader, NNTP, Outlook Express, Posting, Signal-to-noise-ratio, Spam, Spew, Talker, Thread, Usenet*

## Newsreader

A program that allows users to read Usenet newsgroups. Some Web browsers (such as Netscape Navigator) have the ability to read and post articles in addition to browsing the Web. Newsreaders can also be found as part of some e-mail programs, such as Outlook Express and Netscape Messenger. Standalone newsreaders can also be downloaded. Examples of these include Free Agent and NewsWatcher.

*Links: Netscape Messenger, Newsgroups, Outlook Express, Usenet*

## NewsWatcher

A standalone Mac newsreader. It can be configured with users' preferences along with the name of their news server.

*Links: Freeware, Newsgroups, Newsreader, Shareware*

## NFS (Network File System)

A protocol suite that allows computers on a network, no matter what operating system they are running and what type of computers they are, to share disk drives, thereby allowing one computer access to another and its contents as if these files were stored on the computer's own hard disk.
*Links: LAN, LAN server, Network, Protocol*

## Nibble

Four bits or half of an eight-bit byte.
*Links: Bit, Byte*

## NIC (Network Information Center)

A place that handles information for a network. The most famous of these on the Internet is the InterNIC, the largest register of domain names.
*Links: InterNIC, Registering a domain name*

## NNTP (Network News Transfer Protocol)

One of the protocols within the TCP/IP protocol suite. It is the main set of communication rules for the transfer between newsgroups and newsreaders. A newsreader connected to a news server will be using this protocol to read messages.
*Links: Newsgroups, Newsreader, Protocol, TCP/IP*

## NOC (Network Operations Center)

Responsible for the day-to-day operations of the Internet's component networks.
*Links: InterNIC*

## Node

A connection or end point for information transmissions. This could be a computer, a printer or any other device connected to a network.
*Links: ARPANET, Flow control, Hub, LAN, Network, SLIP/PPP, TCP/IP*

**northernlight.com (www.northernlight.com)**
A leading search and research engine with exclusive access to over 6,000 full-text publications. It dynamically groups results into meaningful category folders. Users can then open the folder that most closely matches the type of information they want. It also provides a useful alert facility whereby users are notified by e-mail of changes to Websites of interest.
*Links: Auto-bot, Directory (Internet), Portal, Search engine*

**Norton AntiVirus**
One of the best anti-virus programs. It contains many features including automatic scanning, updating of virus definitions and program through LiveUpdate, messages about product information, upgrades, updates, and technical tips, the ability to create either a Zip Rescue disk or a set of rescue floppy disks, plus the option of customising the program's features.
*Links: Anti-virus program, Freeware, McAfee VirusScan, Trojan, Virus*

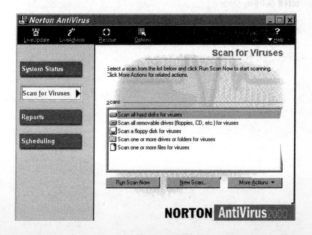

**NSAPI (Netscape Server Application Programming Interface)**
Allows programmers to design Web-based applications that
work better than CGI scripts.
*Links: API, CGI, Script*

**Nslookup**
A program that allows a user to find out the Internet address
(for example, 194.130.58.202) for an entered hostname (for
example iconbooks.co.uk), or vice versa.
*Links: DNS, IP, IP address, PING*

**NT-1 (Network Terminator 1)**
An interface box built into ISDN adapters that converts ISDN
data into something a PC can understand (and vice versa), just
as a modem converts a telephone line's analogue data (and
vice versa).
*Links: High-speed connections, ISDN, Modem*

**NTFS (NT File System)**
One of the file systems for Windows NT in addition to the FAT
file system as used by Windows 95 and 98. However, files in
this system are not accessible from other operating systems.
*Links: FAT, File, Operating system*

# O

### Object linking and embedding
The ability to create objects using one application, then to link or embed them within another.
*Links: Object-oriented programming, OCX*

### Object-oriented graphics
Graphical images (also called vector graphics) that are represented as instructions or mathematical formulae. Examples include lines, circles and squares.
*Links: Object-oriented programming, Raster graphics, Vector graphics*

### Object-oriented programming
A type of programming whereby part of a program is defined as a distinct object with its own data type and set of procedures. This allows each object to work on its own or interact with other objects.
*Links: Object linking and embedding, OCX*

### OCR (Optical Character Recognition)
Electronic recognition of printed or written text characters – for example, a letter can be read on to a computer using a scanner and the text edited using a word processor without the whole letter having to be retyped. The potential of OCR systems is enormous. Current uses include the mail service, where letters are sorted using OCR machines, considerably speeding up mail delivery.
*Links: AI, Fuzzy logic, Scanner*

## OCX

An Object Linking and Embedding (OLE) custom control. It provides functions such as window resizing. There are many files in the Windows directory with the OCX file name suffix. Microsoft now calls an OCX an ActiveX control.
*Links: ActiveX control, Object linking and embedding*

## Offline

Describes a computer that is not connected to the Internet.
*Links: e-mail, Host, Internet, Online*

## OH (Off hook)

A light on a modem indicating that the phone line is open and ready for communications.
*Links: Modem*

## 'On the fly'

Describes Webpages that involve dynamic content. This can be achieved using active server pages or Cold Fusion – every request being individually produced by the server. This is in contrast to 'static' or 'flat' pages, which can only be changed by editing the original HTML file.
*Links: ASP, Cold Fusion, DHTML, Dynamic content, HTML, SHTML*

## Online

Being connected to the Internet. It is also used to distinguish activities performed on the Internet as opposed to the real world – for example, online chat and online shopping.
*Links: Chat, e-business, Internet, Offline, Shopping*

## Open

Reading a file or launching an application, among other things, as in 'Open this file using Microsoft Word', which means the file can be read using Word.
*Links: Associate, Launch*

**OpenGL (Open Graphics Library)**
An API (application program interface) used for defining 2D and 3D graphic images.
*Links: API, Graphic accelerator, MIP mapping*

**OpenTransport**
The connection between a user's Mac and a TCP/IP network. It replaced the MacTCP control panel, and offers many improvements in performance and convenience.
*Links: Macintosh, MacTCP, TCP/IP*

**Opera**
A small and fast Web browser. It is approximately 1.2 megabytes in size and therefore fits easily on a diskette, which makes it ideal for installing on to any PC. It also caters for users who don't have computers powerful enough to run the latest versions of Netscape and Internet Explorer. It doesn't have as many features as the bigger browsers, but it does support many of the advanced features like Java. It can be downloaded and used free for thirty days, after which users must pay to register their own copy. If users decide not to register, they will only be able to view the Opera Software Website once the thirty-day trial period has expired.
*Links: Browser, Shareware*

**Operating system**
The fulcrum of a computer. It is a program that manages all other programs, called applications, on a computer. These applications make requests for services to the Operating system. Examples of operating systems are Windows 95, 98 and 2000, Windows NT, UNIX and the Mac OS 8.5.
*Links: Linux, Mac OS, UNIX, Windows, Windows 98, Windows 2000, Windows NT*

**Optical fibre**
See Fibre optics.

**.org**
A top-level domain name that usually denotes a non-profit organisation.
*Links: Domain name*

**OS/2**
IBM's operating system for personal computers, mostly used by IBM's corporate customers.
*Links: Operating system*

**OSP (Online Service Provider)**
A term normally used to distinguish Internet access providers that have their own online independent content – such as America Online (AOL) – from Internet Service Providers (ISPs) that simply connect users directly with the Internet. In general, companies sometimes identified as OSPs (in this usage) offer an extensive online array of services of their own apart from the rest of the Internet and sometimes their own version of a Web browser. The most popular OSPs are: AOL (America Online), CompuServe and MSN. In reality there is little distinction between ISPs and OSPs.
*Links: Access, Access number, AOL, Churn, CompuServe, Content, Dial-up account, ISP, MSN, POP*

**Out box**
The folder where e-mail is stored before it is sent.
*Links: e-mail, In box*

**Outlook Express**
A piece of software created by Microsoft that can manage a user's e-mail accounts. It resides on a computer's hard drive and enables users to direct their individual e-mail accounts to

one location, where mail can be read and managed centrally. It enables users to sort and organise their e-mails into folders, grouping relevant messages together. It is also possible to read and compose offline, and connect to the Internet only when users wish to send and receive messages.

*Links: Address book, Attachment, cc, e-mail, Mail client, Newsreader*

## Overclocking

The resetting of a computer so that the microprocessor runs faster than the manufacturer-specified speed (for example, setting an Intel 400 MHz (megahertz) microprocessor to run at 450 MHz). This is possible with most good makes of chip (for example, Intel).

*Links: CPU, Intel, Microprocessor, Pentium*

# P

### Packet
Anything – an e-mail, Webpage, multi-media – transferred on the Internet is divided into chunks of data called packets, which are then routed. This is performed by the TCP/IP. As well as information, the packet includes the address of the sender and receiver, error control information and check procedures.
*Links: ARP, Checksum, Chernobyl packet, Data traffic, Fast packet, Header, Latency, Packet sniffer, Packet switching, Router, Runt, SOCKS, TCP/IP, Telnet, Tracert*

### Packet sniffer
A program that is designed to recognise certain groups of numbers or letters – for example, credit card numbers and passwords – in the packets of information that travel across the Internet, usually with malicious intent. This is a main reason for using secure e-mail.
*Links: DSS, e-mail, e-mail security, Fast packet, Packet, Sniffer*

### Packet switching
The method used to send basic units of data (packets) across the Internet. It is quite likely that these packets will take different routes, even if they all regard the same file, and these routes are decided both when they are sent and by computers along the way. When they are received, the TCP layer reassembles these packets in the correct order. It is because of packet switching that so many people are able to use the same lines at the same time.
*Links: SMDS*

**Page**
See Webpage.

**Page requests or Page views**
This is the number of times a Webpage is requested from a server and is a much more accurate way of measuring traffic to a site than hits, which can be misleading.
*Links: Hit, Impressions, Marketing*

**PageMill**
A Webpage editor from Adobe.
*Links: Editor*

**Paint Shop Pro**
A graphic program that can be used for preparing images for use on the Internet. It is able to support most bitmap formats, including GIF and JPEG formats. It is also able to use Adobe Photoshop plug-ins.
*Links: Adobe Photoshop, Bitmap, GIF, JPEG*

**Palm Pilot**
A hand-held personal organiser or PDA (personal digital assis-tant) made by 3Com.
*Links: Hand-held computer, PDA, WML*

**Parallel port**
A connection normally located on the back of a PC. Unlike serial ports, parallel ports are able to send multiple signals because they work using parallel wires, therefore allowing a greater bandwidth. This is particularly relevant when using printers that connect to a computer using this port.
*Links: Flow control, Port, SCSI, Serial port*

**Parse**
To take a string of data and break it up into smaller manageable

pieces that an application program can handle.
*Links: Parser*

## Parser

A program, usually part of a compiler, that receives input which can then be managed by another program – for example, other components in a compiler. A parser may also check to see that all necessary input has been provided.
*Links: Compile, Parse*

## Partition

Part of a hard disk that is treated by the computer as if it were a separate disk drive. Multiple partitions are normally only used with large drives. It is very useful for running more than one operating system – for example, one partition for Windows and another for UNIX.
*Links: Operating system*

## Pascal

The first computer language that many programmers learn.
*Links: C++, Java, Perl*

## Password

A set of keyboard characters needed to logon to a computer system or Website.
*Links: Account, Authentication, Case sensitive, Cookie, IntelliSense, Login, Wallet*

## PC card

Usually used in notebooks or laptop computers, these are devices packaged in a small card (about the size of a credit card). They must conform to the PCMCIA standard and can provide additional memory or modem capabilities for instance. They also provide the ability for hot plugging.
*Links: CardBus, Device, Dongle, Hot plugging, Modem, PCMCIA*

**PCI (Peripheral Component Interconnect)**
A high-speed local bus on the motherboard of a PC that can be used to connect to components – for example, a graphics adapter.
*Links: Bus, Motherboard*

**PCMCIA (Personal Computer Memory Card International Association)**
An industry group that provides the standards for PC cards.
*Links: CardBus, Hot plugging, PC card*

**PDA (Personal Digital Assistant)**
A term used for any small mobile hand-held personal computer. PDAs are often used as personal organisers and as notepads on which files can be created for subsequent transference to larger computers. Some PDAs offer a variation of the Microsoft Windows operating system called Windows CE. The Palm Pilot is an example of a PDA.
*Links: Hand-held computer, Palm Pilot, Windows CE*

**PDF (Portable Document Format)**
A file format that presents documents with all of their formatting on any computer and on any platform. The documents can be printed, navigated, made larger or smaller for viewing and so on. This is extremely useful if a company wishes to show and allow the downloading of, for example, its brochure from the Internet. It is also one of the ways of displaying text and images on an e-book. In order to view PDF documents (distinguished by the file extension .pdf) the user's computer must be equipped with the Adobe Acrobat reader, which can be obtained free of charge by downloading from the Adobe Internet site.
*Links: Adobe Acrobat, ClearType, e-books, Microsoft Reader, PGML*

**Pegasus**

An e-mail program that allows e-mail to be sent and retrieved while other mail is being read or written – that is, it sends and retrieves in the background. The program has been around since 1990.

*Links: e-mail, Mail client*

**Pel**

A contraction of picture element. The term 'pixel' is much more commonly used.

*Links: Active Matrix Display, ClearType, Pixel, Raster graphics, Resolution, TFT screen, Vector graphics, Voxel*

**Pentium**

Produced by Intel, this is the most-widely used personal computer microprocessor. It was introduced during 1993 and quickly replaced the then-common 486 microprocessor as the preferred choice of most PC users. The Pentium Pro includes another microchip containing cache memory that, being closer to the processor than the computer's main memory (RAM), speeds up computer operation. The Pentium II is a Pentium Pro with Intel's MMX technology included. It has a greater Level 1 cache and is suitable for applications that include motion video and 3D images.

*Links: Intel, Level 1 cache, Microprocessor, MMX, Pentium III, Wintel, Xeon*

**Pentium III**

A microprocessor designed by Intel. It is viewed as the next generation of chip after its Pentium II and is faster. It contains a new range of instructions that allows 3D, imaging, streaming video, speech recognition and audio applications to be run more quickly.

*Links: Intel, Microprocessor, Pentium*

**Peripheral device**
Any computer device that is not part of the essential computer (the processor, memory and data paths) but that is situated relatively close by. An example would be a CD-ROM drive or a printer.
*Links: Device, Hardware*

**Perl**
A programming language normally used to create CGI programs, because it is able to efficiently manipulate text. It is a similar language to the C language.
*Links: CGI*

**Petabyte**
A measure of memory or storage capacity. It is approximately 1,000 terabytes.
*Links: bps, Byte, Hard disk*

**PGML (Precision Graphics Markup Language)**
A 2D graphics language created by Adobe, IBM, Netscape and Sun Microsystems to compete with Microsoft's ClearType technology. It allows for the precise control of layout, fonts, colour and printing among other things.
*Links: Adobe Acrobat, ClearType*

**PGP (Pretty Good Privacy)**
An easy-to-use and free program that encrypts and decrypts e-mail over the Internet. It is also possible for users to create their own certificates so that the recipient can verify who the message really came from and know that the message wasn't changed on the way. It can also encrypt files on a computer so those files remain private even if the computer and disks are stolen.
*Links: Digital certificates, e-mail security, Public key, Security*

**PICS (Platform for Internet Content Selection)**

A way of blocking inappropriate Websites. This Internet protocol and technique is associated with labelling a Webpage with
information about that page's content. A user's browser reads
the label and, depending on the criteria set by the user, displays or blocks the page. It is not actually a ratings system
although it is a way of using ratings systems, which are said to
be PICS compliant.
*Links: Censoring Web material, cyberangels.org, Internet Explorer,
Netscape Navigator, NetWatch, RSAC, SafeSurf*

**PINE**

An e-mail client for people using a UNIX shell account.
*Links: Shell account, UNIX*

**PING (Packet INternet Groper)**

A software utility that can be used to verify that the TCP/IP connection with a particular Internet host is working. PING can also
be used to find out the IP address for a particular domain name.
Windows, for example, includes the ping.exe program.
*Links: IP address, TCP/IP*

**Pixel (Picture element)**

One of the individual squares that makes up a graphic image.
*Links: Active Matrix Display, ClearType, Raster graphics, Resolution, TFT
screen, Vector graphics, Voxel*

**PKZIP/PKUNZIP**

One of the most popular Windows programs for compressing
(also known as zipping) and decompressing (also known as
unzipping) files. It can be downloaded in shareware form.
*Links: Compression, Shareware*

**Platform**

The underlying software or hardware used as a base on which

to build something else. Common platforms include PC, Macintosh and UNIX. A platform will consist of the operating system and a microprocessor. The operating system must be designed to work with the particular microprocessor's set of instructions. For example, Windows and Intel's Pentium chips are designed to work together, as are Macintosh and Motorola. A cross-platform is one that can be used on more than one platform.
*Links: Cross-platform, Wintel*

### Player

A program that displays or plays the information in a file. For example, if users want to play MP3 files, they need an MP3 player. Most players can be downloaded from the Internet or are already contained on the Operating system.
*Links: Applet, Digital audio, Flash, Helper application, Plug-in, QuickTime, RealAudio, RealPlayer, Shockwave, Sound player, Streaming sound*

### Plug-and-Play (PnP)

A computer system's ability to automatically recognise and correctly configure devices plugged in to it. However, it doesn't always work smoothly and the configuration may have to be performed manually.
*Links: Device, Hot plugging, USB*

### Plug-in

An accessory computer program that works in conjunction with a larger application providing additional functions. Web browsers like Netscape Navigator and Microsoft Internet Explorer have many plug-ins that provide functions (including moving and animated objects and live audio) and interactivity that use a computer's sound/video cards and can be viewed in real time. For example, a user would be able to listen to online radio, watch video clips or listen to music samples using these controls. Some of the better known plug-ins include Adobe

Acrobat and Shockwave. Most users wait until they need a particular plug-in before they download it; if one is required there is usually a link enabling the download on the same page. Plug-ins are distinct from players in that players work only if the information is stored on a separate file and appear distinct from a browser. Some plug-ins have optional cost upgrades that can be downloaded once a user becomes expert and wants extra functionality. However, the basic versions are suitable for everyday use.

*Links: ActiveX, Browser, Dynamic fonts, Flash, Helper application, Interactivity, Live3D, Media players, Player, QuickTime, RealAudio, RealPlayer, Shockwave, Splash page, Streaming sound, TrueSpeech, VRML*

### PNG (Portable Network Graphics)
Similar to the GIF format, this is also a compressed graphic image file format. CompuServe originally developed the GIF and technically holds the rights to its usage. It is thought by many that the PNG format, which is already supported by many applications (including browsers), will come to replace the GIF format.

*Links: Bitmap, Raster graphics*

### POP (point-of-presence)
The place where ISPs or OSPs can be accessed. Most ISPs have more than one telephone number through which Internet access can be made so they can be said to have more than one POP location. The POP of these services can also describe its IP address.

*Links: IP address, ISP, OSP*

### POP3 (Post Office Protocol)
The latest version of a protocol for receiving e-mail. It is a client/server protocol in which e-mail is received and held for users by their mail server. In effect, a post-box with the supplier

of the e-mail account who keeps e-mail messages until the user collects them. Once messages have been downloaded from the supplier, they no longer reside on the server.

*Links: Auto-bot, Client, IMAP, Mailbox, Mail server, SMTP*

## Pop-up

Used to describe menus or windows that can suddenly appear, prompted by the user clicking a mouse button or passing the cursor over an active icon (called a rollover). An example would be clicking a menu bar item (such as File) and the subsequent list appearing beneath it. A pop-up window must be smaller than the background window or interface, otherwise it's a replacement interface. On the Web, JavaScript (and, less commonly, Java applets) are used to create interactive effects including pop-up and full overlay windows.

*Links: Drop-down menu / Droplist, Menu bar, Mouseover event, Rollover*

## Pornography

There are organisations like the Internet Watch Foundation and the Recreational Software Advisory Council that are working to clean up the Web. In addition, Internet Explorer and Netscape Navigator include a content advisor which allows users to set different levels on language, nudity, sex and violence that can be viewed based on specified ratings systems. There are also software programs (called Censorware) that can monitor browsing. Children, for example, can be pointed in the direction of Websites specifically designed for them like Yahooligans!

*Links: Censorware, cyberangels.org, PICS, SurfWatch*

## Port

A connection for use between a computer and an external device (for example, a printer). Ports are typically located on the back of a computer and types include serial and parallel.

*Links: AGP, Parallel port, Serial port*

**Portability**
Used to describe any piece of hardware or software (or even file) that can be used on more than one type of computer or, more specifically, more than one type of operating system. One example is the .pdf file format, which can be viewed on almost any type of computer as long as it has the Reader software.
*Links: Adobe Acrobat, Applet, Export, Import, Java, PDF*

**Portal**
A gateway designed to be a user's starting point from which to begin a journey around the Internet. (Note: it is not necessarily the service through which the user connects.) There are essentially three types of portal: those that are effectively search engines or major directory lists (such as Excite and Yahoo!); large sites that take a slightly more branded look and direction, but that are still very large in the areas they cover (such as CNET and AOL); and specialised portals such as www.21stcentury.co.uk. Portals invariably offer a range of services such as e-mail, chat rooms and bulletin boards in an attempt to keep users.
*Links: AOL, CNET, Excite, Euroseek, Gateway, Go, Gogettem, Hotbot, Hot list, Keyword, MSN, Specialist search sites, Vertical portal*

**Posting**
Placement of a message anywhere on the Internet – for example, newsgroups and discussion groups.
*Links: BBS, Discussion group, Newsgroups*

**Postmaster**
Similar to a Webmaster, this is someone in charge of e-mail for a particular organisation, whether it be a service provider or a company.
*Links: Webmaster*

### PostScript

A programming language that describes how a printed page will look – that is, the size, position, style and so on of text and graphics on a page. PostScript files have the extension .eps. These files can be opened on most operating systems with PostScript software. Many printers also contain PostScript software, and the language has become an industry standard.
*Links: .eps*

### POTS (Plain Old Telephone System)

The traditional telephone service that many homes use, as opposed to the new telephone technologies. With these new technologies comes the important question of whether and how existing voice transmission for ordinary phone communication can be accommodated. For example, ADSL and ISDN provide some part of their channels for 'plain old telephone service' while providing most of their bandwidth for digital data transmission.
*Links: ADSL, High-speed connections, ISDN*

### PPP (Point-to-Point Protocol)

A set of communication rules that allow a computer to connect to another computer using the TCP/IP protocol over a telephone line. This is what happens when accessing the Internet. A user's computer connects with a server computer via a phone line, giving access to the whole of the Internet.
*Links: Access, SLIP, SLIP/PPP, TCP/IP*

### PPTP (Point-to-Point Tunnelling Protocol)

A set of communication rules required to create a Virtual Private network.
*Links: Tunnelling, Virtual private network*

### Program

A set of instructions for a computer to execute. The computer

gets one instruction and performs it, then gets the next instruction. Typically, the program is put into a storage area accessible to the computer. The storage area or memory can also contain the data on which the instruction operates. (Note: a program is also a special kind of 'data' that tells how to operate on 'application or user data'.)
*Links: Application, Object-oriented programming*

### Prolly

Short for probably.
*Links: Clickly*

### Prompt

A request from a computer for the user to do something, often indicated by a flashing symbol where text is to be typed or the mouse placed. For example, if 'login:' is seen, it usually means a username needs inputting.
*Links: Access, Account, Login, UNIX*

### Protocol

The set of communication rules needed to allow two devices to exchange information with each other. This could be between a computer and a printer. It could also be between two computers, as is the case with the Internet.
*Links: ARP, Communications protocol, Ethernet, FTP, HTTP, HTTPS, IMAP, IP, Kermit, MIDI, NNTP, POP, PPP, PPTP, RSVP, SLIP, SLIP/PPP, SMTP, SOCKS, SSL, TCP/IP, TFTP, UUCP, WAP*

### Proxy server

A server (program) that resides between a client application – for example, a Web browser – and a real server. The most requested content form the Web is held on it, providing quicker access and increased security for users. They are also able to provide direct Internet access from behind a firewall by opening a socket on the server through which data can pass.

*Links: Firewall, Gateway, SOCKS, WinProxy*

## Public key (for PGP)

A user's public key is needed by people sending and receiving encrypted e-mail to the user. It can normally be included by users whenever they send a signed message. Public keys consist of very large numbers.
*Links: Encryption, PGP, Public Key Cryptography*

## Public Key Cryptography/Encryption

When the Secure Sockets Layer (SSL) is used as the protocol for secure Web transactions, these transactions are encrypted using public key cryptography. In this system, messages are encoded and decoded using a public key and a private key. The public key is made known to everyone and the private key is kept secret. When one is used to encode a message, the other is needed to decode it. These are often used in digital certificates and certain versions of Navigator and Explorer contain this type of security.
*Links: Digital certificates, Security, SET, SSL*

## Pull

The Web is traditionally based on pull technologies. For example, a Webpage isn't delivered until a browser requests it. The Internet is working here in reactive manner to a user's demands.
*Links: Push*

## Push

The sending of information without the recipient having actually requested it. Even though examples of push technologies have been around since the start of the Internet (the best example being e-mail), this is probably the area of the Internet that will have the greatest impact over the coming years, particularly with the way businesses will operate. Most forms of broadcasting involve push technologies. Mailing lists are also examples of this in action. This is why companies will often request a user's e-mail address when registering with their site. This shows that there are two levels operating here: pushing to targeted individuals (such as with mailing lists); and general push (which anyone can tune into, such as radio or Webcasting).

*Links: eCRM, e-mail, Helper application, Pull, Webcasting*

# Q

**QoS (Quality of Service)**
As with any industry or business, it is important to be able to
guarantee a minimum level of capability. This is particularly true
of the Internet, especially when dealing with the transmission of
information that can only work above certain bandwidths, such
as multi-media information. This is one reason why when users
request Streaming Video, they may be asked what transmission rate they can use (for example, 28.8 kbps, 55.6 kbps, ISDN
or ADSL) as the video delivered will be tailored accordingly.
*Links: High-speed connections, RSVP*

**Query**
A request for information. This might be performed on search
engine for example.
*Links: Database, Field, Keyword, SQL*

**Queue**
A list of instructions or files waiting to be executed or printed.
Many people queue e-mails they wish to send so that they can
all be transmitted simultaneously. This means they only have to
connect to the Internet once and for a short period of time.
*Links: e-mail*

**QuickDraw**
Macintosh's graphics control language and one of the reasons
for a common look between Macintoshes.
*Links: Apple, Macintosh*

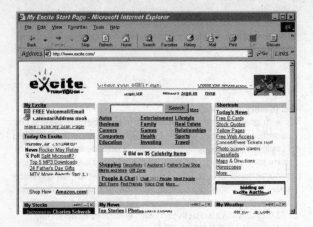

## QuickTime

The standard way of storing multi-media files on the Macintosh. These files can be played (and to some degree controlled) on a QuickTime player. This resides either on the browser or can be downloaded. QuickTime files have the file name extensions: .qt, .mov and .moov.
*Links: Multi-media, Player*

## QuickTime VR

An enhanced version of QuickTime. It can be used to view and rotate a 3D object (which can be created from a series of photographs and need not be computer-generated). The mouse and keyboard are used to vary the viewing of the object. A QuickTime VR plug-in is available for most browsers.
*Links: CAD, QuickTime, VRML*

# R

### Radio button

This is a way of selecting a choice in a list of options. For example, a user may be asked to select which of the following wage brackets they are in:

| | |
|---|---|
| Under £10,000 | ⊙ |
| £10,001–£15,000 | |
| £15,001–£25,000 | ○ |
| £25,001–£35,000 | |
| over £35,000 | ○ |

Each option may have a circle by it and if a user clicks inside the circle it becomes selected – that is, goes from white to black. Normally, only one option from the list can be selected.
*Links: Checkbox*

### RAM (Random Access Memory)

A computer's main working memory. It retains memory for as long as the computer is running. It is where the operating system, application programs and data in current use are kept. RAM makes these much quicker and easier to reach for the computer's microprocessor than if they were on the hard disk, floppy disk or CD-ROM so the more RAM the better. When a computer is turned off, RAM loses its data and when it's turned back on again, the operating system and other files are loaded once more into RAM, usually from the hard disk. RAM comes in several different forms – for example, SRAM, SDRAM and DRAM.
*Links: DIMM, Memory, ROM, SDRAM, SIMM, SRAM, Swap file*

### Raster graphics

Also referred to as bitmaps, these are typically known by their GIF, TIFF and JPEG formats. With these, every point of the image is marked black, white or another colour – that is, they are defined pixel by pixel.

*Links: Bitmap, Vector graphics*

### Readme

Software and Website publishers often make available a file that they consider to contain useful information on their particular service or product. These files often come in the form of plain text files.

*Links: e-text, FAQ*

### Real Name

A way of providing a short cut to a Website by assigning it an easy-to-remember name. An example might be to name the URL http://www.iconbooks.co.uk as 'Books'. This name can then be entered on the browser to go to Icon Book's site. The facility requires that the Real Name extension is downloaded and installed.

*Links: Bookmark, Favorites, Shortcut*

### RealAudio

A continuous or streaming sound technology that supports FM stereo sound quality. To be able to listen to a such a soundfile, a player or plug-in is required. These may come included with a Web browser. Alternatively, they can be downloaded from the RealAudio or other Websites. A suitable server is required to deliver RealAudio sound from a Website. Files of this type have the file name extensions of .ra and .ram.

*Links: Helper application, Media players, Player*

### RealPlayer

A plug-in/ActiveX control that allows the playing of RealAudio-

format audio and video files, including streaming audio. By working in real time, it is much quicker than downloading an entire song or video before listening to or viewing it.
*Links: Helper application, Media players, Player*

### RealSystem
Also called RealAudio. An audio streaming standard.
*Links: RealAudio*

### Reciprocal link
A hyperlink placed on a Website in return for another site having put a link on its page.
*Links: Hyperlink, Website*

### Refresh
To clear a Webpage and reload the information.
*Links: Browser, Cache, Error messages, Load*

### Registering a domain name
There are a number of domain name registering organisations, the largest being Network Solutions' InterNIC Registration

Services. First, check whether the domain name required has already been taken. One way of doing this is to use the whois search box on the InterNIC home page. Once that's been established, simply follow the instructions for registering.
*Links: Domain name, InterNIC, Whois*

## Relational database
A collection of data items organised as tables made up of rows and columns. It might be that the table defines a relation between things in each row. However, this doesn't mean they are restrictive as some databases can be viewed in many different ways. Relational databases are easy to create and access, and have the advantage of being easy to extend. A new data category can be added without requiring that all existing applications are modified.
*Links: Access (Microsoft), Cold Fusion, Schema, SQL server*

## Re-mailer
Also known as an e-mail reflector. A sender's e-mail is kept anonymous and is commonly known as anonymous e-mail.
*Links: e-mail reflector, Mailing list*

## Remote logon
The use of a remote computer over a network as if it were a local computer. This can be achieved using one of several protocols, including Telnet.
*Links: Telnet, Terminal emulation*

## Remote terminal
Any terminal that is not physically on the same site as the computer to which it is attached. Telnet is a terminal emulation program that allows application programs based on it to login to a remote computer. Users of this protocol are therefore able to access their personal files from any location.
*Links: Dumb terminal, Telnet, Terminal, Terminal emulation*

**Resolution**

A measure of the amount of detail that an image contains. For example, an image whose resolution is 300 dpi is more detailed than an image of 150 dpi. But because the former contains more information, it is a larger file and would, of course, take longer to download. The visible difference in resolution might be negligible and a resolution of 300 dpi for a particular image deemed unnecessary. Resolution is also a description of the number of pixels (individual points of colour) contained on a display monitor. This is given in terms of the number of pixels on the horizontal axis and the number on the vertical axis. The sharpness of the image on a display depends on the resolution and the size of the monitor. The same pixel resolution will be sharper on a smaller monitor and gradually lose sharpness on larger monitors because the same number of pixels is being spread over a bigger area.

*Links: Aliasing, Aspect ratio, Bitmap, Colour depth, dpi, Jaggies, MIP mapping, Pixel*

**Response time**

A measurement of the time between a request for information over a network and the network's fulfilment of that request. 'Overall response time' is an aggregate or average measurement of various response times over a particular network or through a particular host.

*Links: Access time, Bandwidth*

**Rich Text Format**

See .rtf.

**Right click**

The clicking of the right mouse button (once) in order to access short-cut options. The equivalent of this on the Mac is obtained by clicking and holding down the button on the mouse.

*Links: Mouse, Pop-up, Shortcut*

**Ripping**

Transferring music from a CD to a computer's hard drive. To be able to do this, a ripper and encoder need to be downloaded.
*Links: MP3, MusicMatch*

**RNIS (Réseau Numérique à Intégration de Services)**

The European name for Integrated Services Digital Network (ISDN).
*Links: ISDN*

**Roaming service**

The ability to use a service in many locations. An obvious example is the use of a mobile phone in a foreign country. The roaming service facility is also becoming more and more common (and important) in relation to the Internet, particularly business users. People travelling abroad may still want Internet access using their conventional method, typically the laptop. And they don't want to have to pay long-distance call charges. There are presently two ways of achieving this. The first is by using an ISP with local access numbers in many countries. (One example is AOL, which is a multi-national service provider.) Another way of achieving a roaming service is through using an ISP that has signed up to iPass, which is an agreement between ISPs worldwide to allow access to their services by members of the co-operative group. Special software and registration are needed.
*Links: AOL, Cybercafé, iPass, Webmail*

**Robot**

See Bot.

**Robust**

A robust product is one that doesn't easily break. For example, an operating system that remains unaffected if any individual

application program fails or a piece of hardware that is very durable would be referred to as robust.
*Links: Hardware, Operating system, Software*

### Rollover
A common use of JavaScript. It refers to a linked image on a Webpage being replaced with another image when the cursor passes over that link.
*Links: JavaScript, Mouseover event*

### ROM (Read Only Memory)
Computer memory containing data that can only be read. Data in ROM is not lost (as it is in RAM) when the computer power is turned off – this makes it the ideal place to have the program that boots up a computer.
*Links: BIOS, CD-ROM, PC card, RAM*

### Router
A device or piece of software that can connect two networks (for example, a local network to the Internet). A router also looks at destination addresses of packets passing through it and determines which route to send them.
*Links: Hub, Node*

### RSAC (Recreational Software Advisory Council)
An organisation that has set up a PICS-compliant rating system – that is, it is a content-rating service. It was originally set up to issue a ratings system for computer games but has since extended this system to the Internet.
*Links: Censoring Web material, Censorware, cyberangels.org, PICS, Pornography*

### RSVP (Resource Reservation Protocol)
A protocol that allows the reservation of routes on the Internet, particularly for the transmission of high-bandwidth messages.

RSVP provides the Internet with a greater ability to support specified Qualities-of-Service.
*Links: Broadcast, Protocol, QoS*

### .rtf (Rich Text Format)
Word processing files are sometimes saved as Rich Text Format. This is useful because it retains the document's formatting but can be opened on a variety of word processing programs or platforms.
*Links: Cross-platform*

### Runt
A packet that is too small to transfer.
*Links: Packet*

# S

### SafeSurf
A PICS-compliant rating system – that is, a content-rating service – set up by a parents' group whose intention is to make the Internet safe for children.
*Links: Censoring Web material, PICS*

### savvysearch.com (www.savvysearch.com)
This is a CNET meta-search tool. Search engines include Hotbot, Galaxy and Lycos.
*Links: CNET, Meta-search tools*

### Scalability
This describes how well a piece of software or hardware adapts to increased demands.
*Links: Hardware, Software*

### ScanDisk
Available on Windows and DOS, this can be used to check a hard disk for errors. It can then repair the damaged areas. It will run automatically if Windows isn't properly shut down, perhaps because it froze or crashed.
*Links: Windows*

### Scanner
An external device that captures images from anything that can be scanned for computer editing and display. Sources could be photographs, books and so on. Scanners most commonly come in the flat-bed form but are also available as hand-held

and feed-in. They can scan images in black and white only or colour and typically attach to a computer using an SCSI.
*Links: Device, Hot plugging, OCR, SCSI, TWAIN, USB*

## Schema
The organisation or structure for a database – that is, whether it is relational or object-oriented.
*Links: Database*

## Screen capture/dump
The copying of whatever is being displayed at the point of capture on to a file or printer.
*Links: Capture*

## Screen saver
The display of an animated image or blank screen after a pre-determined amount of time when there has been no user activity. It was originally introduced to protect display screens against ghosting or screen burn.
*Links: FED*

## Script
A CGI script is a program that runs on a server and processes requests based on input from the browser. Concerning pro-gramming, a script is a program that is carried out by another program rather than by the computer processor.
*Links: Author, CGI, JavaScript, Logon script, Mouseover event, Server script, VB Script*

## Scroll
To move information, be it text, an image, a spreadsheet and so on, and which might be on a Webpage, across a screen so that all of the information on a page can be viewed. Scrolling can be horizontal, vertical or even a combination of the two.
*Links: Frames, OCX, Webpage*

### SCSI (Small Computer System Interface)
Pronounced 'scuzzy'. A parallel interface standard used by personal computers to attach and communicate with peripheral devices. These could be disk drives, CD-ROM drives, printers and scanners. SCSIs are faster and more flexible than previous interfaces.
*Links: ANSI, Device, Parallel port*

### SDK (Software Development Kit)
A set of tools that enables programmers to create their own programs or 'plug-ins', often for another piece of software.
*Links: JDK, Plug-in*

### SDMI (Secure Digital Music Initiative)
A research group comprising more than 120 companies from the music, IT and copyright sectors, whose main aim is to make it increasingly difficult to listen to pirated material. This includes creating a new and more secure MP file format.
*Links: MP3*

### SDRAM (Synchronous DRAM)
A new type of DRAM chip, the output of which is synchronised with the clock speed for which the microprocessor is optimised, making data available to the microprocessor more quickly.
*Links: RAM*

### .sea
A self-extracting file on the Macintosh platform.
*Links: Macintosh, Self-extracting files*

### Seamless tiling
When an image repeats itself across and down a Webpage, adding texture to the page. Only one copy of the image file is downloaded; the user's browser completes the repetition. This

is an extremely effective technique if the background appears to be a continuous surface.
*Links: Webpage*

**Search agent**
See Spider.

**Search engine**
These search the full text of Webpages automatically and are the main means by which users will, initially at least, locate information on the Web. Search engines try to find instances of individual words or phrases (known as the search term). It only takes a matter of seconds for the search engine to deliver a list of Internet sites, ranked by relevance, in which it has identified the presence of the requested search term. In order to reduce the number of hits, the search engine may provide advance search options to narrow or broaden the search by, for example, searching only the Web, or limiting searches to sites emanating from a specific geographical or national region.
*Links: About, Allonesearch, AlltheWeb, Alt text, AltaVista, Archie, Ask Jeeves, Boolean Logic, Bot, Britannica, Buffer page, Copernic 2000, Crawler, Debriefing, Directory (Internet), Dynamic content, Excite, Euroseek, Findwhat, Galaxy, Go, Gogettem, Google, Hotbot, Infind, Keyword, Looksmart, Magellan, Mamma, Meta tag, MetaCrawler, Meta-search tools, MonsterCrawler, MP3, MSN, Multi-search tools, Northern Light, Portal, Query, Savvysearch, Spamdexing, Spider, WebCrawler, Yahoo!*

**Sector**
A track on a disk (for example, a hard disk) that can contain data and is the smallest unit that can be accessed.
*Links: Bit, Byte, Data, Hard disk*

### Secure channel

Any technology that provides secure point-to-point communications, for example between a Web browser and a Web server. This is of particular importance for financial transactions
*Links: Security, SSL*

### Security

One of the most complex issues concerning the Internet. New features – such as firewalls or the Secure Socket Layer protocol – are always being developed that make Web interactions safer. Conversely, there are features such as cookies that, as well as being beneficial, raise security issues.
*Links: Access control, Accessware, Commerce server, Cracker, Digital certificates, DSS, e-business, e-commerce, Encryption, Firewall, HTTPS, Identity hacking, Packet sniffer, PGP, Proxy server, Public Key Cryptography, Secure channel, Security zone, SET, Virtual private network*

### Security zones

The main feature of Internet Explorer's security policy. As the Web is explored, a status bar displays the security zone of the current page. There are four zones: Local Intranet (pages accessed without going through a proxy server); Trusted Sites (sites that a user trusts); Internet (sites that have not been assigned to any other zone); and Restricted Sites (sites a user has decided not to trust). They provide a way of controlling the types of content to which a user's computer can gain access on the Internet. Only rated content that meets the criteria set by a user can be displayed.
*Links: Internet Explorer, Security*

### Select box

A device used by many user-input forms on the Web giving viewers the ability to choose either one or multiple values from a selection. A select box is also very useful when it is not important to show all of the selections at once – for example, a box

giving a list of countries from which just one is selected based on where the user lives.
*Links: Form, Webpage*

### Self-extracting files

A compressed program that, when run, extracts its own data into ready-to-use files. On PCs, these files have the extension .exe (although not exclusively) and on Macs, .sea
*Links: Compression, .exe, .sea*

### Serial port

An interface for serial communication, one transfer at a time, between a computer and another device. This is in contrast with a parallel port, where more than one transfer at a time can take place. The COM port on a PC is an example of a serial port, and this might connect a computer with a modem or even a hand-held device.
*Links: Parallel port, Port*

### Server

A computer that provides services for other computers. Software run by these computers is called server software. There are a variety of servers connected with the Internet. Mail servers handle incoming and outgoing mail. These include POP3 servers and SMTP servers. Web servers store and transmit Webpages and FTP servers store files that can be transferred to and from a user's computer. A client is the requesting program. Web browsers are clients that request HTML files from Web servers. Mail servers service e-mail clients, for example, Outlook Express and Eudora.
*Links: Access, Ad server, Application server, ASP, Back-end, CGI, Client, Client/Server network, Commerce server, Cookie, Dedicated server, Domain name, Dynamic content, e-commerce, Firewall, Gateway, Hit, Host, IP address, ISP, LAN server, List server, Mail server, Page requests, POP3, PPP, Proxy server, Server script,*

*Service space provider, Servlet, SQL server, SSI, SYSOP, Thin client,*
*Upload, URL, Virtual hosting, WAIS*

**Server has no DNS Entry**
The URL entered is an incorrect address.
*Links: Error messages*

**Server script**
A CGI script is a program that runs on a server and processes
requests based on input from the browser.
*Links: CGI, Script, Server*

**Service Space Provider**
Somebody who provides storage space on a server for Webpages for anyone who wants it. Some ISPs provide an amount
of free space as part of their package; there are other organisations that make a charge.
*Links: Hosting, ISP, Website*

**Servlet**
An applet (small program) that runs on a server. Very often, a
servlet is based on user interaction or input – for example,
when accessing a database through a Website. It can execute
more quickly than CGI applications and is therefore especially
useful on servers with lots of traffic.
*Links: Applet, Application, CGI, Server*

**SET (Secure Electronic Transaction)**
A system supported by Mastercard, Visa, Microsoft, Netscape
and others for ensuring the security of financial transactions on
the Internet. A user is given an electronic wallet (digital certificate). A transaction is then made and verified using a
combination of digital certificates and signatures involving the
buyer and the buyer's bank.
*Links: Digital certificates, Security, Wallet*

### SGML (Standard Generalised Markup Language)
An international standard for the organisation and tagging of elements of a document.
*Links: CFML, HTML, PGML, XML*

### Shareware
Software that can be downloaded at no charge but on a trial basis only. The understanding is that if the software is installed and retained, a payment should then be made. Other shareware (sometimes called liteware) is offered with certain capabilities disabled as an enticement to buy the complete version of the program. All shareware programs should be scanned for viruses before opening.
*Links: Freeware, Liteware, Virus*

### Shell account
An account with access to the Internet using UNIX.
*Links: C shell, Command line, HyperTerminal, Ircii, Lynx, PINE, Terminal emulation, UNIX*

### Shockwave
Developed by Macromedia, this is a downloadable Web browser plug-in that displays animated graphics, plays sounds and lets a user interact with a page. It is essentially a group of multi-media players.
*Links: Browser, Interactivity, Media players, Player, Plug-in, Streaming sound*

### Shopping cart
A software technology that allows visitors to browse a Website selling items and to place those items they wish to purchase in an electronic shopping cart. The value of these goods is then given at the checkout.
*Links: Shopping*

**Shopping, online**
The retailing industry is at the leading edge of the most recent
Internet technological developments. With the development of
the SSL protocol, it is possible to send credit card details safely
over the Internet. The Internet offers a number of advantages
over the traditional ways of purchasing goods. It is very easy to
search a retailer's catalogue. It is very easy to compare prices
of products from one retailer to another to obtain the best available price. However, it is by no means certain that prices on the
Web are cheaper than elsewhere. One of the main reasons
people cite for Web shopping is not price benefits, but convenience. It offers door-to-door delivery and is available
twenty-four hours a day, seven days a week.
*Links: Amazon, Auctions, BOL, Calculators, Cookie, e-business,*
*e-commerce, Lastminute, Security, Shopping cart*

**Shortcut**
The creation of an icon, typically on the desktop so that a par-
ticular program or folder can be more easily accessed.
*Links: Desktop*

**SHOUTING**
This is the online (or e-mail) presentation of words entirely in
upper case – for example, HOW ARE YOU? It is considered the
equivalent of vocal shouting and is thought to be rude by most
people. It is one of the rules of netiquette not to shout.
*Links: Netiquette*

**Shovelware**
Content put on the Web so quickly that the look-and-feel of the
site suffers considerably.
*Links: Content*

**SHTML**
A Web file suffix denoting that the page being received has

been produced 'on the fly'. This could be fresh content, for example.
*Links: DHTML, Dynamic content, HTML, On the fly, SSI*

### SIG (Special Interest Group)
A group of people who meet or exchange e-mail messages on a common interest.
*Links: BBS, Discussion group, Message board, Newsgroups*

### Signal-to-noise ratio
A comment on the amount of useful information to be found in a particular newsgroup – for example, 'The signal-to-noise ratio in this newsgroup is high', implies there is a great deal of useful information.
*Links: Newsgroups*

### Signature
Created by the user, this is a short text file that is automatically appended to that user's outgoing e-mail and Internet postings. It provides various bits of information about the sender – for example, full name, favourite quote and so on.
*Links: e-mail*

### Silver Surfer
Describes anyone using the Internet who is over the age of fifty. This is one of the fastest growing groups of people using the Internet.
*Links: Newbie*

### SIMM
A group of RAM chips on a small circuit board with pins that enable it to connect to the computer motherboard. PC owners sometimes expand RAM by installing additional SIMMs.
*Links: RAM*

**.sit**

A Macintosh file that has been compressed using StuffIt and can be expanded using StuffIt Expander.
*Links: StuffIt Expander*

**Site**

See Website.

**Skin**

The surface look of a program. For example, the browser Neo-Planet allows users to change the way it looks. Skins are the graphic images that house the buttons and displays that overlay an application such as a media player or a browser. They are the interface via which content is reached – a bit like the casing and buttons on a hi-fi or mobile phone.
*Links: Media players, NeoPlanet*

**SLIP (Serial Line Internet Protocol)**

A method of connecting to the Internet, although a more common method is PPP.
*Links: PPP*

**SLIP/PPP**

One way of connecting to the Internet. To connect this way, TCP/IP software is needed on the computer. Using this method, a computer becomes a node on the Internet from which client applications can be run.
*Links: Access, PPP, TCP/IP*

**Slot**

A socket in a computer that can accept an expansion board, such as video acceleration, sound or disk drive control. This can be used to increase the capability of a computer.
*Links: Expansion board, Graphic accelerator, Sound card*

**SMDS (Switched Multimegabit Data Service)**

A high-speed public, packet-switched service that enables organisations to connect LANs that are geographically apart into a single Wide Area Network (WAN).
*Links: LAN, Network, Packet switching, WAN*

**S/MIME (Secure Multi-Purpose Internet Mail Extensions)**

A secure method of sending e-mail that uses the RSA encryption system. S/MIME is included in the latest versions of the Web browsers from Microsoft and Netscape, and enables secure messaging between different e-mail clients.
*Links: e-mail security, Public Key Cryptography*

**Smileys**

See Emoticons.

**SMTP (Simple Mail Transfer Protocol)**

The set of communication rules for the sending of e-mail. It works by identifying the server through which a user's e-mail will be sent. Typically used in conjunction with either IMAP or POP3, both of which deal with incoming mail, most mail programs allow users to state both their SMTP server and POP3 server separately.
*Links: e-mail, POP3*

**Snail mail**

Use of the traditional post service or the sending of hard-copy letters.
*Links: e-mail*

**Sniffer**

A tool that is able to monitor networks and therefore help with the control of traffic by identifying potential problems. It can also be used illicitly (see Packet sniffer).
*Links: InContext WebAnalyzer, Network, Packet, Packet sniffer*

### SOCKS
A proxy server protocol that provides a basic firewall by checking incoming and outgoing packets. This allows it to hide the IP addresses of those that use it. FTP, Telnet, Web browsers and so on can still be used by those behind the firewall.
*Links: e-mail security, Firewall, IP address*

### Software
A program that instructs hardware (for example, a computer, a printer) on how it should operate. There are effectively two types of software: application software and system software. The former is what a user might directly use (such as a word processor); the latter supports the former and includes operating system software such as Windows.
*Links: Application, Hardware, Killer app, Operating system, Program*

### SOHO (Small Office Home Office)
Refers to products specifically designed for small businesses – for example, printers, scanners and such like.
*Links: Solution*

### Solution
Implies that a product is addressing the 'problems' that have been associated with a particular type of computer software package or application.
*Links: Application server solution*

### Sort
To put information in a certain order – for example, files could be sorted by date, alphabetically by name and so on.
*Links: Database*

### Sound card
A type of expansion board for PCs, required for audio applications. One of the best known is the SoundBlaster.

*Links: Expansion board, Expansion slot, Graphic accelerator, Media players, Multi-media, Player*

### Sound player
A small application for playing sound files. It can act as a helper application for browsers, allowing a user to listen to sound on the Internet.
*Links: Application, Helper application, Media players, Multi-media, Player, Plug-in*

### Source code
The original form in which a computer program is written. A Webpage, for example, could contain any of the following languages: HTML, JavaScript and Java. These languages may actually call on other scripts or documents that are written in a different code (for example, Perl and C++).
*Links: C++, CGI, Code, HTML, Java, JavaScript, Perl, Script*

### Spam
The electronic equivalent of junk mail, this is unsolicited e-mail or newsgroup postings, often to more than one destination. Usually, these messages are an attempt to sell a service or product. Because the Internet is a public network, it is very difficult to stop spam. Some e-mail services now employ spam-blocking techniques to enable a user to filter out unwanted e-mail, and there are other ways of reducing the amount of spam received. Users should be careful who they give their address to and should establish a spam-friendly account. This would be a separate account to the one used for their normal daily messages, which could be given to anyone from whom there is danger of receiving spam (such as when registering on a Website). The adoption of this word is apparently due to the Monty Python sketch in which each menu item included the tinned meat product Spam.
*Links: e-mail, Marketing, Spamdexing, Webmail*

## Spamdexing

A combination of spam and index, this is information placed in a Webpage or meta tag that results in search engines being 'tricked' into providing misleading results concerning a particular site. This can be achieved in a variety of ways. A keyword can be placed on a Webpage many times, disproportionately weighing the relevance of this page to the subject word. Another method is to include one or more subject words that have nothing to do with the content of the Website solely for the purpose of incorrectly indexing the site. The intention behind spamdexing is that people will visit a Website who wouldn't normally have done so given the correct information. A classic example is the placement of XXX (often used by sexually related sites and as a search term for people wanting to locate these sites) on a site that might sell hot food.
*Links: Auto-bot, Bot, Marketing, Search engine, Spider*

## Specialist search sites

There is an increasing number of specialist search tools and sites dedicated to particular themes or topics, catering to audiences with particular areas of interest – for example, football, philosophy or the stock market. Many of these are driven by commercial concerns. Others include research sites, hobbyist or travel sites. There are also several national and regional search tools, many of them portal sites. As the amount of information to filter and process increases, it is likely that directories with more narrowly defined areas of interest will increase in number. The term 'portal' is often used when talking about specialist search sites.
*Links: Directory (Internet), Portal, Search engine, UKplus, Vertical portal*

## Spew

Relating to newsgroups and chat rooms, this is when one of the participants repeatedly types, or talks, about the same thing.
*Links: Blatherer, Jabber*

### Spider

A program that roams the Internet collecting data and looking for new and updated pages. It contributes its discovery to a database, which can then be searched using the search engine. Spiders are a vital part of search engines because of the huge rate at which new pages are put online – a rate that couldn't possibly be manually indexed.

*Links: Agent, Auto-bot, Bot, Search engine, Spamdexing*

### Splash page

A Webpage that is encountered before a homepage and which usually informs a visitor of optional ways or certain conditions needed to view the actual site. For example, it might be that a certain plug-in is needed, or a certain version of a particular browser, or the visitor might be offered the choice of viewing a frames or non-frames version of the site.

*Links: Buffer page, Homepage*

### Spool (Simultaneous Peripheral Operations Online)

This is to store a program or task in a buffer (special area of memory) so that it can be printed or otherwise processed at a more convenient time. For example, printing jobs that are spooled are put into a queue.

*Links: Buffer*

### Sprite

An animated graphic that can be interacted with. The most common example is a character in a computer game that a player controls (for example, Lara Croft in the Tomb Raider series of computer games).

*Links: Games*

### SQL (Structured Query Language)

A standard query language used in many programs that involve requesting information from a database. A SQL query might be:

Select name, sales from table1
Where sales > 10,000.

This type of command language lets users manipulate data in all sorts of ways. It also includes a programming interface.
*Links: Database, Query, Relational database, SQL server*

## SQL server

A relational database management system that users are able to query using the SQL language. The term also refers to two database management products from Sybase and Microsoft.
*Links: Database, Query, Relational database, SQL*

## SRAM (Static RAM)

RAM that doesn't need to be refreshed, like DRAM does. It is faster and normally more expensive than DRAM, and is used for functions where speed is important, such as in caches.
*Links: RAM*

## SSI (Server Side Include)

A form of HTML comment whereby data is dynamically generated for a Webpage by the server every time one is requested. Webpages that contain SSIs sometimes have an .shtml extension.
*Links: Dynamic content, HTML, SHTML*

## SSL (Secure Sockets Layer)

A protocol used for transmitting encrypted messages therefore enabling secure Web transactions. It helps to protect the privacy of data exchanged by a Website and a user by using public key cryptography to establish proofs of identity. Webpages that require an SSL connection can be identified by their beginning with 'https:' instead of 'http:'.
*Links: HTTPS, Public Key Cryptography, Security*

### Stage directions

Used in chats to indicate vocal inflections, facial expressions or body language. Typically surrounded by < > – for example, < smile > and < shrug >.
*Links: Emotags, Emoticons*

### Static IP

A user's IP address that is the same every time they 'logon' to the Internet.
*Links: IP address*

### Status bar

Both Netscape Navigator and Internet Explorer have status bars. On Navigator, this is found at the bottom of the window and contains the following items: a lock icon that shows whether there is a secure connection; a connection icon that shows whether Navigator is working online or offline; a download bar, which provides the progress of the downloading of a file; a status message area that explains what Navigator is doing. Internet Explorer's status bar also contains a lock icon when there is a secure connection as well as a connection icon and so on. In addition, when a cursor passes over a link in the browser's window the URL of the link appears in the status bar and when a Webpage is being downloaded, the status bar shows the progress.
*Links: Internet Explorer, Netscape Navigator*

### Streaming sound

Sound played in real time – that is, as it is delivered – is unlike sound files that first need to be downloaded in their entirety before they can be played (for example, a WAV file). An example of a media form that works with the former but not the latter is live radio (or indeed any sound that is truly live). Streaming audio requires a plug-in player. This will either already be on the browser or can be easily downloaded. Shockwave and

RealAudio both provide streaming sound players.
*Links: Helper application, Media players, Player, RealAudio, Shockwave*

### StuffIt Expander

A shareware program that is able to decompress most compressed files that can be found on the Internet, particularly those with the extension .sit. It is available for Macintosh and Windows. On the Macintosh, a file can be decoded and expanded simply by selecting it, then dragging and dropping it on the StuffIt Expander icon.
*Links: Compression*

### Style guide

A set of guidelines written by the developers of a particular Website for the purpose of keeping consistent any further site developments. Examples of what this might include are the code, fonts and colours used on the site.
*Links: Webdeveloper, Website*

### Style sheets

Templates in word processing, desktop publishing and Website design that define the layout of a document. Parameters including page size and fonts are specified. These can enable users to define a variety of style sheets – for example, when using a word processor there might be a style sheet for private correspondence, another for work letters and so on. On the Web, a style sheet often refers to cascading style sheets.
*Links: Cascading Style Sheets*

### Subject

A short description of an e-mail provided by the sender.
*Links: bcc, cc, e-mail*

### Submit button

An icon typically found at the bottom of a form on a Webpage

on which users can click to send the information they've entered on the form to the Web server.
*Links: CGI, Form*

## Subnet
Short for subnetwork, this is a self-contained section of a larger network. It is usually identified by its subnet address, which is part of the IP address.
*Links: IP address, Network*

## Subnet mask
A number used to identify a subnet.
*Links: Subnet*

## Subroutine
Part of a program that is 'called' from another part of the program. Often, a well-structured program will consist of a short main routine that calls on many subroutines to do the work. For example, when loading a computer game, the main routine is clicked on which then calls on the rest of the program.
*Links: Program*

## Subscribe
When users add their e-mail address (and possibly other information) to a mailing list or discussion group.
*Links: Mailing list, Marketing, Moderated mailing list*

## Surf
Surfing the Web is the process of clicking on hyperlinks, then following the Web-like formations that are created as users weave their way around the Net linking between sites, each leading from one another.
*Links: Browse, Hyperlink, Navigate*

**Surf monkey**
A Web browser for the PC that adds a new element of fun to surfing. For one, it allows users to 'blow up' any Webpages they don't like.
*Links: Browser*

**SurfWatch**
A Net filtering program designed to monitor children's use of the Internet and prevent them from opening unsuitable sites. It can also be used to prevent people from using the Net for leisure purposes at work. It works by using categories that bar objectionable content.
*Links: Censoring Web material, Censorware, PICS*

**SVGA (Super Visual Graphics Array)**
An SVGA monitor can display up to 1280 x 1024 pixels using over 16 million different colours.
*Links: Aspect ratio, Resolution*

**Swap file**
A storage area on a hard disk for data that is normally held in RAM. This can be used to create virtual memory and the appearance that there is more RAM than there truly is.
*Links: RAM*

**SYSOP (Systems Operator)**
Someone who manages a computer server.
*Links: Webmaster*

**System**
The combination of hardware and software components that run in the computer. These should be chosen carefully to ensure they work well together. For example, Intel Pentium microprocessors are designed to work with the Windows operating system. The operating system is perhaps the most

important software component, and manages and provides services to other programs that can be run in the computer.

*Links: Hardware, Intel, Operating system, Software, Wintel*

# T

### T-1
A leased line connection capable of transmitting information at about 1.5 mbps, the fastest speed commonly used to connect networks to the Internet.
*Links: Backbone, Dedicated line, Leased line, T-3*

### T-3
A leased line connection capable of transmitting information of about 43 mbps. This is more than enough to allow full-screen, full-motion video – although such lines are used mainly by ISPs to connect to the Internet backbone and for the backbone itself.
*Links: Backbone, Dedicated line, Leased line, T-1, VOD*

### Tag
A type of command or instruction, typically relating to HTML or Webpage code. These instructions specify formatting, and are used to add pictures and links to a Webpage. Examples of HTML tags are:

    &lt;P&gt;     paragraph break, and
    &lt;B&gt;     bold.

The instructions always come surrounded with &lt; &gt;.
*Links: CFML, HTML, Meta tag*

### Talker
Similar to a chat room, but traditionally using text only. A user would normally connect via Telnet, although it is possible to

420 | **Part Two: Internet Dictionary**

connect to some using a browser. It can be thought of as the chat version of a MUD – that is, a MUD without the role-playing.
*Links: Chat, MUD*

### Task
A process, one that may be executed at the same time as other processes. Most operating systems support multi-tasking, which allows multiple tasks to run at the same time, taking turns using the resources of the computer.
*Links: Operating system*

### Task bar
The bar in the Windows operating systems that typically runs along the bottom of the screen. It displays the Start button, any programs or windows that are active, plus tiny shortcut icons as well as the time.
*Links: Desktop, Menu bar, Toolbar*

### TCP/IP (Transmission Control Protocol/Internet Protocol)
The standard method for transmitting messages. It works by converting the messages into small data packets when they are sent and reassembling them at their destination (another computer). The sender and recipient don't even have to belong to the same network. The IP takes care of addresses, ensuring that the packets all go to the appropriate places over the multiple nodes and networks. The TCP takes care of keeping track of the packets. TCP/IP is integral to the success of the Internet.
*Links: ARP, Communications protocol, CU-SeeME, Data traffic, DNS, HTTP, IP, IP address, MacTCP, NNTP, Node, OpenTransport, Packet, PPP, Protocol, SLIP/PPP*

### Technophile
A lover of technology.
*Links: Digerati, Net God, Web guru*

**Technophobe**
A hater of technology.
*Links: Digerati, Net God, Web guru*

**Telnet**
Established in 1974, this was the first public packet data service. It enables users to logon to other computers over the Internet by allowing their computer to act as a terminal on the other computer. Its interface is text based, and users usually have to enter their logon name and password before gaining access to the system. It is mostly used for checking e-mail but can also be used for downloading and chatting and so on. It is possible to use Telnet via a Web browser by changing the 'http://' to 'telnet://', then entering in the site's address.
*Links: Firewall, HyperTerminal, Netscape Navigator, Packet, Remote logon, SOCKS, Talker, Terminal*

**Terminal**
A device that enables users to send commands to another computer. An example of this is Telnet.
*Links: Dumb terminal, HyperTerminal, Remote logon, Telnet, Terminal emulation*

**Terminal emulation**
When a computer is made to respond (usually by using soft-ware) like a terminal. It is used to dial in to a UNIX shell account from a PC or Mac. Microsoft's terminal emulator is called HyperTerminal; this comes with Windows 95, 98 and NT. Mac-Terminal is the Mac equivalent.
*Links: HyperTerminal, Remote logon, Terminal*

**Text Editor**
A program that can be used to enter, modify, store and usually print text.
*Links: Editor, Word processor*

**TFT screen (Thin Film Transistor screen)**
A type of active matrix display for laptops. It offers better resolution and contrast than traditional passive matrix displays.
This is because a separate transistor controls each screen
pixel, offering a much quicker refresh rate. For example, the
mouse pointer is not lost when moved quickly.
*Links: Active Matrix Display*

**TFTP (Trivial File Transfer Protocol)**
A more basic variation of FTP.
*Links: Anonymous FTP, Authentication, FTP*

**Thin client**
A small (in file size) program or application that runs on a user's
computer.
*Links: Client, Server*

**Thread**
A series of messages or postings all related to the same topic
on a discussion or newsgroup. It is possible with many newsreaders for a user to follow a thread and therefore a discussion.
This facility is often called a thread selector. One way of identifying a thread is by indentations. A response to an article is
indented compared to the article itself which is directly above
it.
*Links: Article, Conversation view, Discussion group, Follow-up, Hierarchy,
Message board, Newsgroups, Newsreader*

**Throughput**
The amount of data a computer can process over a period of
time.
*Links: Scalability*

**Thumbnail**
A small version of an image, approximately the size of an actual

thumbnail. This smaller-sized image allows for quicker down-loading and the ability to have more text displayed along with it. For example, a page on an online bookstore relating to a specific book would display a thumbnail of a book cover along with the book's synopsis. Thumbnails can often be clicked on for a larger and more detailed version of the image. They provide the ability to display multiple images on the same Webpage at the same time.
*Links: Bitmap, JPEG*

### Tier 1 ISP (First Tier Internet Service Provider)
An ISP with a direct connection to the Internet. ISPs can also be Tier 2, 3 or more whereby they lease their connections from a Tier 1 provider.
*Links: Backbone, ISP*

### TIFF (Tagged Image File Format)
Well supported file format used for still-image bitmaps. These are stored using tagged fields. Application programs can use the tags to accept or ignore fields, depending on their capabilities. TIFF files end with the .TIF extension.
*Links: Bitmap, GIF, JPEG*

### Tin
A popular UNIX newsreader.
*Links: Newsreader, UNIX*

### Title bar
The bar that runs along the top of a window, displaying the title of the window (normally the file name) and the program being used.
*Links: Floating toolbar, Menu bar, Task bar, Toolbar*

### Token Ring network
A Local Area Network (LAN) in which all of the computers are

connected in a loop. In this type of network, the computers can't all send messages at the same time. They can only do so when they hold a token, which is routinely passed round.
*Links: LAN, Network*

## Tool

Used to describe everything from mini actions or functions performed within a larger application (like 'cut and paste') to actual applications themselves (such as editing or graphics applications). It is also used to describe custom-built applications for Websites used to maintain their content (information). It can be used in the plural form ('tools') to refer to a group of programs that do different things.
*Links: Application, Editor, Shortcut, Toolbar*

## Toolbar

The tools usually seen at the top, but also along the bottom or side of the interface of an application or program, designed to make using the application faster. It might be arranged in the form of 'buttons' and is available for use at any time. A toolbar can usually be configured by the user to show fewer or more tools, and whether they appear in text or graphic form.

Tool bars

*Links: Floating toolbar, Menu bar, Nav bar, Tool*

**TOSsed out**

When a user is removed from a chat room for violating its Terms of Service (TOS) agreement.
*Links: AUP*

**Tracert (Trace route)**

A program that follows a user's packets across the Internet. It is useful if data seems to be moving rather slowly because these packets do not go directly from one computer to another and this program highlights the routes taken.
*Links: Multi-homing, Packet, Packet sniffer, Router, RSVP*

**Trackball**

Similar in function to a mouse in that it is a pointing device; it could even be described as an upside-down mouse. Tracker balls are common on CAD workstations and portable computers.
*Links: CAD, Mouse*

**Transparency**

The technique of making graphics look as though they have been produced directly on a Webpage instead of the actual case of being produced on a rectangular background, then pasted on.
*Links: Transparent GIF, Webpage*

**Transparent GIF**

A GIF image to which a particular colour has been assigned so that when the image is displayed, anywhere on the image that contains this colour it allows whatever is beneath to be visible. This proves particularly useful with images that are placed on top of patterned backgrounds.
*Links: GIF, Transparency*

### Travel, online
The Internet is useful for all sorts of travel purposes. Information on a potential destinations can be viewed, the route planned and any reservations made, be they for accommodation or the actual travelling (plane, boat, train). This can significantly save time and money.
*Links: Security, Shopping*

### Triplecast
The simultaneous broadcast of a program on television, radio and an Internet site or channel.
*Links: Broadcasting, MultiCasting*

### Trojan
A computer virus that comes disguised as a program. A user might download or receive this program thinking it is something they wish to open without realising what the program actually contains. This is one reason why people should be wary of attachments from people they don't know.
*Links: Attachment, Virus*

### Tron
When someone can't be contacted except via e-mail or online chat, especially when there are other means of contacting them (for example, phone, in person).
*Links: Key pal, Netizen*

### TrueSpeech
A Netscape Navigator plug-in that enables real-time audio to be listened to.
*Links: Netscape Navigator, Plug-in*

**Trumpet winsock**
A TCP/IP stack that enables a computer using Windows 3.1 to connect with the Internet.
*Links: TCP/IP*

**Tunnelling**
A way of allowing the Internet to operate as if it were a private network.
*Links: PPTP, Virtual private network*

**TWAIN (Technology Without An Interesting Name)**
A driver for scanners that enables users to scan an image directly into the application they wish to use it in. This application doesn't have to be a graphics application. It could be Microsoft Word, for example.
*Links: Device driver, Scanner*

# U

### ukplus.co.uk (www.ukplus.co.uk)
This is a UK-centric directory portal owned by the publishers of the *Daily Mail* and *The London Evening Standard*.
*Links: Directory (Internet), Portal, Search engine*

### Undernet
A Website with a large network of Internet Relay Channels (IRCs).
*Links: Chat, IRC*

### Unicast
Similar in meaning to Point-to-Point communication. It is the transfer of data between a single sender and a single receiver.
*Links: PPP*

### Universal network
It is the long-term aim of many that a single network should be able to carry all our communications facilities such as the phone, video, Internet and so on, with the result that they merge.
*Links: Network*

### UNIX
An operating system first made available to researchers and students in 1973 and on which many of the Internet's communication software protocols were developed. It is still very much used by today's web developers.
*Links: Operating system, Shell account*

**UnPC**
Not politically correct.
*Links: e-mail shorthand*

**UnZip**
A program for unzipping ZIP files.
*Links: Decompression, UnZipping*

**UnZipping**
The extraction of files from the Zip format. These are invariably compressed and the unZipping includes decompressing them.
*Links: Compression, Zip drive, Zip file*

**Upgrade**
A new version of a piece of software or hardware that is designed to replace an older version of the same product. With software, upgrades are commonly a lot cheaper than buying the software afresh. For example, it is possible to upgrade the

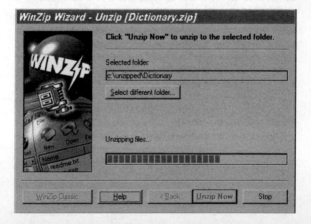

Windows 95 operating system to Windows 98.
*Links: Backwards compatible, Hardware, Software, Upgrade fever*

**Upgrade fever**
The intense desire to upgrade hardware and/or software when
there is no real need.
*Links: Upgrade*

**Upload**
Copying a file from a computer to a server. It is the opposite of
download.
*Links: Downloading, FTP*

**Upper case**
See Case sensitive.

**UPS (Uninterruptible Power Supply)**
Should there ever be a power failure, this is a device that uses
batteries to continue providing electricity to a computer for a
short while. It also helps protect a computer from power
surges.
*Links: Device*

**URL (Uniform Resource Locator)**
All Websites have URLs. These describe the location and
access method of a resource on the Internet. For example, the
URL http://www.iconbooks.co.uk shows the type of access
method being used (http) and the server location that hosts the
Website (www.iconbooks.co.uk). As most URLs are very long,
many Web browsers contain a bookmark feature, which allows
a user to save a URL if so desired by the user.
*Links: Address, cgi-bin, Companies, Country codes, Domain name, Hot
spots, HTTP, IntelliSense, Meta tag, Status bar, URL minder, Webpage,
Website*

### URL minder
An agent that notifies a user when a Webpage they've specified has changed, by periodically checking it. The robot can tell whether it has been updated and if so notifies the user by e-mail. One example of this is NetBuddy.
*Links: Agent, Auto-bot, Bot, NetBuddy*

### USB (Universal Serial Bus)
A 'plug-and-play' interface between a computer and add-on devices, for example a Zip drive or scanner. Consequently, a device can be added to a computer without having to add an adapter card or even turn the computer off. Some ADSL modems are able to take advantage of the USB port.
*Links: ADSL, Hot plugging, Plug-and-Play*

### Usenet
A bulletin board system where each collection of posted notes is known as a newsgroup. These newsgroups have descriptive names and the prefix of a newsgroup name indicates the subject category or hierarchy into which the newsgroup falls. Most browsers, including Netscape and Microsoft, provide access to any selected newsgroup. Subject categories or hierarchies include alt. and sci.
*Links: BBS, Hierarchy, Internet Explorer, Netscape Navigator, Newsgroups, Newsreader, Thread*

### Username
The name sometimes needed to access a computer system, or the name by which someone is known on the Internet. It is usually the first part of someone's e-mail address before the @ sign but can also be a chat nickname. Most users can specify their username, although most Websites or systems will *not* allow the same username to be assigned to two different people.
*Links: Address, Authentication, Chat, Handle*

**Using a previously cached copy instead**

When a Webpage that has been visited before can't be accessed, Netscape Navigator or Internet Explorer will default to a copy of the page from the previous visit, if available.

*Links: Cache*

**UUCP (UNIX-to-UNIX Copy Protocol)**

A method of communication between different UNIX systems for the copying (sending) of files and sending commands to be executed on another system.

*Links: Protocol, UNIX*

**UUENCODE/UUDECODE**

A UNIX utility program that provides a way of converting binary data into ASCII. This can be used for posting to Usenet or e-mailing with non-MIME compliant mail clients.

*Links: ASCII, Binary file, MIME*

# V

### VAN (Virtual Area Network)
A network on which users will be able to meet 'face to face' and which requires broadband transmission. This concept will prove extremely useful to many different areas, including remote medical diagnosis, legal consultation and conferences.
*Links: Broadband, Video-conferencing*

### Vanilla
The basic version of a software or hardware product – that is, one with no extra features.
*Links: Hardware, Liteware, Software*

### VBNS (very high-speed Backbone Network Service)
An experimental WAN in the United States consisting of super-computer centres.
*Links: Backbone, WAN*

### VBScript (Visual Basic Scripting Edition)
Similar to JavaScript. It is a simpler version of Microsoft's Visual Basic programming language.
*Links: JavaScript, Script, Visual Basic*

### vCard
An electronic business (or personal) card that can include images and sound as well as text. Some applications allow the viewing of vCards and the ability to drop them into an address book.
*Links: Address book*

## Vector graphics

Images that consist of lines and shapes that are outlined and filled with colours. Creation of these images is undertaken by using geometrical formulae that place lines and shapes in a given two-dimensional or three-dimensional space. The file is saved as a sequence of vector statements. This can result in a much smaller file than a bitmap image. Another advantage of vector graphics over raster graphics (bitmaps) is that they can be enlarged or reduced without any loss of sharpness because the picture is not a fixed number of pixels. Most sophisticated graphics systems such as animation software use vector graphics. However, many output devices, including laser printers and visual monitors, can only display raster graphics, so vector graphics must first be translated into bitmaps for these devices.
*Links: Bitmap, CAD, Raster graphics*

## Veronica (Very Easy Rodent Oriented Netwide Index to Computerised Archives)

Can be used to find out what is on Gopher sites. It looks through the network of Gopher sites for what has been specified in a user's search request.
*Links: Gopher*

## Vertical portal

Generally used to specify a niche portal.
*Links: Directory (Internet), Portal, Search engine, Specialist search sites*

## VGA (Visual Graphics Array)

A VGA Monitor can display 640 x 480 pixels using 16 different colours or 320 x 200 pixels using 256 colours. These colours can be chosen from a table of up to 262,144 colours.
*Links: SVGA*

### VI (Visual Interface)
A UNIX-based text editor. The system is controlled by using the keyboard rather than the normal use of both mouse and keyboard.
*Links: Text Editor, UNIX*

### Video-conferencing
The ability of two or more people at different sites to communicate visually by using a network such as the Internet to transmit video. It is typically performed using a video camera, microphone and speakers as well as the user's computer. Video-conferencing software programs currently available include CU-SeeME and Conference.
*Links: Broadband, Broadcasting*

### Virtual
A simulation of the real thing. This has great currency in technology at the moment. For example, the Internet is seen by many as a Virtual World.
*Links: Virtual circuit, Virtual hosting, Virtual memory, Virtual organisation*

### Virtual circuit
A connection between a user and an Internet site (or more specifically two computers) that acts as though it is a direct connection.
*Links: Virtual private network*

### Virtual hosting
Used to describe Web space that is hired, as opposed to owning the Web server host. Many companies and individuals hire a host because the cost of ownership can often not be justified.
*Links: Dedicated server, ISP, Service Space Provider*

## Virtual memory

A way of increasing the size of a computer's memory by using a disk file to simulate additional memory space.
*Links: Memory, RAM, Swap file*

## Virtual organisation

An organisation or company whose members are geographically apart yet appear to be all together in one real and physical location. This is becoming more and more common, and is possible with the growth of the Internet.
*Links: LAN, WAN*

## Virtual private network (VPN)

By using the PPTP protocol and various security procedures, it is possible to create a private network using the Internet. This can result in huge savings for a company because it provides a much cheaper alternative to a system of leased or owned lines between offices. The most obvious benefactors of VPNs are small businesses.
*Links: PPTP, Security, Virtual circuit, Windows 2000*

## Virus

A program designed to replicate itself from one computer to another and corrupt those computers in some way. Macro viruses are among the most common viruses, although they tend to do the least damage. The most famous virus to date was the 'I Love You' virus of May 2000, which was estimated to have caused around US$6 billion worth of damage. The virus spread so quickly and with such devastation because when opened it forwarded itself to every person in a user's e-mail management software's address book.
*Links: Anti-virus, Attachment, Freeware, Macro virus, McAfee VirusScan, Norton AntiVirus, Shareware, Trojan*

**Visual Basic**
A programming language that allows the creation of Windows applications in a very short time and which is ideal for making prototypes. Users are able to use a Graphical User Interface to bring all the necessary building blocks of a program together.
*Links: Graphical User Interface, VBScript, Windows*

**VOD (Video-On-Demand)**
A technology that enables Internet video broadcasting and desktop video-conferencing on the Internet and over telephone lines and private networks.
*Links: Broadband, Broadcasting, Intranet, Video-conferencing*

**Voice recognition**
The ability of a computer equipped with a sound card and the appropriate software to recognise words and commands given to it by a user's voice. This might include instruction on what the computer should do (for example, 'Connect to the Internet') or dictation to a word processor.
*Links: Sound card*

**Voxel**
The three-dimensional equivalent of a pixel, and therefore a unit of graphic information. It is defined by x, y and z co-ordinates.
*Links: Pixel*

**VRML (Virtual Reality Modelling Language)**
A language that can be used to create three-dimensional (3D) worlds on the Internet, and which can be interacted with. It can be thought of as the 3D equivalent of HTML and has great potential for the future. One example of its use might be the ability to be shown around a house anywhere in the world without having physically to travel there. A VRML browser or

plug-in is required to view VRML files. Such files have the .wrl extension.

*Links: Avatar, HTML, Interactivity, Live3D, MIP mapping, Plug-in, QuickTime VR, VRWeb*

## VRWeb

A browser able to view 3D objects created using the Virtual Reality Modelling Language (VRML).

*Links: Browser, VRML*

# W

### W3C (the World Wide Web Consortium)
A group of organisations that exists to develop standards and enhance the World Wide Web.
*Links: WWW, XML*

### WAIS (Wide Area Information Server)
A system that allows a user to retrieve content on the Internet by using natural language searches and indexed searching.
*Links: Boolean Logic, Meta-search tools, Multi-search tools, Search engine*

### Wallet
One method of facilitating online shopping. It is a small program to which has been added the necessary credit card and address data of the user. This data is stored in an encrypted and password-protected form on the user's computer, so that when they wish to make a purchase they can select a card from their list of cards and provide the relevant password along with the shipping address. The wallet program establishes a secure connection with the seller and transmits the information. Examples of wallet programs include Microsoft Wallet and CyberCash.
*Links: Decode, Decryption, Digital certificates, Security, SET, SSL*

### Wallpaper
This is the background of a desktop. It is possible to use almost any image or pattern as the background. Most graphic files such as GIF and JPEG images can be used as wallpaper.
*Links: Bitmap, GIF, JPEG, Skin*

## WAMBAM (Web Application Meets Brick And Mortar)
Used to define the online efforts of traditional brick and mortar stores, such as bn.com
*Links: e-commerce, e-tailing*

## WAN (Wide Area Network)
A network that connects computers over a large geographic area – as opposed to a LAN, which is typically confined to an office or building.
*Links: LAN, Network, Virtual organisation*

## WAP (Wireless Application Protocol)
The world standard permitting mobile phones to access the Internet. WAP technology will bring Web functionality to specially designed mobile phones. At the time of writing, these services provide only limited Internet access, covering channels for news, sports, share prices, weather, TV listings, entertainment and e-auctions. WAP phones have bigger display screens to allow a user to read the Web through a microbrowser and are fitted with special software. One of the drawbacks is that WAP displays a cut down text-only version of Websites, and that Websites need to be written using WML.
*Links: GSM, Protocol, WML*

## Warez
It is possible to come across software on the Internet that has been cracked and made available to anyone who wants to download it. This software is often called 'warez'.
*Links: Cracker, Freeware, Hacker, Software*

## WAV (Wave file)
A Windows sound file.
*Links: Media player, Player*

### Wavetable

A table of real recordings of musical instruments that have been digitised and are available for playback. These recordings are stored on the memory of a computer's sound card but this can be complemented by software.
*Links: MIDI, Sound card*

### Web guru

A term used to describe someone with a great deal of Internet knowledge.
*Links: Denizen, Digerati, Net God, Technophile*

### Webcams

Cameras that are placed at strategic sites around the world and that beam their images in real time on the Net. These images could be of anything – for example, from the top of a ski resort enabling visitors to see the conditions before they go, wild life in the jungles of Africa, the traffic in Trafalgar Square, or someone's bedroom.
*Links: Broadcasting, Webcasting*

### Webcasting

The use of the Web to broadcast information, including live or delayed versions of sound or video broadcasts. Webcasting is an example of a push technology on the Internet (unless the information is archived and hence needs to be pulled).
*Links: Broadcasting, Push, Webcams*

### webcrawler.com (www.webcrawler.com)

A Web search engine that indexes Webpages by title and URL.
*Links: Directory (Internet), Portal, Search engine*

### Webdesigner

The person responsible for the look-and-feel of a Website.
*Links: Look-and-feel, Webdeveloper, Webpage, Website*

## Webdeveloper

The person responsible for the architecture, or the nuts and bolts, of a Website. This person produces the programming that allows a particular Web product to work.
*Links: Architecture, Cold Fusion, Webdesigner, Webpage, Website*

## Webmail

The service provided by an ISP e-mail address and a computer-based e-mail management system such as Outlook Express, available from one source. Web-based e-mail allows people to check their e-mail from any computer – they don't even have to own one. As a consequence, Webmail is highly popular with people on the move, such as frequent travellers. Another advantage is that a user should be able to have an e-mail address for life, which can't be guaranteed with ISP and business e-mail. However, there are also disadvantages. A user has to be online to use the service and Webmail systems offer only limited storage. Examples of Web-based e-mail include Hotmail, BigFoot and Another.
*Links: Another, BigFoot, Cybercafé, e-mail security, Hotmail, Roaming service, Spam*

## Webmaster

A person who manages a Website. This person *might* be responsible for making sure everything works, replying to queries, monitoring traffic and so on.
*Links: Postmaster, Tool*

## Webpage

These make up a Website and will contain text, graphics, animations, and perhaps even multi-media elements like video options and sounds. The pages are often the same size and dimensions as the screen viewing them, but they can be bigger. Scroll bars on the right-hand side and sometimes at the bottom of the screen can be used to view larger pages. A unique Web address or URL is allocated to each Webpage and it is this that enables a browser to locate it.

*Links: Active, ActiveX, Applet, Ad banner, Alt text, Anchor, Architecture, ASP, Body, Bookmark, Broken link, Browser, Buffer page, Cache, Cascading Style Sheets, CFML, CGI, DHTML, Dynamic fonts, Electronic publishing, Form, Frames, Hit, HTML, Hyperlink, Internet Explorer, Java, JavaScript, Load, Meta tag, Nav bar, Netscape Navigator, On the fly, Page requests, PICS, Pull, Refresh, Rollover, Scroll, Seamless tiling, Search engine, Select box, Server, Spamdexing, Splash page, SSI, SSL, Submit button, Tag, Thumbnail, Transparency, URL, Webdesigner, Webdeveloper, Website, WWW*

## Website

The key to the Web. It is a specific location on the Internet managed by an individual, group, or company that provides information or services concerning specific areas of interest, products general knowledge and so on. A Website contains many Webpages. Every Website will comprise an opening or homepage, which should provide a sitemap or content listing. Every Website's URL comes in the form www.domainname.domain (e.g. www.iconbooks.co.uk).

*Links: Address, Application server, Architecture, Authentication, Beta testing, Broadcasting, Censorware, Channel, Clickstreams, Cobweb site, Cold Fusion, Content, Content provider, Country codes, Domain name, Down, Dynamic content, e-commerce, Electronic publishing, Eyeballs, FAQ, Flash, Frames, Ghost site, Hit, Homepage, Hosting, Hot list, HTTP, Keyword, Lag, Launch, Live, Log, Look-and-feel, Mappucino, Microsite, Mirror site, PICS, Readme, Reciprocal link, Search engine, Service Space Provider, Spam, Spamdexing, SSL, Style guide, Style sheet, URL, URL minder, WAP, Webdesigner, Webdeveloper, Webmaster, Websmith, WML*

## Websmith

A person who builds a Website.

*Links: Webdesigner, Webdeveloper, Website*

## WebTV

A way of accessing the Internet from a TV, without the need for a computer. Webpages look a little different on a TV than when viewed on a computer. WebTV (or something of its type) is seen as the future of the Internet as the number of potential users is very much higher, so the potential of home shopping, banking and so on could be realised.
*Links: Broadcasting, WAP, Webcasting, Website*

## Welcome page

See Homepage.

## Whois

A way of finding out information about a domain name or IP address – for example, the name and address of the name's owner.
*Links: Domain name, InterNIC*

## whowhere.com (www.whowhere.com)

A personal directory Website where user scan search for someone's e-mail address, or phone and address, by entering his or her name and location.
*Links: Directory (Internet), Search engine*

## Wideband

A communications path capable of speeds between 64 kbps and 1.5 mbps. Examples include ADSL, Cable modem and T-1.
*Links: ADSL, Cable modem, T-1*

## wildcard or *.*

A symbol that represents any other symbols or characters. In DOS and Windows the asterix (*) is a wildcard that stands for any combination of letters. For instance a*.exe would refer to all files starting with 'a' and ending with 'exe'.
*Links: Windows*

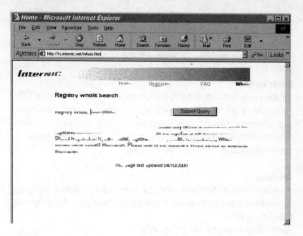

### WinAmp

A popular piece of software that allows users to play MP3 and numerous other audio format files. It can be downloaded free of charge.

*Links: Helper application, Media players, MP3, Player*

### Windows

An operating system produced by Microsoft. It dominates the personal computer market. Indeed, many versions have been created – including Windows CE designed for hand-held computers and Windows 2000.

*Links: Operating system, Windows CE, Windows 98, Windows 2000, Windows NT*

### Windows 95

Released in 1995, this was the operating system produced by Microsoft designed to replace its previous Windows 3.1. DOS was removed as the underlying platform together with all the

associated limitations, and a new graphical user interface was introduced. The system marked a major advance over the previous version.
*Links: Windows, Windows 98, Windows 2000*

## Windows 98

To the user, this appears to be almost identical to Windows 95. However, a number of new features were introduced, including the integration of Internet Explorer into the operating system. The desktop itself is able to operate as if it were a Webpage.
*Links: Windows, Windows 95, Windows 2000*

## Windows CE

A version of the Microsoft Windows operating system designed for mobile and other space-constrained devices – for example, hand-held PCs.
*Links: Hand-held computer, HDML, PDA*

## Windows NT

An advanced Microsoft Windows operating system. It is designed for anyone, including businesses, needing advanced capability and supports multi-tasking. There are two versions of Windows NT: Server and Workstation. The latter has been designed for desktop computers.
*Links: Windows, Windows 2000*

## Windows 2000

Based on the NT operating system, this is designed by Microsoft for the professional user as well as the larger business market. It is also seen as the next step after Windows 98 in the evolution of its operating systems. It provides the ability to set up a Virtual private network as one of its new features. There are four Windows 2000 products in all, the least expensive being Professional, which is aimed at individuals as well as businesses.

*Links: Operating system, Virtual private network, Windows,
Windows NT*

### WinGate
A product that allows all users on a LAN to share a modem on
one computer, and even one Internet account.
*Links: LAN*

### WinProxy
Has the same function as WinGate.
*Links: LAN, WinGate*

### WinSock (Windows Sockets)
An API that enables any TCP/IP client application (for example,
a browser) to communicate with other machines via the TCP/IP
protocol (in other words, use the Internet and all its features).
*Links: API, Client, TCP/IP*

### Wintel
A contraction of Windows and Intel used to describe the hardware and software combination of an Intel microprocessor
running Microsoft Windows. Often used with the word 'platform' in opposition to the UNIX or Macintosh platforms, and
also sometimes in a pejorative manner to imply the monopoly
powers that Intel and Microsoft have.
*Links: Intel, Windows*

### WinZip
A program that can be used to decompress most files
downloaded on the Internet. It is the Windows equivalent to
Macintosh's StuffIt. WinZip interfaces to most virus scanners
helping to provide protection from any infected files unwittingly
downloaded.
*Links: Compression, StuffIt, PKZIP, Zip file*

**Wired**
The state of being connected online. In capitals it is also a popular Web magazine.
*Links: Online, Zine*

**WML (Wireless Markup Language)**
A language that allows WAP devices to use the Net. Websites have to be translated from their normal HTML to WML in order for WAP devices to be able to view them.
*Links: HDML, WAP*

**Word**
Developed by Microsoft, this is a popular word processor with many features, including the ability to save a document as a Webpage.
*Links: Word processor*

**Word processor**
A computer program that can be used to prepare (through creating, editing and printing) written documents. The term is used to suggest that the program is more than just an 'editor'. The most popular word processors are WordPerfect and Microsoft Word.
*Links: Application, Bitmap, OCR, Software, Style sheet, Text Editor, Voice recognition*

**Workstation**
A typical term to describe a computer used for applications that require a fair degree of capability, particularly concerning power and graphics. Examples of areas of use are science and engineering where complex calculations may need to be undertaken.
*Links: CAD, Desktop publishing*

**World Wide Web**
See WWW.

**WORM (Write Once Read Many)**
A device used to write information on to a disk which, once written, is permanent. There is also the worm virus such as 'I Love You', which was prevalent during May 2000.
*Links: CD-R, Device*

**WS_FTP**
A FTP client program with a graphical user interface.
*Links: Client, FTP, Graphical User Interface*

**WWW (World Wide Web)**
The resources and users on the Internet that use the Hypertext Transfer Protocol (HTTP). Websites are at the heart of Web.
*Links: Communications protocol, HTTP, HTTPS, Protocol, TCP/IP, URL, Website*

# X

### Xeon
A Pentium microprocessor from Intel based on its Pentium II. It is designed for use in 'mid-range' servers and workstations.
*Links: Intel, Pentium*

### XML (eXtensible Markup Language)
A similar language to HTML, although it offers features unavailable to HTML. It is a standard developed by W3C especially for Web documents, but any document tagged in XML can also be formatted for publication in CD-ROM and printed book form. Its power derives from the fact that it is a language for writing languages and therefore allows greater explanatory powers. Consequently, a choice of how data is presented can be offered to a browser. XML describes *how* information is presented rather than *what* information is presented, and allows for the description of the same information in many ways at the same time.
*Links: Dreamweaver, HTML, Markup language, SGML, W3C*

# Y

**Yahoo! (Yet Another Hierarchical Officious Oracle) (www.yahoo.com / www.yahoo.co.uk and so on)**
A directory of Websites started in 1994, which quickly came to be one of the most visited sites on the Net. There are many country and regional Yahoo!s offering users the ability to search more precisely. If a search query doesn't lead to a Yahoo! topic page, it will still normally lead to results from the search engines to which Yahoo! links.
*Links: Directory (Internet), Multi-search tools, Meta-search tools, Portal, Search engine*

**Yahoo! Mail**
A Webmail facility provided by Yahoo!
*Links: Webmail*

**yahooligans.com (www.yahooligans.com)**
The Yahoo! search directory for kids.
*Links: Yahoo!*

# Z

### Zine (electronic magazine)

Any Website that publishes content in a magazine format and which derives most, if not all, of its revenue from ad sales. An example of a famous zine is *Hotwired*.

*Links: e-journal, e-zine, Magazines, zine.net*

### zine.net (www.zine.net)

A Website containing information on independent zines. It is an excellent starting point for viewing electronic magazines.

*Links: Magazines, Zine*

### Zip drive

A small, portable disk drive with a high storage capacity developed by Iomega Corporation. There are two sizes currently available, a 100 MB size and a 250 MB size, the former being the equivalent of about seventy floppy disks. Zip drives are ideal for backing up, archiving, storing unusually large files (particularly graphic images), exchanging large files with someone and putting a system on another computer.

*Links: Archive, Back up, Hard disk*

### Zip file/Zipping

A compressed file format. On the Internet large files that would normally take a very long time to download are usually first compressed into Zip files before being made available. After a file is downloaded, a decompression software program is required to 'unZip' the file. This is a very straightforward operation. Zip files are extremely useful when sending any large

file to another person by e-mail – for example, photographs.
*Links: Compression, .exe, PKZIP, UnZip, UnZipping, WinZip*

### Zmodem
A file transfer protocol for modems that sends data from an Internet host to a PC. The data is sent without acknowledgement from the computer receiving the data.
*Links: Modem, Protocol*

# APPENDICES

## Shorthand

These are commonly used phrases reduced to the acronymic form.
They are designed to make messages quicker to write.

| | |
|---|---|
| A/M | Above Mentioned |
| A/S/L | Age/Sex/Location |
| ADN | Any Day Now |
| AFAIK | As Far As I Know |
| AFK | Away From Keyboard |
| AKA | Also Known As |
| AMBW | All My Best Wishes |
| AOLer | A member of AOL |
| ASAP | As Soon As Possible |
| AYSOS | Are You Stupid Or Something |
| B4 | Before |
| BBIAB | Be Back In A Bit |
| BBL | Be Back Later |
| BCNU | Be Seein' You |
| BD | Big Deal |
| BFD | Big F***ing Deal |
| BFN | Bye For Now |
| BIF | Basic In Fact |
| BITD | Back In The Day |
| BM | Byte Me |
| BRB | Be Right Back |
| BTSOOM | Beats The Shit Out Of Me |
| BTW | By The Way |
| CID | Consider It Done |
| CIO | Check It Out |
| Cof$ | Church of Scientology |

| | |
|---|---|
| CUL8R | See You Later |
| CYA | See Ya |
| DILLIGAS | Do I Look Like I Give A Shit |
| DLTM | Don't Lie To Me |
| EML | Evil Manic Laugh |
| F2F | Face to Face |
| FUBAR | F***** Up Beyond All Recognition |
| FUD | (Spreading) Fear, Uncertainty, and Disinformation/Doubt |
| FWIW | For What It's Worth |
| FYA | For Your Amusement |
| FYI | For Your Information |
| GDM8 | G'day mate |
| GG | Good Game |
| GL | Good Luck |
| GMTA | Great Minds Think Alike |
| GR&D | Grinning Running And Ducking |
| GR8 | Great |
| GTG | Got To Go |
| GTGB | Got To Go, Bye |
| GTSY | Glad To See Ya |
| HAGO | Have A Good One |
| HTH | Hope This (or That) Helps |
| IAE | In Any Event |
| IC | In Character |
| IDKY | I Don't Know You |
| IDST | I Didn't Say That |
| IDTS | I Don't Think So |
| IFU | I F***** Up |
| IMHO | In My Humble Opinion |
| IMNSHO | In My Not So Humble Opinion |
| IMO | In My Opinion |
| IOH | I'm Outta Here |
| IOW | In Other Words |
| IRL | In Real Life |
| IYSS | If You Say So |
| IYSWIM | If You See What I Mean |

| KIT | Keep In Touch |
| L8R | Later |
| LMAO | Laughing My Ass Off |
| LOL | Laughing Out Loud -or- Lots Of Love |
| LTNS | Long Time No See |
| MHOTY | My Hat's Off To You |
| MorF | Male or Female |
| MOTD | Message Of The Day |
| MOTSS | Members Of The Same Sex |
| NBIF | No Basis In Fact |
| NFW | No F***ing Way |
| NP | No Problem |
| NRG | Energy |
| NRN | No Reply Necessary |
| NW | No Way |
| OIC | Oh, I see |
| OOC | Out Of Character |
| OOTB | Out Of The Box -or- Out Of The Blue |
| OTOH | On The Other Hand |
| PBT | Pay Back Time |
| PLS | Please |
| PMFJI | Pardon Me For Jumping In |
| POV | Point Of View |
| ROTFL | Rolling On The Floor Laughing |
| RSN | Real Soon Now |
| RTFM | Read The F***ing Manual |
| RTM | Read The Manual |
| SITD | Still In The Dark |
| SNAFU | Situation Normal, All F***** Up |
| SOL | Sooner Or Later |
| SorG | Straight or Gay? |
| SUYF | Shut Up You Fool |
| SWDYT | So What Do You Think |
| TANSTAAFL | There Ain't No Such Thing As A Free Lunch |

| | |
|---|---|
| TARFU | Things Are Really F***** Up! |
| TEOTWAWKI | The End Of The World As We Know It |
| TIA | Thanks In Advance |
| TIAIL | Think I Am In Love |
| TIC | Tongue In Cheek |
| TTFN | Ta Ta For Now |
| TTT | To The Top |
| TTYL | Talk To You Later |
| TX | Thanks |
| TYVM | Thank You Very Much |
| unPC | unPolitically Correct |
| WAG | Wild Ass Guess |
| WB | Welcome Back |
| WCA | Who Cares Anyway |
| WDYS | What Did You Say |
| WEG | Wicked Evil Grin |
| WTF | What The F***? |
| WTG | Way To Go! |
| WYRN | What's Your Real Name? |
| WYS | Whatever You Say |
| WYSIWYG | What You See Is What You Get |
| WYT | Whatever You Think |
| YA | Yet Another |
| YDKM | You Don't Know Me |
| YSYD | Yeah, Sure You Do |
| YTTT | You Telling The Truth? |
| YW | Your Welcome |

# Emoticons (aka Smileys)

Emoticons are a sequence of ASCII characters originally meant to represent emotion in e-mail or news (which they still do, but there are also 'emoticons' that represent things other than emotions) and usually follow after the punctuation (or in place of the punctuation) at the end of a sentence. They can be 'seen' better if the head is tilted to the left – the colon represents the eyes, the dash represents the nose and the right parenthesis represents the mouth. It should also be pointed out that they look best in the Times New Roman font.

Below is a selection of the many emoticons that have been invented. These have been split into categories depending on what they are intended to display to make them easier to view. Most are rarely used but give a strong impression of the power of the imagination and indeed the need to stay human in computing. If you are hungry for more, a search on any decent search engine should deliver the results to satiate any appetite.

## *States of mind*

| | |
|---|---|
| :-) | Smile |
| ;-) | Smile with a wink |
| :-\|\| | Angry |
| :-( | Sad |
| :-)) | Really happy |
| :-D | Big grin |
| :-o | Surprise/shock |
| $-) | Greedy |
| :-/ | Perplexed |
| ?:-/ | Puzzlement or confusion |
| =:O | Frightened (hair standing on end) |
| =8O | Wide-eyed with fright |
| :-} | Embarrassed smile |
| ;-^) | Tongue in cheek |
| %*@:-( | Hung over |
| #-) | User partied all night |
| <:I | Dunce |

| :-\| | Non-committal |
| (-_-) | Secret smile |
| >:) | Perplexed look |

## Physical descriptions

| :-)<///////> | User wearing a necktie |
| :-'\| | User has a cold |
| :-~) | User has a cold |
| :-{} | User wearing heavy lipstick |
| :-)8 | User is well dressed |
| 8:-) | Glasses on forehead |
| {(:-) | User is wearing a toupee |
| (:-I | Bald person |

## Actions

| :-* | A kiss |
| :-P~ | A lick |
| X= | Fingers crossed |
| :-P | Sticking out a tongue |
| X-) | I see nothing |
| :-X | I'll say nothing |
| :~~~ | Drooling |
| ...---... | SOS |
| :'-( | Crying |

## People/characters

| (_8-(\|) | Homer Simpson |
| C\|:-= | Charlie Chaplin |
| =\|:-)= | Abraham Lincoln |
| *<:-) | Father Christmas |
| (:)-) | Scuba diver |
| *#:-) | Scotsman |
| 0:-) | Angel |
| :-[ | Vampire |
| +-:-\| | Religious person |
| ]:-) | Devil |

## Objects/animals

| | |
|---|---|
| [:-|] | A robot |
| (:V) | A duck |
| 3:-o | A cow |
| @]-'---,-- | A rose |
| :8) | A pig |
| 8) | A frog |
| >[] | A television |
| (::[]::) | A plaster/bandaid (can indicate help or assistance) |
| 0>> | Ice-cream cone |
| <3 | A heart |

## Assicons

These are a variation on the emoticon theme and involve a particular part of the body. Likewise, they are intended to be fun, offering a modicum of relief to those involved in the drudgery of text messaging.

| | |
|---|---|
| (_!_) | a normal ass |
| (__!__) | a fat ass |
| (!) | a tight ass |
| (_._) | a flat ass |
| (_o^^o_) | a wise ass |
| (_E=mc2_) | a smart ass |
| (_13_) | an unlucky ass |
| (_$_) | money coming out of his ass |
| (_?_) | a dumb ass |

# Error messages

When receiving any error messages, it is always worth attempting the action again one or two times. Another option is to try refreshing the page.

| ERROR MESSAGE | MEANING | ACTION |
|---|---|---|
| 400 – Bad request | Incorrect URL entered. Either the server doesn't recognise the document, the page no longer exists or access is unauthorised. | Check the entered URL for any typos. Is the address case sensitive? |
| 401 – Unauthorised | Either the user is unauthorised or the password they entered was incorrect. | Re-enter the password. |
| 403 – Forbidden | User is not permitted to access the document. A password may be needed. | Re-enter the password. |
| 404 – Not found | The host server is unable to locate the file entered at the given URL. Either it has been entered incorrectly or no longer exists. | Check the entered URL for any typos. Check the site that is supposed to contain the file still exists. |

| | | |
|---|---|---|
| **550 – ????? is not a known user** | A sent e-mail wasn't recognised by the recipient mail server. Either the username part of the e-mail was incorrect or an account is no longer held with that server. | Check the e-mail's username for any typos. Is it case sensitive? |
| **Bad file request** | The form being accessed either contains an error or is not supported by the user's browser (very rare). | The user should try using a different browser. |
| **Failed DNS lookup** | The URL requested couldn't be translated into a valid Web address. | The system might've made a mistake (common) so a simple reload would correct this. Check the URL for typos. |
| **Host unavailable** | The host server may be offline or down. | Try the server again and if unsuccessful, try again later. |
| **Unable to locate host** | As above or the user has lost connection. | Re-connect if necessary and follow the instructions above. |
| **Unable to locate server** | The URL entered is either incorrect or no longer exists. | Check the URL and try again. |

| | | |
|---|---|---|
| **Host unknown** | Either connection has been lost somewhere or the URL is incorrect. | Re-connect if necessary, click the Reload button or check the URL for any mistakes. |
| **NNTP server error** | An error message associated with newsgroups. Either the user's server software is not working properly or the newsgroup doesn't exist. | Check the URL and try again. If unsuccessful a number of times, the user should contact their ISP as the problem is possibly their's. |
| **Too many users** | Some sites set a limit on the number of users allowed to access it at any given time. This is to avoid slow transfer rates. | Try again when there is less traffic. |
| **Helper application not found** | The user's browser is unable to recognise the file that it is trying to download. | The option 'save to disk' should be presented. It might be possible to open the file from the computer. |
| **File contains no data** | There are no Web pages on the requested site. | Try again later and check the URL for any errors. |

# File extensions

The group of letters after a period or 'dot' in a file name is called the
file extension. This extension refers to the type of file it is. Below is a
list of file extensions including applications that can open them.

| | |
|---|---|
| .au, .aif, .aiff, | These are all sound files and can be played on most decent audio or media players such as RealAudio. |
| .avi | Video for Windows. These files can be large and need to be downloaded in their entirety before they can be played. A good windows media player, like RealPlayer, should be able to view these files. |
| .bmp, | Bitmap graphic formats; can be viewed by any decent graphics viewer or even within a browser. |
| .doc | This is an MS Word document file and can be opened in MS Word or Wordpad. |
| .eps | A postscript image. A file format used to import images into programs such as PageMaker and Quark. |
| .exe | This is a self-executing Windows or DOS program. |
| .gif, .jpg, .png, | These are all types of bitmap graphic .jpeg, images, which can be opened by any decent graphics program or even viewed from within a browser. |

| | |
|---|---|
| .html, .htm | Web-documents written using HTML. Can be viewed using a browser. |
| .hlp | Windows help files. |
| .hqx | This is a Mac BinHex file that can be opened by BinHex or StuffIt Expander. |
| .mov, .qt | This is a QuickTime video file originally used with the Macintosh and now used with Windows. It can be played using QuickTime. |
| .mpeg, .mpg, .mpe, .miv | MPEG (Motion Pictures Expert Group) file, which is a compressed video format. These files can be opened using a video viewer such as RealPlayer. |
| .mp3 | MPEG audio file that can be played using any MP3 player such as WinAmp or Sonique. |
| .pdf | Adobe Acrobat hypertext format. Files saved as .pdf retain their original formatting and can be viewed using Adobe Acrobat Reader, which can be downloaded from the Internet for free. |
| .ps | This describes a Postscript document. These can be read by programs such as PageMaker and Quark. |
| .ram, .ra | These are real audio files and can be opened using RealAudio. |

| | |
|---|---|
| .rtf | This is a word processing file saved as Rich Text Format. It is useful because it keeps the document's formatting but can be opened in a variety of word processing programs. |
| .sea | Macintosh self-extracting file. |
| .sit | Macintosh file compressed using StuffIt, which can be opened using StuffIt Expander. |
| .tif, .tiff | Tagged Image Format, a type of bitmap graphics format that can be opened using any decent graphics viewer including a Web browser. |
| .txt, .text | This is a text file and can be opened using any word processor or text editor. |
| .wav | This is a Windows sound file. It can be played using Windows Media Player as well as any decent media player. |
| .wrl | A VRML (Virtual Reality Modeling Language) file that can be viewed on browser with a VRML plug-in usually available at sites using VRML. |
| .zip | Windows file compressed using a ZIP utility such as PKZIP and WinZip. It can also be opened using these utilities. |

# Newsgroups

Newsgroups are groups of people getting together on the Internet to discuss a particular subject. They consist of messages, and users are able to 'post' and 'reply to' messages from other users. Newsgroups are divided into topic areas by category name or hierarchy, indicating the very broad subject matter they cover. The category name appears at the beginning of the newsgroup's name. In order to access a newsgroup, a user needs a news server address and a newsreader program.

Category names and their style of content include

| | |
|---|---|
| alt. | stands for alternative. This was set up in response to the controls that were imposed on some Usenet groups. An alt. newsgroup can be started by anyone. They tend to cover some of the more wayward sites, including pornography groups. |
| biz. | business products and services. |
| comp. | discussions relating to computers and technology, including consumer advice. |
| humanities. | both professional and amateur discussions relating to the humanities and the arts. |
| misc. | miscellaneous discussions about anything not covered by the other categories. |
| news. | information about the Usenet network |
| rec. | recreational sports, hobbies, music and so on. |
| sci. | professional and lay scientific iscussions. |
| soc. | social issues, society and socialising. |
| talk. | topical debates about current issues. |

# Website listing

Hopefully this book has enabled you to go about finding sites you are interested in. However, it is always useful to have a few pointers so we've listed below some of our favourite websites under various subject headings.

| | |
|---|---|
| **Art, Literature & Writing** | http://eserver.org |
| | www.artchive.com |
| | www.moma.org |
| | www.poetrysoc.com |
| | www.poets.org |
| | www.wwar.world-arts-resources.com |
| **Auction sites** | www.ebay.com |
| | www.ebid.co.uk |
| | www.icollector.com |
| | www.qxl.com |
| **Books & Music** | www.addall.com |
| | www.alphabetstreet.co.uk |
| | www.amazon.com / www.amazon.co.uk |
| | www.bn.com |
| | www.bol.com |
| | www.bookfinder.com |
| | www.bookshop.co.uk |
| | www.dotmusic.co.uk |
| | www.dymocks.com.au |
| | www.freebase.com |
| | www.mp3.com |
| | www.music.com |
| | www.napster.com |
| | www.thebookplace.com |
| | www.waterstones.co.uk |
| **Business** | http://finance.uk.yahoo.com |
| | www.bloomberg.com / www.bloomberg.co.uk |
| | www.thedeal.net |
| | www.womenconnect.com |

| | |
|---|---|
| **Computing** | www.cnet.com |
| | www.eeggs.com |
| | www.freestufffactory.com |
| **Education** | www.bbc.co.uk/education/ |
| | www.britannica.com |
| | www.novelsguide.com |
| | www.schoolbytes.com |
| | www.study24-7.com |
| | www.studyfree.com |
| **Employment** | http://employment.yahoo.com |
| | www.careersonline.com.au |
| | www.monster.com / www.monster.co.uk |
| **Fashion, Beauty & Health** | www.avon.com |
| | www.beautyscene.com |
| | www.designersdirect.com |
| | www.drann.net |
| | www.easyshop.co.uk |
| | www.healthfinder.gov |
| | www.intofashion.com |
| | www.mwsearch.com |
| | www.nhsdirect.nhs.uk |
| | www.synergy-health.co.uk |
| **Films** | www.film.com |
| | www.filmgeek.com |
| | www.mtv.com |
| **Food** | www.askachef.com |
| | www.foodchannel.com |
| | www.ichef.com |
| | www.organicdelivery.co.uk |
| | www.organicsdirect.co.uk |
| | www.simplyorganic.net |
| | www.waitrose.com |
| **Gardening** | www.cooksons.com |
| | www.e-gnome.com |

| | |
|---|---|
| | www.garden.com |
| | www.hdra.org.uk |
| | www.plants-magazine.com |
| | www.rbgkew.org.uk |
| **Holidays & Travel** | www.bargainholidays.com |
| | www.expedia.com |
| | www.holidayauctions.net |
| | www.lateseats.com |
| | www.lonelyplanet.com |
| | www.rolholidays.co.uk |
| **Kids** | www.beano.co.uk |
| | www.bonus.com |
| | www.cyberteens.com |
| | www.disney.com |
| | www.familyplay.com |
| | www.kidpub.org |
| | www.kidsonline.co.uk |
| | www.sesamestreet.com |
| | www.yahooligans.com |
| **Science & Environment** | www.chem4kids.com |
| | www.nature.com |
| | www.newscientist.com |
| | www.sciencedaily.com |
| **Silver Surfers** | www.ageofreason.com |
| | www.lifebegins.net |
| | www.thirdage.com |
| **Sport** | www.itv-f1.com |
| | www.sportal.com |
| | www.sportlive.net |
| | www.sportstalk.com |
| | www.teamtalk.com |
| | www.totalsports.net |
| **Women** | www.beme.com |
| | www.femina.com |

# INDEX

## A